Dec-06

Mel!

♡ Harmony

Bar Codes

Law and Society Series
W. Wesley Pue, General Editor

The Law and Society Series explores law as a socially embedded phenomenon. It is premised on the understanding that the conventional division of law from society creates false dichotomies in thinking, scholarship, educational practice, and social life. Books in the series treat law and society as mutually constitutive and seek to bridge scholarship emerging from interdisciplinary engagement of law with disciplines such as politics, social theory, history, political economy, and gender studies.

A list of the books in this series appears at the end of this book.

Jean McKenzie Leiper

Bar Codes: Women in the Legal Profession

UBCPress · Vancouver · Toronto

15   14   13   12   11   10   09   08   07   06   5   4   3   2   1

Printed in Canada on ancient-forest-free paper (100% post-consumer recycled) that is processed chlorine- and acid-free, with vegetable-based inks.

Library and Archives Canada Cataloguing in Publication

Leiper, Jean McKenzie, 1938-
    Bar codes : women in the legal profession / Jean McKenzie Leiper.

(Law and society, ISSN 1496-4953)
Includes bibliographical references and index.
ISBN-13: 978-0-7748-1319-8 (bound); 978-0-7748-1320-4 (pbk.)

    1. Women lawyers – Ontario – Social conditions. 2. Sex roles in the work environment – Ontario. I. Title.

HD6054.2.C3M34 2006   305.43'349713   C2006-903733-7

Canadä

UBC Press gratefully acknowledges the financial support for our publishing program of the Government of Canada through the Book Publishing Industry Development Program (BPIDP), and of the Canada Council for the Arts, and the British Columbia Arts Council.

This book has been published with the help of a grant from the Canadian Federation for the Humanities and Social Sciences, through the Aid to Scholarly Publications Programme, using funds provided by the Social Sciences and Humanities Research Council of Canada.

UBC Press
The University of British Columbia
2029 West Mall
Vancouver, BC V6T 1Z2
604-822-5959 / Fax: 604-822-6083
www.ubcpress.ca

Contents

Acknowledgments

I am indebted to The Social Sciences and Humanities Research Council of Canada for their generous financial support (Strategic Research Grant 816-98-0028). Their funding has allowed me to move beyond the local level and broaden the scope of this study immeasurably. I also thank the staff at the Law Society of Upper Canada for supplying computerized records of women practising law throughout the province.

The project has been a cooperative venture, made possible by the contributions of many people. It deals with a topic that has intrigued me for a long time, but because I was busy with other work or, more to the point, unsure about how to begin, it did not take shape until 1993 when I received a letter from my daughter, Janet Leiper. She had contacted nineteen of her legal colleagues and they had all agreed to take part in a study of women lawyers. She had assured them that they would remain anonymous and had told them to expect a call within six months. Thank you, Janet!

I am also very grateful to Kim Twohig, a long-time friend and general counsel in the Crown Law Office of the Ontario Ministry of the Attorney General. At my request, she called a network of senior women in the legal profession, generating a sampling base that would have been impossible to build without her initiative.

Many people have been involved in the research process over the life of this study. I thank Dana Harrison for helping me launch the project when funds were limited. I also thank my research assistants at King's University College at the University of Western Ontario – Colleen Dragunevicius, Jana Fear, Michelle Ingratta, Julienne Patterson, and Beverly Paul – for their superb work. I am particularly indebted to Gale Cassidy, a wizard with NUD*IST qualitative software and SPSS programs. She coordinated the programs and provided a level of methodological sophistication that is, I believe, quite rare. I thank Phyllis Fidler and Samantha Pearson for their clerical expertise and their willingness to tackle any task.

I express my gratitude to colleagues, family, and friends for listening to my ideas, reading portions of the completed work, and offering valuable suggestions. The members of the Research Group on Women and Professional Education provided strong support and an opportunity to discuss issues surrounding legal education. Jeff Cormier read early drafts of the work, and David Paul contributed wit and wisdom at every turn.

Chapter 3 is a revision of an article reprinted with permission of the University of Ottawa Press from *Learning to Practice: Professional Education in Historical and Contemporary Perspective*, Ruby Heap, Wyn Millar, and Elizabeth Smyth, eds., "Gender, Class and Legal Education" 239-63, © 2003. Chapter 5 is a revision of an article reprinted with permission of Elsevier from *Minding the Time in Family Experience: Emerging Perspectives and Issues*, vol. 3, Kerry J. Daly, ed., "Gendered Views of Time and Time Crunch Stress: Women Lawyers' Responses to Professional and Personal Demands" 251-80, © 2001. I wish to thank both these publishers for their cooperation.

I also acknowledge the support provided by UBC Press. Two anonymous readers gave me excellent suggestions for revisions to the preliminary draft. Randy Schmidt guided the project from its inception and Darcy Cullen administered the details of copy editing and production. I am grateful for their unlimited store of patience and encouragement.

I am most indebted to the women in this study for the gift of their time and their trust. For the past twelve years I have thought of them as "my lawyers" and I will miss the contact with them.

Finally, my deepest appreciation is reserved for Doug Leiper, my patient, intelligent, and good-humoured partner.

Bar Codes

1
Introduction: Recognizing the Codes

> You asked me why I ventured into this career. I guess probably
> that ... maybe just for Dad predominantly ... My father was a
> lawyer ... my father's father was also a lawyer and subsequently
> a judge ... so I guess to some extent it's always been a factor.[1]

This woman came from a well-established legal background. When her
father practised law in the post-war years, he would have had very few
women as colleagues. Her grandfather would have been part of an even
more exclusive men's club, anchored in earlier legal traditions that reflected a nineteenth-century world where elite members of the profession
were drawn from colonial families of high social standing. Schooled in
Latin, Greek, and the classics, these "professional gentlemen" were well
acquainted with the science of law and their status as barristers set them
apart from their lower order colleagues, the attorneys.[2]

In spite of these professional class distinctions, law and legal practice
were masculine domains and would remain exclusively male until Clara
Brett Martin was called to the bar in 1897. Her entry was seen as a vic-
tory by early feminists, but the profession was to continue along a male-
dominated path throughout most of the twentieth century.[3] Undoubtedly,
the first women law students faced a hostile environment and, although
the sexism is less obvious now, women in law still enter an arena where
many of the leaders are men who endorse the practices and values of a
very traditional profession. The climate is often adversarial, many of the
cases are cast in masculine terms, and, until recently, law school classes
were still addressed occasionally as "gentlemen."

The image of the learned gentleman lingers in the Ontario legal profession. It is perpetuated in the faces of founding fathers on the walls of
Ontario's law schools and in the corridors of the Law Society of Upper
Canada. To some extent, partners in the large law firms lining Bay Street
in Toronto and senior members of the judiciary still belong to a prestigious gentlemen's club where masculine values prevail in spite of the rapid
influx of women.

The woman cited earlier is in many ways unique. Very few of the women
in this study can lay claim to such prestigious roots. In fact, they are a
disparate group, the daughters of middle-class families or one generation

removed from their immigrant roots. Some of them moved quickly through the educational system while others entered law school as mature students. A few of them began their working lives as secretaries or law clerks or nurses, several of them were housewives in a previous life, and some of them were the first members of their families to attend university. One woman said that when she called the Ministry of Education to inquire about law school she was greeted by derisive laughter. Another woman was told by a guidance counsellor that she would make a good farmer's wife.[4] The miracle lies in the fact that they persisted in spite of such rude treatment. They are definitely not members of an exclusive group born into affluence, but, together, they provide a portrait of the changing face of the legal profession in Ontario.

I began contacting them when the study was in its formative stages, late in 1993. By the time it was completed in 2002, 110 women practising law throughout the province of Ontario had taken the time to sit down and talk to us, sharing their thoughts about their professional and private lives. Since they typified the first generation of women in a profession that had been male-dominated for centuries, their views were critical to an understanding of women's experiences as lawyers. Why did they choose law in the first place? How did they view their law school and articling experiences? How had their careers taken shape in light of their family and community interests? What were their achievements and disappointments? Would they choose law if they had a chance to start over or would they encourage their daughters to pursue legal careers? These were some of my concerns in the initial design of the study, but the interview process opened up many more topics, providing a rich store of anecdotes and opinions about life in the legal profession.

Why are their stories important? Taken together, these women are not exceptional. They represent a broad cross-section of ages and social backgrounds, many of them have children and, like other groups of women, they vary in terms of their marital status, race, ethnicity, sexual orientation, and other distinguishing characteristics. In fact, their heterogeneity makes them ideal candidates for research as law societies and bar associations work to accommodate the needs and interests of increasingly diverse groups of new lawyers. Descriptions of their lives are also valuable for women contemplating legal careers because, in spite of rosy media accounts, women face unique challenges within the profession, particularly if they add parenting responsibilities to their load of legal duties.[5]

Do their lives resemble those of women in other male-dominated professions? In many ways they do. Most of the women in these professions have acquired specialized training, enhanced occupational prestige, and the potential to generate high earnings. The money and career advancement, however, are often contingent on a willingness to work exceptionally long hours, and recent findings suggest that these patterns are exacerbated by rising expectations for performance in law, academia, and senior managerial ranks. Women in these professions often postpone marriage and family in the pursuit of career goals such as tenure, executive positions, or partnership status. Women in corporate management or medical practice sometimes have access to flexible working hours, but permanent part-time work or extended periods of leave are usually seen as barriers to professional advancement. Generally, women with children register high levels of work-family conflict, and their career progress lags in comparison with the achievements of childless women and men. Even though they may be productive, committed professionals, organizational and professional norms assign them second-class status.[6] Women now enter the professions in greater numbers than men, but a two-tiered profile is evident: men are more likely to advance to senior, decision-making levels while women often remain in the lower ranks, doing the diligent day-to-day work.[7]

Although these patterns are evident in male-dominated professions generally, they are particularly pronounced in the practice of law where time-keeping is meticulous. Individual practitioners record their billable hours in six-minute segments, and, if they work in large firms, they are expected to meet demanding standards for performance. Many of these firms have gradually increased their requirements, establishing time norms that have slowly seeped into other types of practice.[8] Private law firms are businesses driven by profits, so the most promising lawyers are also expected to be rainmakers, seeking out new clients and keeping in touch with old ones. Since collegiality is important, many of the informal aspects of legal practice require unlimited amounts of time for networking, both on and off the job. Women with families often lack this kind of free time because their tightly drawn schedules include family activities and household organization. They are typically very efficient workers, committed to their professional careers, but because most senior partners violate accepted time norms, they view motherhood as a professional liability.[9]

These women constitute a first wave – an avant-garde – in a profession designed by men, for men, and grounded in the assumption that they can be released from family commitments at will. Their encounters with this culture and their strategies for dealing with multiple demands on their time provide some answers and raise more questions about the kinds of time stresses that have become extreme in the lives of many Canadian women. In law, as in other elite professions, many policy-makers are still wedded to the idea that men should develop their careers while women deal with family caregiving. These norms prevail in Canadian society generally, even though most women with young families are employed outside the home. Since they are more pronounced in pressure-cooker environments such as legal practice, studies such as this one highlight these results and suggest ways of addressing work-family conflict in general. Although women are the focus of my study, families also stand to benefit from the ideas generated by this kind of research. It is part of a much larger movement to resolve work-family issues in Canada, the United States, and other industrialized countries.[10]

Bar Codes

Civil and criminal codes are the most obvious cornerstones of legal doctrine, a dynamic body of knowledge that promotes justice and provides the underpinnings for social order. However, codes extend into every corner of legal practice. The profession is built around written codes of conduct – expectations for the fair treatment of clients and appropriate moral behaviours. Lawyers who fail to meet these standards are summoned before their respective law societies and, in some cases, disbarred from practice because they are deemed to have violated the profession's code of honour. In many ways, legal prose is expressed in code, presented in arcane language or Latin terms that are relevant only in the context of case law.[11] Dress codes are also part of the legal experience, particularly in the courts of Commonwealth countries; legal robes are considered *de rigueur*, providing an established standard of dress and emphasizing status differences among judges and lawyers. These kinds of codes are formalized in rules and laws grounded in expectations for compliance, on the part of both professional practitioners and other members of society. The gowned lawyer represents legal expertise but other coded meanings can remain hidden from the general public. The women in this study have been instrumental in drawing our attention to some of these codes. Their anecdotes and reactions have exposed less obvious facets of legal practice, giving me an opportunity to examine the impact of these customs on their professional and personal lives.

In spite of the presence of codes, informal norms can evolve over time, leading to patterns of behaviour apparent only to members of the inner circle. Legal education, the practice of law, and day-to-day courtroom activities are replete with norms that are confusing for neophytes. These cultural contradictions reflect a set of unwritten codes that can be particularly problematic for women (expectations about hours on the job, access to the best files, informal meetings, or unspoken views about pregnancy and childbirth). These norms become codes in themselves, guarded by established members of the profession and open only to persistent outsiders who succeed in deciphering the signals. Women who either fail to crack the codes or choose to ignore them can remain committed members of the bar but they are distanced from the powerful centres of legal practice. This study highlights powerful connections between the formal codes and those that sometimes escape detection, shedding light on the ways in which women's legal careers hinge on their access to social and cultural capital.

Central Themes in This Study

The interviews for this study ranged across landscapes that I had not imagined when I embarked on the venture. On a bleak January day in 1994, I walked into a small law office in downtown Toronto and found a young criminal lawyer struggling to keep her practice alive. As we talked, she described her anxieties about court appearances and told me about the relief she experienced when she traded her professional dress for casual clothes at the end of a working day. She had raised a subject that I had not considered relevant to the study – the importance of professional clothing in projecting an image. When she mentioned her feelings of inadequacy under the cover of her legal robes, images of Portia flooded through my mind, and I began to wonder if women, more than men, needed the protection of robes to convince others of their value as lawyers.

As a result of this conversation, Portia's story became increasingly important to my understanding of women's experiences in the profession. The robes convey professional status, leading the women, like Portia, down a path to professional legitimacy.[12] As a result, Portia assumes centre stage in Chapter 2, and her brief flirtation with the law provides a pivotal organizing metaphor for the book.[13] The image of a small, "unlessoned" girl emerging from the cocoon of femininity as a learned doctor of laws through the simple act of robing is a powerful one. In spite of her youth and her lack of legal training, Portia still serves as a convincing role model for women entering the legal profession. Her story has inspired feminist legal scholars and, for some, she has assumed iconic proportions.[14]

The gowned lawyer has always been a key player in the drama of the courtroom, projecting an image of professional credibility that sets him apart from clerks, clients, and other courtroom functionaries. The act of robing is heavy with the weight of symbolism and tradition, born of a patriarchal culture. Legal robes are also part of a larger history. Like religious dress, they were initially designed for men but they are curiously androgynous. As Margaret Thornton has observed, in any other setting they would constitute women's dress but, paradoxically, they would be devoid of authority.[15]

Women who enter law are caught between these competing visions – the unlessoned girl and the respected professional gentleman. They cross the boundary between these two images when they robe for court, signalling to others that they are ready to do their job. They have acquired the knowledge and credentials they need to act as respected professionals, but they are relative newcomers in a historical sense. In this chapter, their accounts are anchored in a discussion of theories of the professions, stressing the importance of the specialized knowledge that distinguishes members of the legal profession and enables them to set exclusionary boundaries.

Until recently, women were targets of these exclusionary practices so the robes hold particular significance for them. They still face contradictory norms about appropriate professional dress, and so, like Portia, they run the risk of appearing "unruly," vaguely sexual, and potentially disruptive to the system. Michel Foucault's theories of disciplinary practices are relevant in this chapter, along with the suggestion that women must learn to tame themselves, to become docile, if they are to succeed in the practice of law. In spite of these lingering undercurrents, women report that their professional identity is enhanced when they wear the robes. Their self-confidence grows, but they feel the weight of their responsibility and deep inside they may feel a sense of confusion about their own identity. Many of the women in this study expressed mixed feelings about their robes, best summed up by a judge who said: "I like putting on my robes because I like – not – being me." The androgynous character of the robes can also lead to confusion. Women are used to wearing long, flowing garments, but the tight vest and white tabs are definitely masculine attire. These contradictions are discussed at some length in Chapter 2, casting light on the importance of professional dress in conveying legitimacy and the sometimes fragile face that members of a profession present to their clients and adversaries.

Portia's influence threads its way through successive chapters of the book, reminding readers that women in the legal profession never quite fit in. Like medieval and Renaissance women, hampered by the constraints of Salic Law, they remain, to some extent, impostors in a culture imbued with masculine values.[16] They encounter the norms of the legal culture when they enter law school and repeatedly throughout their careers – in everyday practice, in the courtroom, and in other encounters with the system generally. Traditionally, these institutions have been inhabited and controlled by men who spoke a common language. Many of them were the sons or grandsons of lawyers, and they moved easily in legal circles where the customs required no explanation. Women who lack these kinds of connections have been baffled by many of the practices they have encountered. In hindsight, they appear to have been incredibly naïve, but they were a pioneering group, understandably ignorant of the hidden assumptions and the *lingua franca* of legal practice.

Chapter 3 is devoted to a discussion and analysis of women's experiences in law school, opening with a description of Clara Brett Martin's attempts to gain entry to the profession. As the first woman in the British Commonwealth to be accepted for legal training, she provided a strong model, but women in other jurisdictions faced even more formidable barriers. Since law schools reflect the views of legal scholars and practitioners alike, this chapter also incorporates a discussion of legal culture and the potential for shifting attitudes and practices in response to the entry of women. Although their numbers have increased dramatically in recent years, the profession remains resistant to women's requests for a more inclusive approach to legal affairs. The positive effects of feminization will only be manifested when courses such as family and employment equity law are elevated in status, and law firms adjust their focus to accommodate lawyers' needs for family time. Without progress in these areas, occupational segregation will become more entrenched and existing gender-based disparities in earnings will continue to grow. These disparities are rooted in informal patterns that favour lawyers without ongoing family responsibilities – time for forging client networks, developing collegial relationships, and generally building a profile of loyalty to the firm. Pierre Bourdieu's theories of social and cultural capital provide conceptual guidelines here, identifying the subtle ways in which women are often excluded from professional circles.[17]

Portia's example is evident again in a discussion of women's styles of practice, linking their purported commitment to an "ethic of care" to her concern for mercy in the administration of justice. The debate about Carol Gilligan's "differences" hypothesis generates a battery of questions about accepted stores of professional knowledge and their apparent failure to address the interests of many women students.[18] These concerns set the stage for a description of changes in legal training in Ontario over the past two hundred years, taking note of differing opinions about the balance between theory and practical knowledge and accepted methods of instruction.

Women's entry to law school represents the most recent event in a chronology marked by dissent. It is an important part of the historical record because feminist critiques of the system represent a challenge to long-standing educational practices and visions of the law itself.[19] From the beginning, the legal profession has incorporated an elitist bias. Ontario farmers' sons with professional ambitions rarely became powerful urban barristers, black lawyers were uncommon, and the profession was riddled with anti-Semitism.[20]

On a contemporary note, I examine the experiences of women in law school, comparing the recollections of the women in this study with widespread reports of alienation and silencing that have marked the law school years for women in large American universities. Since feminist issues can sometimes cloud the effects of less obvious inequities, Chapter 3 also includes a brief discussion of the barriers that can distance women from each other – social class, colour, sexual orientation, and physical disabilities. These factors influence a woman's law school options, her treatment by professors and peers, and her legal practice. The chapter concludes with a glimpse of the future – the inequities that persist in the timed escalation of tuition fees and the paths to career success offered by the most prestigious schools. Race, ethnicity, and social background are powerful mediators in this process, and they deserve in-depth treatment. I regret that this book does not include this kind of focus, but, given the amount of space devoted to gender inequities in the profession, the addition of a single chapter dealing with racial issues would constitute a disservice to racially marginalized groups. Other authors have produced first-rate work in this area, and the literature will be enhanced by future studies of the effects of race on lawyers' lives.[21]

Many women report that discriminatory practices follow them into legal practice and are heightened with the births of their children because constraints on their time prevent them from taking part in many of the less formal aspects of practice. Consequently, the theme of time is a strong feature in this book. Chapters 4 and 5 deal with their daily routines and the ways in which they view their temporal commitments. The experiences of these women are also fundamental to an understanding of time pressures at broad societal levels in Canada, the United States, and across many international borders. When women began moving into the labour force in significant numbers during the 1960s, the ideal North American family was headed by a male breadwinner, and his back-up support came from a homemaking wife. A nostalgic vision of this family ideal has persisted in spite of dramatic changes in divorce rates, family patterns, and women's levels of participation in the paid labour force. The impact of these broad social patterns on the lives of busy families has emerged slowly, beginning with women's reactions to the pressures of their overlapping roles and extending to include the time stresses affecting all family members. Scholarly work in this area has developed from a slow trickle of articles and an occasional book in the mid-1980s to a deluge of publications covering all aspects of the work-family connection. Governments and private foundations in all industrialized countries have now committed massive amounts of funding to research dealing with the crisis in family time pressures.[22]

Time-use scholars debate long-term trends in working hours, but all agree that the burden of time stress is heavier for some groups than for others. Men still work longer hours than women on average, but parents of young children experience the most extreme time crunch.[23] Without exception, researchers report that the majority of women take responsibility for the "second shift" at home, in many cases stretching their precious time to the breaking point.[24] These trends, discussed in more detail in Chapter 4, are used to introduce a discussion of time crunch stress in the lives of women lawyers. Well-educated professionals are among those groups working the longest hours so the women in this study are a valuable target group for research on time. If they have children, they are even more likely to feel extreme stress. Until women began to enter the profession in significant numbers, many men practised law secure in the knowledge that their wives would manage their busy households and support them in their career ambitions. Law was seen as a two-person career so these patterns laid the groundwork for the "long hours culture" that came to define good legal practice. Most of the women in law lack this kind of support. In fact, many of them are responsible for family and household organization in addition to their legal duties, and, if they are single parents, the load becomes even more burdensome. Their strategies for dealing with time pressures are important because they can provide models for new generations of professional women, they can help to reshape the temporal organization of law firms and courts, and they can alert policy-makers in general to problems that arise when women (and men) work excessive hours.

Chapter 4 summarizes findings from a quantitative analysis of the lawyers' scores on an index of time crunch, modelled on questions from Statistics Canada's General Social Surveys on Time Use. Their scores are compared with those of other employed women, with a focus on the lawyers who reported the highest levels of time crunch stress. Recurring themes from their interviews are dovetailed with items from the index, sharpening our image of the most common temporal problems in their lives – lack of time for family and friends, a tendency to cut back on their sleep, and constant stress in the face of overloaded schedules. The chapter ends on a positive note by turning to the stories of women who have managed to overcome some of their time-related stress.

Chapter 5 examines the multidimensional nature of time in women's lives, opening with a critique of the dualistic theories that draw clear conceptual lines between quantitative clock time and the cyclical patterns often identified as women's time. Once again, Bourdieu's theories are relevant. Social capital is a precious resource, providing access to the informal contacts and networks necessary for successful legal practice, but time itself is also a critical part of social capital.[25] Without ready access to unclaimed time, women are often left in the margins, professionally speaking, because their tightly scheduled family commitments must be met. The metaphor of the robes can also be invoked to describe these patterns: to the casual observer, women appear to be on equal footing with their male colleagues but, without adequate time, they never quite reach performance expectations. Some senior partners see women with small children as akin to Portia, playing at practice but not entirely committed to the profession.

Feminist theories frame my discussion of time in the lives of the lawyers in this study by identifying the temporal conflicts inherent in the organization of their public and private lives. Julia Kristeva's glorification of motherhood provides a starting point for this discussion, sparking a debate about the inconsistencies between women's cyclical time and the demands of a capitalist economy. Recent feminists also wrestle with gendered labels used to describe different kinds of time, concluding that terms such as "masculine" and "feminine" time are distortions viewed through a normative lens. When the discussion turns to the realities of women's lives, scholars readily acknowledge the complex workings of women's daily time commitments, but the most telling comment lies in Karin Jurczyk's observation that women remain, sadly, "in-between times," powerless to change either family times or professional schedules.[26]

Qualitative material gleaned from the interviews is particularly enlightening in this chapter, confirming many of the patterns identified in these theoretical visions. Clock time competes with less structured time in the complex daily lives of these women and provides a continuous linear metric as they struggle to fill their quota of billable hours on the job. This chapter also documents the frustrations experienced by women who have attempted to reconcile the demands of motherhood with increased pressure to perform in law firms where partners fail to appreciate the importance of family time. Kristeva's idealized vision of motherhood is soured by the expectations of employers who see pregnancy as a liability and, in some cases, as an opportunity to replace a woman with someone they regard as more productive. This chapter also acknowledges the punishing hours worked by women without families. Several of them described the levels of commitment they maintained before being summarily dismissed or simply recognizing that the job had taken its toll in other ways.

Since attitudes and practices within the legal culture can affect the profiles of women's career paths, Chapter 6 centres on these issues – the subtle and not so subtle ways in which careers are modified, reshaped, and, occasionally, sabotaged. Like day-to-day patterns of activity, career paths also reflect visions of time, inviting theoretical representations that summon up a range of time-space metaphors. They can be strong, straight, upward bound, and linear or they can be twisted, broken, misshapen, and cyclical. Most economists would agree that the unbroken linear path represents the ideal career.[27] However, this career model is a stagnant reflection of men's careers in the mid-twentieth century, aptly described as part of an outdated "career mystique" that leaves no room for alternative career lines.[28]

It is true that many successful men have followed this kind of career trajectory and continue to do so, but women's careers are often quite different. Are they less valuable? Are they more realistic? Is there room for alternative models of career shaped by the interruptions that characterize the working lives of many women? If so, what are the implications of these new career paths for law and other professions? Are there men who would enjoy the freedom to pursue different careers? These are some of the questions that can introduce fresh perspectives, challenging the rigid "career regime" that has institutionalized the classic male career as the only way to organize a working life.[29]

Theoretical career models can be expanded to include patterns that deviate from the traditional linear path, particularly those that incorporate breaks for pregnancy and parental obligations. This vision casts careers in the context of a comprehensive *curriculum vitae*, providing a view of temporality across the life course that lends a new dimension to the employment-centred image of career. Creative scholars have proposed alternative career designs, but they are justifiably suspicious of current language. For example, the metaphor of balance suggests that family concerns deserve equal time with work, but it rests on the assumption that women will be responsible for balancing, leaving established career patterns intact.[30] These general concerns about career styles apply to a range of occupations, and they have recently received widespread attention in the scholarly literature.[31] They are particularly relevant in the legal profession because marked gender differences in advancement have been documented: women face multiple barriers as they proceed down the tenuous path to partnership.[32] To some extent, the successful ones adapt to the culture, fitting in with existing expectations for performance, but they are few in number.

In this chapter, I examine the career paths of a sub-sample of the lawyers in the study by visualizing them along a continuum, beginning with women whose careers best emulate the traditional model. From this benchmark, I examine the careers of women whose lives depart from the straightforward linear route, whether by choice or by chance. This strategy illustrates the effects of pregnancy, parenthood, illness, and other events on the careers of many women who have chosen to practise law and, perhaps, to leave the profession. Their image in the eyes of colleagues may be like Portia's fleeting legal career – a dalliance with the law that leaves them "unpracticed" at some level because they will never achieve complete career success, given their competing responsibilities.

In the concluding chapter, I have tried to pull together the strands of their lives to set their stories in a larger context. Clara Brett Martin gained entry to the profession a full century before we sat down to interview our group of women, at a time when women in Canada constituted a mere 16 percent of the paid labour force.[33] Middle-class women were expected to eschew higher education, marry well, and leave the business of making money to their husbands. In this kind of climate, the prospect of divorce was unthinkable. In many respects, the women in this study inhabit a different world and the rate of change can only accelerate as communications technologies advance and global forces mark the opening of the new millennium. It is my hope that the experiences of the women in this study will provide some initial clues to the changing norms and patterns that lie ahead.

Research Design and Methodology
We listened with fascination to the women in this study as they told their stories, one by one, in the first person singular.[34] The tapes contain laughter, tears, thoughtful pauses, the background chatter of children, and, in one case, the contented purr of a nursing baby. They are much more personal and revealing than the blended voices that shape the statistical generalizations of survey analysis. However, because they sometimes expose women's

fears and frustrations, they raise issues of privacy and anonymity. They are therefore grounded in trust, and I have promised the women that their identities will remain hidden.[35] I think the interviews provide a unique window into the lives of the women who generously agreed to take part in the study. They are located in cities and towns across Ontario and, with one or two exceptions, they were all practising law when we approached them for their initial interviews.

The interview period stretched from January 1994 to August 2002, incorporating two tape-recorded interviews with the majority of the women in the study. The interviews were forty-five minutes long on average, and they were supplemented by a questionnaire recording information about each lawyer's family background, education, year of call to the bar, practice type, family responsibilities, and responses to time pressures. The questionnaires used in the follow-up interviews were shorter but were designed to record changes in the women's legal careers and family arrangements over a four-year period. Most of the women are still acting as lawyers or judges, but thirteen of them have left the profession: one woman has retired and another woman died recently. The others have taken breaks to be with their families or have moved into different fields of work. The remaining women dream of new pursuits as they go about their legal duties. As the study drew to a close, I contacted as many of the women as I could reach, either by e-mail or letter, asking for an update on their lives. Many of them responded, and I have made repeated attempts to find the remaining women but several of them have vanished. The findings from these contacts are summarized in the appendix ("Where Are They Now?").

Plans for the original study were modest. I began the sampling process late in 1993 with lists of Toronto lawyers, provided by two women practising law in the city.[36] My intent was to generate a small quota sample of women, reflecting various types of practice. The initial list developed into a referral sample augmented by contacts provided by some of the women in the study. I interviewed thirty women in the Toronto area in 1994 and repeated the process with an additional thirty women in London two years later, using similar sampling techniques. The profile of the London sample was quite different from the distribution of practice types in the Toronto sample, but it was an accurate reflection of women's patterns. The Toronto women tended to specialize in criminal, corporate, and tax law, while women in London were over-represented in family law practice.[37]

In 1998, the study became much broader in scope when I received funding from the Social Sciences and Humanities Research Council of Canada. With the help of several research assistants, I was able to re-interview the original sixty women and add fifty more women from communities across the province. Using a stratified random sample drawn from the Law Society's membership list, we began by contacting women from suburban Toronto and Ottawa because large percentages of lawyers practise in these two regions. We eventually travelled north as far as Kirkland Lake and criss-crossed the province from Windsor and Lake Huron on the west to Kingston on the east, interviewing women of all ages and practice types, representing a broad range of racial and ethnic backgrounds.[38] Over a six-year period four of the research assistants accompanied me to the interview sites, and, as they gained confidence, each one in turn assumed respon-sibility for some of the interviews. I am grateful that I had a chance to meet and interview almost all of the women in the study at least once be-cause the memories of these visits have made the writing process enjoy-able and, I hope, have contributed to the authenticity of my account. I have also listened to the tapes many times, sometimes laughing out loud or feeling their sadness as I commuted to and from the university.

The first sixty interviews were transcribed and entered into an Ethno-graph program for a qualitative analysis.[39] However, after several years of interviewing, we had amassed transcriptions of approximately two hun-dred interviews and a corresponding bank of quantitative data so we turned to more refined analytical tools. A very complicated NUD*IST qual-itative program yielded blocks of information organized by topic, and these topics were used in turn to cross-reference the qualitative findings with SPSS data sets incorporating the findings from the questionnaire data.[40]

People sometimes ask why men were not included in this study. In fact, I chose to interview women because, without doubt, their experiences dif-fer from those of most men engaged in the practice of law. Some of these women are confused by the teaching methods employed in law schools, and women in general are less likely to find role models or mentors than their male peers.[41] If they choose to combine parenthood with legal prac-tice, they face problems that are beyond the comprehension of many men.[42] My goals were not well defined when I began the study, but I knew that I wanted to link the everyday experiences of women lawyers with their long-term career patterns. I also wanted to see if the entry of women to the legal profession had had a profound impact on the values and cus-toms of the profession. They are a heterogeneous group and their responses were varied but together they describe experiences that paint a rich canvas portraying the complexity of their lives and their views of the profession.

Have women as a group effected change in the teaching and practice of law? Perhaps, but they are still pioneers in uncertain territory. This first wave of women has already left its imprint on law schools, in the courts, and on the informal practices prevailing in law offices. However, they inhabit a world where social norms are in flux – both within the legal community and in the larger society. We may have to look to their daugh-ters and granddaughters for evidence of profound change in a profession bound by centuries of masculine influence.

2

"The Portia of Our Chambers": Voice, Robes, and Reputation

> *Portia.* You see me, Lord Bassanio, where I stand
> Such as I am ...
> ... But the full sum of me
> Is sum of something – which, to term in gross,
> Is an unlessoned girl, unschooled, unpracticed;
> Happy in this, she is not yet so old
> But she may learn; happier than this,
> She is not bred so dull that she can learn;
> Happiest of all, is that her gentle spirit
> Commits itself to yours to be directed,
> As from her lord, her governor, her king.[1]

When Shakespeare produced *The Merchant of Venice* at the turn of the seventeenth century, he chose Portia, a young wealthy heiress as one of the key figures in the plot.[2] As the play opens, Portia's father has just died, leaving instructions for the selection of a husband to manage her fortune. The successful suitor, Bassanio, borrows money from his friend Antonio to woo Portia, but Antonio in turn is forced to borrow the money from Shylock, the moneylender. Shylock has agreed to forego interest on the loan, but, if the money is not repaid within three months, he claims the right to cut off a pound of Antonio's flesh. When Antonio defaults on the loan, Shylock demands his pound of flesh but Portia intervenes, plotting in secret to disguise herself as Balthasar, a respected doctor of laws. Her waiting woman, Nerissa, disguised as a clerk, produces a letter from Portia's cousin, Bellario, legitimizing her legal credentials. A hearing is scheduled to resolve the dispute, and Portia, in the role of judge, provides a brilliant solution: "Therefore prepare ye to cut off the flesh. Shed thou no blood, nor cut thou less nor more but just a pound of flesh. If thou tak'st more or less ... Thou diest and all thy goods are confiscate."[3]

Why is Portia's story relevant to a study of women lawyers late in the twentieth century? She provides a fitting role model because, as many scholars have noted, she is one of Shakespeare's strongest women. In Alice Arnott Oppen's words, "Portia is a twentieth-century representation of what we wish to believe women are. Finding her in Elizabethan Shakespeare, still transmitting beams of wisdom, power and gentleness after four hundred years, is a feminist critic's ideal and temptation."[4] She has wealth and property, confidence, intelligence, cunning, and, with some clever manipulation, access to learning.[5] When she makes her first appearance in the play, she presents herself as diminutive and tired, weighed down by the burden of her father's deathbed order. We see a very submissive Portia, prepared to give over her inheritance to Bassanio and comply with all his wishes, but this Portia is part of a larger masquerade in the drama that will ultimately be played out in the courtroom. It is this new, stronger Portia who serves as a model for women in law.

The process of transformation itself may also resonate with contemporary women lawyers. Portia's metamorphosis from an apparently fragile, "unlessoned" girl to a wise, ostensibly male, judge is a fascinating progression, but some Shakespearean scholars suggest that her brilliance in the courtroom scene represents the true Portia, overriding the modest claim that she is "unschooled" and "unlessoned."[6] Others suggest that she understands her power very well because, in spite of her apparent subservience to Bassanio, she reminds her audience that she has enjoyed the status of managing a large household.[7] I think that Shakespeare deliberately casts her as a meek, submissive woman before he surprises us with a very different Portia in the court scene. She is "unlessoned," "unschooled," and "unpracticed" in the conventional sense, but she assures us that she has the potential to learn the ways of married life. This statement assumes new meaning when we consider her role in the courtroom and her command of legal reasoning. The use of the word "unpracticed" suggests sexual innocence, but it is also relevant to her role as a lawyer. Portia's apparently contradictory comments reflect her position in a society where fathers held absolute authority over their families and marriage was the only vehicle that could remove a daughter from her father's legal control, his *patria postestas*.[8] However, some social historians suggest that privileged Venetian women such as Portia enjoyed much more financial independence than their English counterparts because, although fathers had the right to arrange their daughters' marriages, daughters could exercise their right of refusal.[9] Portia may be presented as an obedient model for Elizabethan women when she honours her dead father's wishes in the choice of a husband. If this is so, Shakespeare defies the norms of Elizabethan society by unleashing a very strong Portia in the ensuing scenes.

Whatever the reasoning, Portia has endured as a symbol of professional success for women lawyers, and references to her abound, both in scholarly writings and in popular fiction. As Daniel Kornstein has observed:

> Portia defies the codes of her milieu by assuming a commanding position of authority and respect as a lawyer and judge in a man's world. She is skillful, witty and learned ... Portia's name has become synonymous with eloquence and wisdom in a female attorney or judge. John Mortimer, the English lawyer and writer, has his fictional London barrister,

Horace Rumpole of the Bailey, often refer admiringly to his female colleague Phillida Trant as "the Portia of our chambers." And at least one
colleague on the [US] Supreme Court has complimented Justice Sandra
Day O'Connor – She Who Really Must Be Obeyed – as "the Portia that
now graces our court."[10]

Portia's story held widespread appeal for feminist scholars interested in
women's impact on the legal profession because her apparent concern for
mercy suggests that women have the potential to bring a more caring
perspective to the practice of law.[11] Critics of essential feminism have
rejected many of these earlier arguments, disputing the validity of the so-
called "Portia myth" and asserting that Portia was little more than a mouth-
piece for the patriarchal legal order of her time. Her role, according to
Ian Ward, was not to bring a woman's vision to the legal arena but to appear
as a "desexed Portia," stabilizing a situation that was highly charged with
emotion.[12] More recently, Erika Rackley has refuted these views, elevating
Portia to iconic levels. Her story can be understood as a myth, but, according to Rackley, Portia is not simply a model to be emulated or an object
to be admired. She serves instead as a window, illuminating the path to
more humane ways of administering justice.[13]

How strong are the parallels between Portia and women practising law
four hundred years later? At first glance, the links appear tenuous because
Portia was not a lawyer, the story of her deception is an amusing but unbelievable tale, and few women today would present themselves in such
a coy, subservient way, even in jest. However, it is the reference to schooling and practice that makes her speech an intriguing one. Women embark-
ing on legal careers are certainly not "unlessoned" or "unschooled," but
they do lack the practice that only years of experience can provide. They
have acquired theoretical knowledge and learned the complex paths of
legal reasoning, but they must first convince themselves and others that
they are legitimate members of the profession. Like Portia, they may need
to don the robes to demonstrate that they can translate their educational
credentials into professional acumen.

Credentials such as degrees, diplomas, and certificates, which are often
displayed prominently, are the most obvious indicators of professional
status, but formal dress, technical language, authoritative manner, prestigious office space, and the cultivation of professional reputations are
also considered necessary to gain the respect of colleagues and foster the
trust of clients.[14] Women's access to these symbols has been constrained
by their delayed entry into the most prestigious professions. Many of these
professions took root during the nineteenth century when scientific knowledge was prized by the developing capitalist world, but women's knowledge, traditionally confined to the practicalities of domestic life, was lost

in the tide of scientific discovery and formal logic. As the market for knowledge and expertise expanded, the professions developed as male-dominated institutions, making it difficult for women to gain entry.

These historical processes provide the backdrop for this chapter, illustrating the ways in which women have been excluded from the professions through their lack of access to the knowledge and credentials deemed necessary for professional status.[15] This discussion leads logically to an examination of women's experience in the practice of law, emphasizing the critical role of professional knowledge and, more importantly, its outward manifestations in establishing them as credible members of the profession. Academic credentials on their own are not a guarantee of professional acceptance; a successful lawyer must also incorporate less obvious signals of competence in her professional persona. Since clothing is critical in conveying legitimacy, legal robes are mantles of professionalism that help to authenticate women as convincing interpreters of legal theory in the courtroom.

Portia's lasting image is, in many ways, reflected in the comments of the women in this study, particularly in their views of the legal robes as signals of their competence as defence lawyers, prosecutors, or judges. By examining the effects of the robes in altering their sense of identity, we can see that both their professional legitimacy and their personal confidence are enhanced by the robing experience. These changes in identity are apparent throughout their careers: the mixture of pride and uncertainty that they felt when they robed for graduation ceremonies or on first entering the courtroom surfaces in the lingering doubts, the awareness of responsibility, and the feelings of inadequacy that they occasionally feel as experienced lawyers. Their views of the courtroom environment are also relevant – their psychological preparation for its adversarial culture, their perceptions of the courtroom as theatre, the importance of robes to their clients, and the dignity inherent in the rituals of the court. Underlying this analysis is the idea that women lawyers operate in an unfamiliar culture because the robes are part of a long patriarchal tradition. They were designed for men, but women, as relative newcomers to the profession of law, often rely on them to enhance their credibility within the profession.[16] Of course, there are always dissenters within the ranks. Some of the women in this study expressed distaste and, at times, contempt for an archaic system of justice, seeing the robes as part of the charade. Theirs is a minority voice, but it is an important part of the completed picture.

Professional Knowledge and Exclusionary Tactics

Rational, formalized, scientific knowledge provides the epistemological base for the professions, and the legal profession has depended on this kind of knowledge to confirm its legitimacy since its inception.[17] Lawyers draw on both theoretical and practical knowledge throughout their careers to demonstrate the expertise that sets them apart from other occupational groups, but they must also convince their clients and colleagues that their knowledge is unique.[18] Early theories represented the professions as ideal-types with such socially functional traits as theoretical knowledge, autonomy, altruism, and authority over clients.[19] These theories provided a useful classification scheme for professional groups, but they ignored the dysfunctional aspects of professional organization, prompting more recent theorists to focus on the power wielded by many professions.[20] Magali Sarfatti Larson, for example, argues that professions create and control markets for their expertise by translating their specialized abstract knowledge and skills into social and economic rewards. Professions are interest groups engaged in competition for control of the market, relying on their knowledge and qualifications to generate both earnings and prestige. If they can maintain a scarcity of specialized knowledge, then they can garner a monopoly of both expertise and status.[21] Since the professional "product" is intangible, the success of professions rests on the trust of those requiring their services. According to Keith Macdonald, "[T]he professional's possession of knowledge and expertise can be warranted by diplomas, certificates and degrees, but only up to a point. Thereafter, trust becomes extremely important and *trust will be accorded to those whose outward appearance and manner fits in with the socially accepted standards of repute and respectability*."[22]

A major transformation of knowledge occurred between the fifteenth and seventeenth centuries. With the dawn of the Enlightenment, societies had become much more complex and knowledge had developed as an empirical, value-free alternative to the morally sanctioned knowledge of earlier times. This new knowledge was both abstract and utilitarian. Where previous forms of knowledge had been practical, rational knowledge gave people the tools to translate abstract ideas into applied areas and develop specialized areas of expertise, laying the groundwork for the modern professions.[23]

More recently, Eliot Freidson has proposed a "third logic" as the foundation for a generalized ideal-typical model of professionalism, arguing that professionalism thrives on the belief that some kinds of work require specialized training and experience that cannot be standardized. Freidson contrasts the "discretionary specialization" of the professions with the "mechanical specialization" of less skilled work, claiming special status for discretionary specialization because it involves the exercise of discretionary judgment with each new task. According to Freidson, this kind of specialization is believed to rest on a body of knowledge acquired through special training.[24] He contends that members of a profession control their own work because their access to theoretical knowledge and its attendant skills elevates them to a privileged position:

> While skill is itself a kind of knowledge, namely, of the techniques for using or applying substantive knowledge, it is *facilitative* in character. Thus, to solve an abstract problem, one must not only have command over the body of knowledge connected with the problem, but also the rules of discourse (that is, logic, mathematics, rules of evidence), and the capacity or skill to employ them so as to arrive at an acceptable solution.[25]

Freidson also stresses the role played by credentials, both formal and informal, in gaining entry to the labour market. While prospective employers may be influenced by extraneous factors such as an applicant's gender or racial background, evidence of an appropriate educational background remains the most essential attribute for candidates seeking entry to the professions.[26] Max Weber recognized the importance of education when he characterized professional knowledge as certified and credentialed. In Weber's view, it was the key to professional exclusivity, allowing groups of people with common characteristics to pursue a collective interest by restricting access to their knowledge, education, credentials, and markets. Thus, by defining itself as a "legally privileged group," a profession is designed to exclude those whom its members see as "outsiders."[27] Weber's successors take the argument a step farther, seeing the professions as manipulative bodies, acting in deliberate, strategic ways to exclude individuals deemed to be unsuited to professional practice.[28]

Since many professions achieved formal status within eighteenth- and nineteenth-century patriarchal societies, women were routinely denied access to their ranks. The exclusion of women was based, at least in part, on the nature and value of their knowledge. Pre-industrial knowledge reflected roles and statuses associated with activities within specific social institutions, so women's domestic knowledge was valued. Defined as "status knowledge" in contrast to its masculine counterpart – scientific knowledge – it had definite practical utility.[29] As industrial society took shape, many women moved out of the home, becoming factory labourers or assistants to their husbands in small family businesses. Their domestic knowledge lost much of its former value and their attendant statuses faded. Within this patriarchal environment, men were free to act as entrepreneurs in the new knowledge-based occupations that would evolve into professions.[30] Scientific knowledge had become a valuable commodity in the market economy, but women's knowledge was often dismissed as folk wisdom. Their status was further degraded by exclusionary tactics that kept them from acquiring the education and training needed to gain professional status.[31]

The rise of the legal profession was based on these patterns of exclusion. Women were formally barred from legal training and practice in most industrialized countries until late in the nineteenth century, and informal methods of exclusion were exercised until well into the twentieth century.[32] It is only within the past twenty-five years that women have gained access to law schools on equal footing with men, but they now enter the profession armed with the necessary credentials in greater numbers than their male counterparts. Are they accepted by their colleagues, their clients, and court officials as competent, knowledgeable practitioners of their craft or are there other factors at work that prevent women from participating fully in the practice of law? The answers to these questions lie with the women themselves, their perceptions of the trust and respect accorded them by others and their views of themselves as effective professionals.

The wearing of legal robes sends an immediate signal to people who encounter a lawyer: they are a dramatic outward manifestation of professional identity and status. Do they help to establish a lawyer, especially a woman lawyer, as a credible practitioner? Since legal robes became an intriguing topic early in this study, I decided to focus on their significance in transforming women's identity in their own eyes and in the eyes of their audiences. Like Portia, many of them see the robes as widely recognized markers of their status as lawyers.

Portia's Influence

In spite of her modest presentation initially, Portia uses the disguise to convince her audience that she is a distinguished judge. When she divulges her plan to Nerissa, she assures her that their husbands will see them "in such a habit that they shall think we are accomplished with that we lack."[33] This statement raises the issue of deceit and suggests that Portia's knowledge may be counterfeit. Her professional status is temporary and her knowledge, like her disguise, is borrowed.[34] By modern standards, her credentials do lack substance. The letter from Bellario legitimates her knowledge all too easily, presenting her as a learned doctor of laws and convincing the court of her expertise. Only the most gullible observer would accept her legal credibility based on his assurance that "[w]e turned o'er many books together. He is furnished with my opinion which, bettered with his own learning, the greatness whereof I cannot enough commend."[35] However, the letter is necessary as a mechanism to further the plot because it confirms Portia's grasp of abstract legal knowledge, but astute readers will see a sexual theme behind her legal front. Lisa Jardine argues that, while Portia is portrayed as a very strong character, the play also reflects contradictory views of learned women that were characteristic of Renaissance society. Portia symbolizes the inflated power of a woman in a man's role when she makes use of her legal knowledge but there is an underlying view of her knowledge as "sexual knowingness" or unruliness.[36]

Cultural ambivalence towards learned women is less pronounced now but it has not disappeared entirely from the legal profession. Until recently, professors, mentors, and judges have been predominantly male, and the hierarchies of many large law firms still reflect a strong male presence in senior positions. In this environment, especially in formal settings, legal robes help women lawyers to convey the message that they are real lawyers who understand the proceedings in the courtroom and are capable of acting effectively. The disguise is crucial to the plot in Shakespeare's play, but is it as critical in the lives of contemporary women lawyers? The responses of the women in this study suggest that, like Portia, they gain confidence and a sense of their own authority when they appear in their robes.

Shakespeare occasionally dresses his heroines in men's clothing to turn the tables on convention. It is a mischievous conspiracy that he initiates with his audience, inviting us to examine the world from a different perspective. In this respect, Shakespeare is like the modern sociologist. For the actor involved in the disguise, however, the change in clothing can be a liberating experience. It offers her a chance to step outside her usual roles, to assume a new or enhanced identity, and to enjoy an altered view of reality. When Portia dons the legal robes, several interesting things happen. The most obvious effect is the concealing of her true identity as she moves from unlessoned girl to respected judge. Yet what is really happening here? Paula Berggren argues that a Shakespearean heroine in disguise moves beyond a simple submerging of her identity and is allowed to confirm her full identity by "activat[ing] the masculine resources with the normal feminine personality without negating her essential femininity."[37] She suggests that women cross these gender boundaries with relative ease. They are adept at making these adjustments because they can disguise their gender more easily than their male counterparts. Women also heighten their status by moving into men's roles. If Berggren's thesis is valid, then Portia's identity is enhanced in several ways: she retains her feminine side, she draws on masculine resources, and, by convincing the court that she possesses great learning, she becomes a very powerful figure when she dresses as Balthasar.

The act of changing gender identity also alters a woman's view of her sexuality, both in her own eyes and in the eyes of others. Portia in legal robes is no longer seen as a potential wife or mother. She has abandoned the world shaped by women's knowledge and entered the realm of abstract thought. By freeing herself from the constraints of women's clothing and putting on men's breeches, she enters a world where the expectations are quite different. Portia demonstrates her understanding of male sexuality when she boasts to Nerissa that she will swagger like a young man:

Portia. I'll ...
... turn two mincing steps
Into a manly stride, and speak of frays
Like a fine bragging youth, and tell quaint lies
How honourable ladies sought my love[38]

Despite this display of bravado, the theme of women's sexual unruliness is not far from the surface when Portia parades in men's clothing.[39] As the play draws to a close, she teases Bassanio about her true sexuality and her dual role:

Portia. Let not that doctor e'er come near my house.
... I'll not deny him anything that I have,
No, not my body nor my husband's bed.[40]

This passage emphasizes the sense of fun that characterizes Portia's new role. The adoption of male dress has given her entry to an arena where she would normally be excluded as a woman, and this experience is exhilarating. She can hide behind her disguise, playfully innocent and yet serious about the impact of her altered persona. She is intoxicated by her venture into the heady realm of abstract knowledge.[41] The gender transformation also gives her voice in a forum where she would not have been allowed to speak as a woman.[42] In a private conversation with Nerissa, she jokes about her "reed voice" and says that she will "speak between the change of man and boy."[43] Her observation implies that a male voice, however immature, still carries more weight than a woman's voice.

Portia's robing is a temporary transformation, allowing her to make a decision that is crucial to the outcome of the play. For career lawyers, however, the process of robing is a much more serious and permanent act. It marks a rite of passage from student to professional status, which is formalized by the call to the bar. Women who go on to pursue careers in litigation wear their robes for many of their court appearances. The robes are a permanent part of their professional image. However, these women share some of Portia's experiences when they robe for court. An examination of their responses to the robes is designed to shed some light on the effect of the robes in altering their identities.

Becoming Lawyers: The Transforming Power of the Robes

The first lawyer I interviewed told me that she always took off her working clothes and put on her sweats when she returned home at the end of a day in the office. She added that this made her "feel like a teenager again," suggesting that she had shed her legal image and her adult responsibilities along with her formal clothing. Her comment sparked my interest in the effects of clothing generally, and court robes in particular, so I asked her to tell me how she felt when she put on her robes. Her response was so intriguing that I decided to include a question about the robes wherever possible in the interviews that followed.[44] Her description of the robing process departs dramatically from the powerful image created by Portia, but it may reflect the divided nature of women in robes:

> It's stressful putting on those robes because you look important and you feel like you know something and I feel like I'm sixteen and I think: "I'm a fraud. This is – I don't know what I'm doing"... I'm still feeling like a teenager and even though I know more than I knew two years ago ... (Criminal lawyer, sole practice, called to the bar 1991)

The women in this study do not appear in disguise, but many of them, like Portia, experience an altered sense of identity, both in their own eyes and in the eyes of other people. When they put on their robes, they feel that their personal confidence is elevated and their professional legitimacy is strenghtened. These two processes reinforce each other as the women work to develop their own professional styles. One experienced lawyer summed up this process of mutual feedback eloquently:

> I like the robes and I hope they never get rid of them. Because, just like I think policemen should wear uniforms and people in the army should have theirs, I think there's a role for uniforms. It delineates – it kind of – *it helps you know who you are and it helps other people know who you are.* I don't like to see them used in an authoritative way and in a demeaning, disempowering way, but I think sometimes that it can help in that sense as in *when you put them on you feel like a lawyer.* And courtrooms are serious places and serious things happen in them and so people should feel a certain solemnity and a certain respect for what goes on and hopefully the people that are entrusted with those responsibilities will carry them out with that same sense of responsibility [italics added]. (Family lawyer, medium-size firm, called to the bar 1986)

She touches on a number of pertinent themes in this quote, both from the perspective of an individual lawyer and in the context of her larger professional world. In personal terms, she talks about the importance of robes in establishing "who you are" as a lawyer and in identifying you as different in some way from other people. The "uniform" is an important part of this process, not as a tool for intimidating other people but simply as a way of helping to establish your credibility. At a broader level, she acknowledges the importance of decorum in the courtroom, suggesting that legal robes convey a sense of dignity and responsibility by acting as powerful symbols of justice. Many of the women expressed similar views. Their most frequent response was that the robes made them feel like real lawyers, and some of them observed that the robes placed them on equal footing with their colleagues. They also reported a sense of personal empowerment that was especially important during their early years in practice when many of them appeared, like Portia, to be too small and too young to act effectively in the courtroom.[45] They recalled mixed feelings on first donning the robes, but, in general, they found that their personal and professional identities were enhanced. While a few women suggested that robes were intimidating symbols of an elitist system, the majority saw advantages to robing as a way of signalling competence in the courtroom and reinforcing the formality of the process.

Fiona Cownie identifies similar themes in her discussion of the importance of appropriate dress for legal academics, emphasizing the links between clothing, identity, and culture. Drawing on Entwistle's description of fashion and embodiment, she characterizes dress as "the visible envelope of the self ... a visual metaphor for identity ... structured by social forces and subject to social and moral pressures."[46] Like Cownie's academics, many of the women in my study rely on their robes as a cover that provides entrée, however tenuous or transparent, to the culture of the profession.[47]

Establishing Professional Identity

All lawyers need to develop a strong sense of their professional identity early in their careers, and the legal robes helped to provide this confidence for many of the women in this study. They used adjectives such as "proud," "strutting," and "special" to describe their initial reactions to the robing experience, but my favourite comment came from a very quiet woman who said spontaneously: "I thought I was hot shit!" Another woman told me that it was really fun when she wore her robes for the first time because she became a lawyer when she was working on a murder trial with senior counsel. She said: "[O]ne day I was sitting at counsel table not robed and the next day [the senior lawyer] introduced me and said: 'Ladies and gentlemen of the jury, you may notice that Ms. _____ has been sitting beside me this entire time and was not robed and today she's robed. She became a lawyer on Friday.'" A third woman remembered the sheer pride that she felt at her convocation, especially because she appeared in her father's robes. The image of a petite woman, cutting the hem off her father's robes to make them fit, is reminiscent of Portia in men's clothing:

> I feel proud, I feel very proud to be able to put on my gowns. In fact, the first time I ever did this was of course at graduation and I used my

dad's gown ... I actually had to have it shortened so I cut it and I felt absolutely wonderful in it. I really felt a connection with him, I felt proud of the profession and I still do when I wear it. And I think for all the talk of abolishing that, I think it would be a mistake because, although it is symbolic, I think it's a very important symbol.[48] (Corporate lawyer, large firm, called to the bar 1988)

This woman identified a strong personal link with her father, as both a loving parent and a respected practitioner, reinforcing the power of the masculine image in this characteristically patriarchal profession. Other women touched on issues of gender and size when they noted that the robes helped to compensate for their youthful appearance and their small size. Presentation of self is a central concern for many women, and they have found that qualities that are prized in other settings can work against them in the courtroom. The image of the little girl in adult clothing appears in the remarks of a young family lawyer who said: "As a first year lawyer I remember feeling, probably a little out of place. I think I probably look younger than I am so I had that ... I always called it my lawyer costume [thinking] that I would be transformed but I don't think that I did have a feeling of real transformation. I felt probably like I was in somebody else's shoes." Another woman said: "[M]y problem is I'm – is you look young and you're kind of cute and people don't necessarily take you seriously ... and you're small and everything else. But when I've got a robe on they know: 'Well, she's not a student and she's not a clerk. She's a lawyer!'" Her comments evoke images of the diminutive Portia as she makes her initial appearance before being transformed in the eyes of her audience. Her reference to being "cute" suggests that some people might see sexual appeal in a woman decked out in men's dress.[49]

These women are deservedly proud of their achievements in a profession committed to masculine values. As Margaret Thornton has noted, the law is grounded in rational thought so women often encounter contradictory norms when they first appear as legal practitioners. Faced with this dilemma, they learn that they are expected to retain their femininity but to dress conservatively, hiding any hint of sexuality that would be disruptive in the masculine world of law. Women who do not achieve this neutral balance are seen to be somehow "out of control" or, like Portia, to be guilty of behaving in an "unruly" fashion.[50] Thornton draws on the theme of the "disorderly woman" as evidence of firmly ingrained views of women as carnal creatures with the potential to disrupt the masculine social order.[51] This vision of woman as a threat has deep historical roots. Carole Pateman traces its modern origins to the rise of liberal individualism, particularly as it is explained in Rousseau's interpretation of contract theory. Women are by nature "disorderly," so they should not be allowed to disrupt public life. They are naturally subordinate to men and their rightful place is within the family, a justifiably patriarchal institution.[52]

Thornton sees the lingering effects of these views in expectations for the personal grooming of women lawyers – their clothes, their hair, and every other aspect of their bodies. Their dress codes are much more explicit and demanding than those for men in the legal profession, and, if not obeyed, they have serious implications for a woman's sense of authority. According to Thornton, "women lawyers must be marked through dress by both gender and authority. They must be clearly differentiated from men, while covering and subduing sexual characteristics, but, simultaneously, they must convey a modicum of authority. The suppression of the sexual and the presentation of the self as conventionally attractive and feminine are intended to appeal to clients."[53]

Perhaps it is for this reason that many of the women in this study recalled feelings of vague uneasiness when they wore their robes for the first time, saying they felt "kind of funny," "conspicuous," "out of place," "exposed," "scared," "stupid," or unsure of their roles. In contrast, some women seemed to find an entirely new identity when they put on their robes, which served either to mask their image of themselves or to enhance their status in the eyes of other people. One of them drew an interesting parallel between her robes and her make-up, seeing the process as a masquerade:

> I think you can hide behind them. I think you could have the same kind of – they could give you the same type of façade that putting a full face make-up on does. You know, sometimes when you really are going out somewhere, you'll do the whole face make-up thing and you can actually – I mean – I can remember in younger years where the more make-up I put on – it was almost like it wasn't me there ... And I think the robes could do the same thing. (Tax lawyer, small firm, called to the bar 1991)

Her use of the make-up analogy describes a stereotypically feminine act, one that signifies a rite of passage from childhood to adult status. It also raises images of a woman's body as an "ornamented surface," subjected to the discipline of cosmetic control.[54] Both Sandra Lee Bartky and Margaret Thornton pursue this theme, invoking Foucault's theories of disciplinary practices in the lives of women who learn to be docile and to submit to the rigours of transformation in law school, in legal practice, or in any other sphere where men hold the levers of power. Bartky searches widely for the source of this disciplinary power behind women's feminine bodies, concluding that it is "everywhere" and "nowhere."[55] It is not limited to the women who choose to practise law, but they are at risk simply because they are women.

When the woman in the earlier quotation said "it's almost like it wasn't me there," she appeared to have erased her image of herself and replaced it with the lawyer's presence. A second woman expressed similar misgivings about her real identity when she said emphatically: "I like putting on my robes because I like *not – being me –* believe it or not." She went on to say that she feels like a little girl (using the diminutive of her name several times) until she puts on her robes and added: "When I put my robes on I ... I feel like I'm Ms. _____ and I *know* I can do my job ... *I like being robed. I like it!* ... I've never liked being described as 'the one who looks like a cheerleader, the bouncy blonde' so I would far rather dress this way and look less like a bouncy blonde." Like Portia, she has left behind the little girl in favour of the wise counsel. Her rejection of the "bouncy blonde" look suggests that she has found a sense of authority by dressing in a manner that is similar to that of her male peers.

Professional identity is such a powerful concept that people who leave the profession may experience a period of confusion. This process can be especially problematic for women who feel caught between their professional and parenting identities. One woman talked candidly about the anguish she felt when she left legal practice almost twenty years after being called to the bar: "For weeks I wouldn't go outside because I didn't know who I was. I was afraid of seeing people who might ask me what I was doing or how was work. I wasn't 'Claire-downtown-lawyer' anymore, nor was I 'Claire-superb-stay-at-home-mom' like the other moms. I was just Claire. At first I hated going to pick the kids up at school because I didn't know what to say to people. I was so embarrassed and ashamed!"[56]

Real Lawyers

Women who appear regularly in court count on their robes to heighten their confidence as practising members of the profession, sending a signal that they have become "real lawyers." Even the most experienced women in the study confirmed the power of the robes in this respect. One of them recalled her early reservations about her professional competence but concluded that several years of practice had helped her to overcome most of her concerns as she adapted to the culture of the courthouse. Her comments suggest that she has attempted to measure up to a prevailing masculine ideal:

Quite apart from what you look like, are you a real lawyer or not? I mean you've got all these people down at the courthouse, male and female, though predominantly male, that have been practising for umpteen thousand years and they do all of these things so easily and they know all the ins and outs and the way it works and you feel like: "Oh my god, I don't know how to do that!" (Family lawyer, small firm, called to the bar 1993)

The process of becoming a real lawyer suggests that neophytes must learn to fit in visually with their colleagues at the bar by camouflaging gender differences in dress. One woman told me that she looked around at her colleagues in dark suits at a hearing and was amused by the fact that she was the only lawyer wearing pink. In a second case, the vision of a lone woman in a sea of suits[57] underscores the power of the masculine presence:

Somehow I felt I preferred to be in robes if I was in court than not in robes. Because I did some construction lien work, for example, and I remember going in there and being the only woman in about forty blue suits and I was – I think I wore bright blue that day and I just felt like – I don't know – you know those pictures that are all black and white and there's one thing painted? That's what I felt like.[58] (In-house lawyer, called to the bar 1996)

The act of fitting in is marked by a feeling of differentiation from people outside the profession. This "difference" theme was apparent over and over again in the course of our interviews. One woman told me that, in spite of her feminist views and her earlier rebellion against professional traditions, she had grown to like wearing her robes:

I first put them on when I was called to the bar and I was in a very rebellious state and I didn't like them. I thought they were symbols of patriarchy at that point and I hated them for that but now I actually like them because – I don't know – I like having that uniform. I like being a lawyer. I like dressing up like a lawyer and I like being differentiated from other people in the courtroom because of the uniform. (Family lawyer, sole practitioner, called to the bar 1986)

Some other women saw the robes as an expression of equality in the courtroom, placing all lawyers on equal footing by hiding expensive suits and neutralizing unpleasant personalities. One of the family lawyers said: "I don't know the reason behind wearing robes but for me it's – when we wear robes ... every lawyer is dressed the same. You're all equal and it's all in the way you present your case and you represent the client." A second woman was much more direct in her observations, saying: "[W]hen I put on my robes and walked into a courtroom, I just wanted to whisper ... and also, looking across at your adversary whom you feel is an asshole and is there in the same robes that you are, you're all equal before the law."

Finally, for many women, the robes signal a sense of personal empowerment, which is tempered in some cases by an overwhelming awareness of the responsibility that they carry. These patterns were evident among many of the criminal lawyers. One of them evoked a picture of an enhanced self, perhaps with masculine overtones, much like the transformed Portia, saying, "[W]hen you put on the uniform in the high court, it's a very positive feeling and I see it as a powerful thing ... It gives you bigger shoulders and your robe flows as you walk along. I find it a very empowering thing and I really enjoy it" (criminal lawyer, small firm, called to the bar 1983). A second woman said that she felt untouchable and empowered in her robes, adding: "I feel like I'm the lawyer. It's like you become the image that you've always thought of when you think of a lawyer." A third woman recalled the elation she felt when she robed for the first time but then stopped to consider the weight of her responsibility to her client. She said: "Those robes for some reason do empower you or give you a boost. And it fills me with fear because there's a lot of responsibility under those robes. Usually when you're in the robes it means you're into really serious business and someone's looking at some serious time so they frighten me. They're on the back of my door and I look at them. It's an awesome responsibility" (criminal lawyer, sole practice, called to the bar 1992).

On balance, legal robes appear to heighten the confidence of the women in this study, especially if they are small or young. Although some of them acknowledge feelings of inadequacy or a sense of masquerading beneath the cloak, most of them see their legal dress as a confidence-building passport to credibility in the courtroom. However, when they say repeatedly that they feel "like real lawyers," it is important to define their images of the "real lawyer." Theirs is a profession established by men and the robes were designed along masculine lines. Why then would women look to them for personal enhancement at the expense of their own gendered selves? Perhaps they have no other choice.

Assuming the Mantle: The Lawyer's Identity in the Eyes of Others
Self-confidence is important to the successful practice of law, and the robes do allow women to experience a transformation of their identity. However, identity is also enhanced or diminished by the responses of others so the reactions of the audience in the courtroom are critical in this respect. For many of the women in this study, legal competence rests on their ability to convince others that they can deal with the abstractions of the law – the statutes and precedents – and convert these into a reasoned argument, but court appearances involve psychological preparation

and the act of robing is an important part of this process. Several women used terms such as "garbing," "gearing up," and "girding yourself" to describe the physical transition from their everyday law practice to the courtroom atmosphere where the adversarial system often prevails. One woman expressed the progression clearly:

[W]hen I'm fully dressed for court I'm dressed for battle and there's a process of garbing up that gets your mind ready for the task that you're going to undertake which is different from all the other tasks you do. Everything else I do in the practice of law is cooperative based. It's problem solving ... When you are in the courtroom ... you are in a very specialized adversarial environment where there are rules of gentility and civility and standards of behaviour and conduct that are expected of you. (Family lawyer, small firm, called to the bar 1991)

The adversarial climate in the courtroom represents a culture that many women find foreign so the robing process gives them a way of putting on their "battle dress" in preparation for entry into the arena. One woman told me that loss of control is not considered to be a feminine quality so she likes to remain calm under attack in the courtroom, adding: "I like to have that fence that I don't lose control. Like I love it when a crown can lose *his* control ... when you lose control, it's like the mind shuts off." Her view confirms Berggren's thesis that women in robes can use their feminine socialization in an environment where the norms of a male-dominated culture prevail. Another woman appeared comfortable with the military language used by some family lawyers when she described her courtroom tactics: "[T]here's one lawyer who's just totally litigious, who just pulls stunts, does dirty things ... when I've gone to court I've just had to *battle* this guy to the ground and I just think it's great when he's *bleeding*. [Are the robes part of the battledress?] Oh yeah. Oh yeah. It's a lot easier when you're in your robes to go in and cross-examine someone" (family lawyer, small firm, called to the bar 1975). She went on to talk about the adversarial tradition, indicating that she was not entirely comfortable with it but that she saw it as a role-playing exercise – a learned behaviour that had allowed her to survive in the courtroom for many years. She has since embarked on a career in mediation law, turning her back on the tradition of litigation that served her well as a family lawyer.[59]

The Courtroom as Theatre

Shakespeare's stage provides a fitting analogue for a study of lawyers because the courtroom is often seen as a theatrical setting. Fiona Cownie pursues this theme when she describes the dress of legal academics. She acknowledges the importance of the costume in any performance and cites Erving Goffman's theories of dress as being critical to the management of identity.[60] Many of the lawyers in this study made specific references to role playing and their costumes. One woman emphasized the importance of her robes in this process, saying: "It feels good. It's like any kind of theatrics – easy to get into the part if you've got all the accessories and the trappings." Another woman recalled a situation in which she saw her own image through the eyes of spectators on the street:

> It was a costume. I mean, I've worked in theatre ... when we used to have our office quite close to the court I would run over, carrying the gown outside with the rest of my uniform on. And I remember one time running across the street and a couple of people looking because they could clearly see that, hey, I was identified as a lawyer, and kind of snickering to myself and thinking: "Well, isn't that funny! I mean, who'd have thought it? You know? I guess there's a certain status to this" ... But it really is a – it's a uniform, a costume. (Family lawyer, small firm, called to the bar 1982)

People play various roles in the courtroom, and the lawyer's robe distinguishes her in the eyes of other participants. Some of the women in this study mentioned the responses of judges and juries, but their overwhelming concern was with their clients' reactions. Although clients have sometimes expressed disappointment at the prospect of dealing with women lawyers,[61] the women in this study had apparently not encountered much resistance in this respect. One woman said: "I don't want them [her clients] saying: 'Why does my lawyer have to be the one who looks like she just crawled out of bed?'" and a second woman saw her robes as a means of conveying her legitimacy to her clients:

> [The robes] elevate you ... in the eyes of your client without question ... the clients really like that because it's very official. It's silly. It's like some lawyers still use red seals whenever possible, or gold seals, even better, because it gives the clients the sense that this is really worth what they're paying. But for me it's just – it's a psychological lift. (Family lawyer, medium-size firm, called to the bar 1987)

Her comments are interesting because she touches on the idea of professional legitimacy in her mention of the legal seals and relates this notion to the professionalism that is inherent in the robes. She also recognizes that by enhancing her image in the eyes of her client, she gives herself a psychological boost.

Women who practise family law are particularly aware of the effect of their robes on their clients. One of the family lawyers said: "[A] couple of weeks ago I was in court and I had a woman who was a client and it seemed like she didn't have a lot of self-esteem. And I could see that she liked having me, you know, acting for her and looking as authoritative. And I think it was – to have, you know, a woman wearing these robes." A second family lawyer was equally impressed by the effect of her robes, saying: "[M]y clients view me differently and I've had clients say that, you know: 'Like gosh, you came in there in those robes and it was just like, Wow! – you know.' And I represent a lot of women and I think they feel empowered to see their lawyer, you know, dressed up just like the judge."

The clients of criminal lawyers may not have much respect for their lawyers or for the system in general, but they are often impressed by the decorum of the courtroom and the seriousness of their situation. A young criminal lawyer in this study said: "I don't generally find that clients treat you with an enormous amount of respect until you prove to them that you deserve their respect. And I think for women, one of the best things you can do is put on a gown. I've had a lot of clients say, 'Wow!' ... Most women I know love to wear their robes." Many of the lawyers in this study expressed admiration for the judicial system and saw their robes as part of a time-honoured British tradition of justice. One of them stated these views at her first interview and reinforced them in her second interview, after she had become a judge:

> I'm also a great believer in rising through the ranks and respecting author-
> ity and experience. So I've always believed that more senior counsel should
> be called before more junior counsel and the longer I practise, the more
> perks I'm entitled to ... [And the robe itself – do you think it's impor-
> tant?] That represents tradition and formality and the whole British sys-
> tem, which I really like. And I also think it makes the law seem very
> important and serious. I don't like the little provincial courts that are in
> strip malls, you know, where your client gets his doughnut and walks in
> the back door. And I think that the more impressive and majestic the
> justice system is, the more of an impression it makes upon the people
> who pass through it. (Criminal lawyer, small firm, called to the bar 1983)

The women who became judges during the interim between interviews were very committed to the formality of the courtroom, but they described contradictory images, often emphasizing the casual nature of the clothes beneath the formal red sash that set them apart from other court officials. The woman in the previous quotation, like Portia, appeared pleased with her ability to move from her street clothes to her judicial robes very quickly:

[Tell me about what it's like to wear the judge's robes.] Well, what I like about it is that I go to work in my jeans ... I go in the back door because I'm wearing a uniform at work ... I'm a quick change artist and so it'll be less than three minutes. Sometimes I go roaring through the police office looking like a university student and I come back out two minutes later fully gowned ... I have a pair of court stripes and ... a white shirt and the vest and the tabs and the robe and the red sash. And I wear pants all the time so I wear ankle socks. I haven't worn pantyhose in three years. (Provincial court judge, called to the bar 1983)

A second woman provided an interesting slant on her progression from the bar to the bench. In a curious twist, she had shed her need to appear in the requisite knee-length skirt and had become quite cavalier about her approach to judicial dress:

I have a whole comedy routine I could do about the robes. They're the stupidest things in the whole world ... they're hot. There are so many layers you can't imagine ... there's a skirt or there are pants ... Until I was a judge I never once set foot in a courtroom in pants ... I always wore a skirt and I never wore a short skirt. It was always just a little below the knee ... because I acted for very unpopular causes, very radical, out there, left wing. The last thing they needed was somebody who looked a little odd. You know, I was traditional, perfect, courteous, kind of very old-fashioned ... But it's very uncomfortable ... So as soon as I became a judge, I thought: "Well ... Who cares? I'm wearing pants. I don't care if they can see it or not! I'm the judge. I can wear whatever I want." (Judge, called to the bar 1980)

"In Such a Habit": Robes, Gender, and Tradition
All costumes can be uncomfortable and constraining at times. Indeed, many of the women described their robes as "a pain," and others said that they were "uncomfortable," "a nuisance," "hot," "smelly," "silly," or "ugly." One woman said: "[T]he gowns are very hot and very awkward ... you're buttoned up to your neck and you've got wool all over you and – so from that perspective, especially if you're doing a trial in one of the outlying districts that don't have any air conditioning, it's not exactly, you know, pleasant." A second woman, unaccustomed to litigation, felt awkward in her robes but was able to laugh about her predicament when she was called upon to fill in for her partner, a family lawyer:

[A]t that point I had never darkened the door of a courtroom and I was just panicked about the idea of ever having to do it. And you had to robe for that court at the time ... So I robed up ... And I went to court that day and got all the uncontested divorces okay. They didn't refuse to give them but I think the judge had a smile on his face the whole time because every time I had to go up to the court clerk and hand in a marriage certificate as evidence, I kept catching the sleeve of my gown on this microphone that was sticking out in the front desk area and I just about disrobed my-self every time I tried to come back to the table. And it was quite obvi-ous that I was so nervous that I could hardly even function. My clients didn't seen to notice, amazingly. I think they were nervous about being there too so I think that it was just part of the package. (Wills and estates lawyer, small firm, called to the bar 1974)

Discomfort is a minor irritation for most lawyers, but the masculine tradition of legal dress poses larger issues for many women. Some scholars contend that civil courts replaced ecclesiastical courts in western Europe at the end of the thirteenth century, and, while judges' robes were initi-ally fashioned after the robes of the nobility, one of the most prominent historians of legal dress, W.H. Hargreaves-Mawdsley, contends that con-temporary legal dress has its roots in the lay dress of medieval men.[62] More recently, J.H. Baker has argued that the modern British barrister's gown was originally a mourning gown adopted on the death of Charles II in 1685.[63] In spite of their origins, the robes incorporate androgynous features. The tailored shirt and wing collar, the tightly fitting vest, the dark pants, and the tabs or "bands" parallel stylistic changes in men's cloth-ing, but the flowing robes can just as easily be seen as women's clothing. Margaret Thornton argues convincingly that all the trappings of the court – wigs, robes, and ermine – are "quintessentially masculine symbols of authority," but she goes on to note the paradox inherent in this situa-tion since these items are decidedly feminine accoutrements in any other setting and, more to the point, they are not associated with authority.[64]

Until recently, legal robes have been particularly problematic during preg-nancy. Although the flowing gown looks like a perfect cover for an expand-ing belly, the vest underneath is designed to fit very tightly, and some judges have been strict about enforcing dress codes in their courts. Sev-eral lawyers in a small Ontario city told me that the widow of a local lawyer used to circulate his outsized vest among pregnant lawyers. One of them told me a very funny anecdote about her experience with "the vest":

I was the first woman in the area to get pregnant ... I was huge when I was pregnant so I went to the judge's secretary ... and said: "Could you please ask his honour if"... I said: "What I'd like to do is just get a little tunic like the convent dresses, you know, and just stick that underneath my robes. Could you just ask his honour?" ... [T]he message that came

back was: "If you can't dress to come to court, don't come to court" ...
So – I remember distinctly – I had this appeal ... I got the first two but-
tons [done] and then of course, it kind of went like this. Right? [She
demonstrates.] And I managed to get the vest and I'm standing there.
Well, of course I've got a backache, so I'm in the middle of this appeal
like all afternoon and I'm tired and all of a sudden I go like this and this
button goes ping! And he's staring at my stomach. And he says: "You have
ten minutes and everybody takes a recess!" And I thought: "Oh good,
your honour!" ... because you see what happens if you undo the first but-
tons under the vest. It was just my bare skin. I thought that had to be
the best revenge. And of course after that everyone got to wear little black
dresses. (Family lawyer, small firm, called to the bar 1975)

Robing companies have only been producing a maternity version of the
vest for a few years so many other women have been forced to impro-
vise by looking for corpulent men and asking to borrow their vests. One
small pregnant woman told me cynically that the official maternity dress
comes in one size only – extra large:

Well, it's a big jumper, although in fairness they don't actually have
blouses that go under it. What they do have are little dickie things that
you're supposed to stick around your neck. But then of course you have
nothing on your sleeves, which is a small issue that I'm still trying to
deal with because when I did it at that time I just rented the gown itself
and it had sleeves in it because for maternity ones you get fake sleeves.
But the one I have now has no fake sleeves so it's just going to be stupid. I don't know what I'm going to do. (Family lawyer, small firm, called
to the bar 1993)

Aside from the discomfort of wearing legal dress, a small percentage of
the women in this study expressed reservations about the formality of
the system and the roles that they were required to play within the courts.
Some of them saw the judicial system as excessively elitist, while others
felt that respect for the law would exist without the tradition of robing.
One woman said that she felt uncomfortable about being "different," and
went on to express her distaste for the values inherent in the courtroom
setting:

I think part of what the gowns say is that we are superior. That's not the
word, but we are set in a different place than other people because of
our education and our experience and because of what we do and I don't
believe that to be true. I mean the other huge part of the system, and I
think the part the gowns address, is that the kind of complete deference

or respect for the court – and you know it although you can never say it in court – I certainly don't have that. I don't believe that the judges are the people they think they are. I think there are a lot of problems in the way the judges are chosen and the way they behave on the bench, and I don't have the kind of respect for the court that the gowns seem to indicate that I should have. (Criminal lawyer, small firm, called to the bar 1994)

A few women said that the robes and court formality were unnecessarily intimidating to clients, especially if they were poor or if they were young offenders:

They're not the most comfortable things to wear and I'm not sure that they're necessary, especially in the family court because it draws a line between you and the clients and I think that it can be intimidating. Not all that we do down in court takes place in a courtroom and you're off in little rooms trying to negotiate and when we're sitting there all dressed up and the client's sitting there often in ragged clothing – because a lot of the clients that we deal with are poor – I think that it just – it widens the gap between us. I really don't think that it adds to anything and if the respect for the court is there, it will be there, regardless of how we're dressed. (Clinic lawyer, called to the bar 1987)

Another woman dismissed the robes as "pretentious" and unnecessary as a tool for creating respect for the court, while one of the last women to be interviewed summed things up with a sparkling sense of wit:

I don't know that we're serving our clients when we prance around in all our robes. I think we're distracting ourselves. I think the idea of the solemnity of the – the only justification for the role of keeping them – is that they do something to the process that is beneficial ... That's the only justification for keeping them. Why on earth do you have to wear seventeenth-century clothing? ... I just think they're silly. (Criminal lawyer, sole practice, called to the bar 1981)

Her reference to seventeenth-century clothing brings us back to Portia and the suggestion that robes are powerful agents of transformation. The majority of the women in this study who wear their robes regularly rely on them to enhance their presence and their image of themselves in the courtroom setting. Many of them find the robes uncomfortable at times, but, on the whole, they are committed to a system of justice that operates in a formal, dignified setting. When they dress in their legal robes and enter the courtroom, they see themselves as actors in a serious drama.

Like Portia, they use their costume and their props to demonstrate their grasp of legal theory and to act as effective professionals.

Conclusion

The Merchant of Venice has long been one of Shakespeare's most popular plays, and Portia's robing experience provides a powerful image of gender transformation. When the play is done well, audiences willingly suspend their disbelief on seeing Portia, cast initially as meek and dependent, transformed into a wise doctor of laws. Women who choose legal careers today are far more learned than Portia was, but many of them find that they also need to present visible proof of their competence before they are accepted as legitimate professionals. Like Portia, they have entered a world inhabited by men where the norms and practices are foreign so they need to find ways of fitting in. Portia's court appearance is fleeting, but they are there for a professional lifetime so public evidence of their legal ability is even more critical.

Access to a unique body of knowledge is an essential aspect of professional status. This knowledge is both abstract and utilitarian so it becomes a powerful tool in the hands of a skilled practitioner. It is acquired in accredited schools and manifested in a set of credentials – the degrees and diplomas needed for entry to any profession.[65] However, access to this credentialed knowledge is not universally available. Professional bodies can safeguard their precious knowledge, allowing only selected groups to join their ranks. The most prestigious professions have exercised these exclusionary practices for many years, barring women and members of other marginalized groups from entry.[66]

The legal profession has followed these general patterns of exclusion in the past, identifying the most promising contenders by their access to specialized knowledge. Since the profession has been grounded in a patriarchal world, the early founders placed high value on rational scientific knowledge and characterized it as men's knowledge. This designation was sufficient to exclude women for many years because their knowledge was deemed to be practical in nature and, therefore, unacceptable in a profession committed to principles of abstract reasoning. By the turn of the twentieth century, a few determined women had gained entry, and, with increasing emphasis on high undergraduate marks and strong LSAT rankings, the proportions of women entering law school has grown dramatically. Now that these standards are firmly in place, women graduate in slightly higher numbers than men. Without doubt, they have demonstrated their capacity for dealing with abstract principles.

In this chapter, I have been concerned with indicators of professional knowledge that are less formalized than diplomas and degrees but equally important in establishing professional credibility. Legal dress is one way of conveying legitimacy. When lawyers robe for their court appearances, they declare their professional status. Do the robes also demonstrate that a lawyer can use her skills to incorporate legal theory into a reasoned argument? The evidence from my study suggests that the robes fulfill a very useful purpose in this respect. Women lawyers reported an enhanced sense of identity when they appeared in their robes. Many of them felt that their professional legitimacy was strengthened and their personal confidence was elevated.

While some of them recalled having mixed feelings on first wearing their robes, most of them felt a sense of pride in their accomplishment. Feelings of uncertainty, self-doubt, and an awareness of their responsibility to clients surfaced for some women from time to time, and such feelings are understandable, given the persistence of contradictory views of women as "unruly" or "disorderly" creatures in a profession committed to the ordered pursuit of justice. The robes are also the product of masculine tradition so they can be less than accommodating for women's bodies, especially during pregnancy. On the whole, however, the robes authenticate their legal knowledge and expertise, allowing the women to move beyond the everyday duties of their practices as they prepare themselves for the adversarial climate of the courtroom.

Most of these women also believed that their robes had a strong positive impact in court. They made them feel like "real lawyers," legitimating them in their clients' eyes and reinforcing the idea that the courtroom is a formal, dignified setting where serious issues receive a fair hearing and justice prevails. By bringing formal credentials to the practice of law, these women have surpassed Portia's definition of herself as "unlessoned" and "unschooled." They are well schooled in the theory of the law. However, like Portia, many of them see disadvantages in being young or attractive in a setting where the main actors have traditionally been male. In many cases, the robes have helped them to overcome any notions that they might be "unpracticed" and allowed them to share the stage with professional gentlemen.

3
Educating Women in the Law: Becoming Gentlemen?

> Slowly have the temples of learning been unlocked to her, one
> by one they swung their heavy doors open and bid her enter,
> until finally, the temple of law and justice itself welcomed her
> within its portals – to help humanity to get its rights. And
> woman, as before, in other professions, has shown ready
> appreciation of the educational advantage law offered her
> and the practical use she could make of it.[1]
>
> – *Women Lawyers' Journal*, 1911

> This afternoon Miss Clara Brett Martin was presented to the
> Judges at Osgoode Hall and was sworn in as a barrister. She
> wore a black gown over a black dress and the regulation white
> tie and bore her honours modestly.[2]
>
> – *Toronto Telegram*, 2 February 1897

Modesty was expected of women in Clara Brett Martin's position. At the close of the nineteenth century, she became the first woman in the British Commonwealth to enter a thoroughly male world – Ontario's prestigious legal profession. The benchers who controlled the Law Society of Upper Canada had resisted her previous attempts to embark on legal training, fussing about the problems that would ensue if women were to join their ranks and appear in bloomers or hats, apparently threatening the dignity of the court.[3] Like Portia, women entering this arena were expected to wear legal robes and the "regulation white tie," but, unlike Portia, they were expected to express their femininity by avoiding trousers. As Mary Jane Mossman has aptly noted, women were different. Clara Brett Martin's success would demonstrate women's suitability for legal practice, but the law itself was anchored in male values, "the idea of 'lawyer' was male, both in terms of legal theory and in the ideas of most members of society ... By accepting maleness as the standard for being a lawyer, moreover, women who became lawyers did so on the understanding that their acceptance as lawyers depended on their conformity to such a standard."[4]

The profession has traditionally selected recruits from a narrow range of elite backgrounds, leaving many would-be lawyers in a disadvantaged position. Class, race, and ethnicity have provided convenient filters for legal gatekeepers, but gender barriers have probably been the most effective tools for excluding large numbers of potential members, both in North America and abroad.[5] Arabella Mansfield was admitted to the Iowa State bar in 1869 and Ada Kepley was granted an accredited law degree a year later, but many other American women were less successful in their attempts to gain entry.[6] In fact, women were not admitted to Harvard's law school until 1950, and some law schools continued to exercise gender discrimination until the early 1970s.[7] Ada Evans was admitted to the University of Sydney's law school in 1898 but only because the dean was on sabbatical leave and unable to prevent her entry.[8] In England, women were excluded from the profession until after the First World War in spite of several attempts to enter. Bertha Cave's application for barrister's training at Gray's Inn was rejected in 1903 and a second woman was declared ineligible to train as a solicitor.[9]

When the benchers of the Law Society of Upper Canada admitted Clara Brett Martin to the bar in 1897, they made legal history, albeit reluctantly. Her acceptance marked a turning point in the profession, but her path to law school had not been easy. She graduated from Trinity College in 1890, taught school for a year, and then petitioned the Law Society of Upper Canada for registration as a student. She was denied access on the grounds that the society's statutes gave them the authority to admit "persons," but women's legal status as persons was a matter of some dispute. She sought support for her cause from influential members of the Ontario legislature and women's rights activists, and, by 1892, the legislature passed a bill ruling that "persons" included women as well as men.[10] The benchers of the Law Society continued to oppose the admission of women but were forced to abandon their stand under pressure from one of Clara Brett Martin's strongest allies – the provincial premier, Sir Oliver Mowat.

Clara Brett Martin was accepted as a candidate for legal training on 26 June 1893, but her success did not signal immediate change in the gender profile of the Ontario legal profession.[11] A handful of women were admitted to the bar over the next two decades, but, by mid-century, they still comprised less than 4 percent of the first-year student body. The profession was destined to remain male-dominated until the final decades of the century.[12] In the late 1950s, women made up 2.2 percent of lawyers called to the Ontario bar, and, by 1990, 41 percent of the candidates were women. By the turn of the twenty-first century, they comprised 50 percent of the bar admission class, and, in May 2005, 57 percent of the bar admission students were women.[13]

What are the implications of these changing gender patterns for legal education? Answers to this question can be found by examining the ways in which the image of the nineteenth-century professional gentleman has been perpetuated, both in the content of legal knowledge and in the pedagogical practices employed in law schools. If the environment reflects the interests of learned gentlemen intent on replicating themselves, then how do candidates who fall short of this image fare when they encounter the law school culture? Some women find the law school environment intimidating and foreign, but social class, race, age, sexual orientation, and disabilities can also work to shape the law school experience in unique ways.

Clara Brett Martin had entered a world controlled by professional gentlemen whose manners and breeding reflected their superior social position.[14] These men were properly socialized and "regularly educated," bearing impeccable credentials and the respectability required for entry to a learned profession. They were schooled in legal matters, but they had also studied classics, mathematics, history, and philosophy. As the sons of an aspiring ruling class, they were a privileged group – the latest generation of professional gentlemen committed to aristocratic British traditions.[15] These "regular" gentlemen understood the unwritten rules of the profession that were replicated in the norms of the law school culture. By default, prospective candidates from all other social groups were deemed irregular and unacceptable. Although evidence suggests that the early benchers tried to include "farmers' sons and country school teachers" in the student body, an Osgoode Hall education was an impossible dream for most sons of the lower classes.[16] Ethnic and racial discrimination also kept many good candidates from practising law, both at the law school entry level and at the door to articling positions.

Christopher Moore documents the Law Society of Upper Canada's resistance in the face of Clara Brett Martin's request for admission, but he leaves his readers with the impression that the benchers operated in a fair and non-exclusionary way in their efforts to establish legal education in Ontario, glossing over the elitism and exclusionary practices that have always characterized legal education.[17] A century later, the profession still has not come to terms with women's presence, in spite of the fact that they are now entering law in greater numbers than men. Men and women are still unsure of their respective roles in many situations, and, as Mary Jane Mossman has noted, women, as newcomers, are still regarded as "outsiders." Women's marginal status may give them a clearer vision of the systemic inequities and outdated practices, but it does not necessarily enhance their standing in a profession where many of the norms continue to reflect men's lives.[18]

Accounts of law school cultures in other jurisdictions confirm similar contradictions. Women were thwarted in their attempts to enter the profession in other Canadian provinces, notably New Brunswick, British Columbia, Manitoba, and Quebec.[19] Margaret Thornton describes gendered patterns of exclusion in Australian legal circles, arguing that admission to law school is not enough to guarantee that women will be viewed as legitimate "knowers" because they still take second place to their male counterparts, the "benchmark men."[20] These men, like the Ontario gentlemen, are predominantly middle-class, white, heterosexual, able-bodied, and politically conservative.

In a similar vein, Helena Kennedy describes her bizarre experiences as one of the first women students in the British Inns of Court where students were required to eat a prescribed number of dinners in the Inn's Hall, purportedly to engage in scholarly discussion of the finer points of the law, but dinner at the hall was invariably an occasion for schoolboy pranks and sexist jokes. According to Baroness Kennedy, prominent London barristers still dine regularly at the Inn where the atmosphere is as stuffy and exclusive as that found in the best men's clubs in the city.[21] Increasing numbers of women have joined the prestigious ranks of the London bar, but many more are found in low-level professional positions. Students from low socioeconomic ranks rarely gain access to barristers' legal training, and members of racial and ethnic minorities are embarrassingly underrepresented in high-ranking positions.[22]

Exclusionary tactics have also been documented in American law schools, often as firsthand accounts provided by women.[23] Mona Harrington summarizes the situation aptly in her description of academic life at Harvard Law School where she recalls that, in spite of the growth in women's numbers "in the inner life of the school, at its intellectual center, a male identity persisted, a sense that the place belonged to men, a sense that women, even as their number rose dramatically, were still outsiders. It is a sense, not at all restricted to Harvard, that the presence of women is somehow out of keeping with the workings of the law."[24]

The law remains the preserve of a particular group of white men whose views have shaped both legal practice and the prescribed routes to professional acceptance. In this respect, the experiences of today's university-trained law student differ very little from those of the nineteenth-century apprentice in the learned gentleman's office. According to Harrington, commitment to this male-centred view of the law ensures that women and members of racialized communities are often barred from full access to the knowledge base that informs legal reasoning. They are disadvantaged before they move into the practice of law because the legal culture does not accommodate their needs or interests.

These concerns about the law school environment, its knowledge base, and its pedagogy merit closer scrutiny, but, at the most fundamental level, we need to consider the cultural underpinnings – the norms and values of the profession itself and the ways in which they affect legal training. The rapid influx of women is germane to this discussion. While many of them find prevailing attitudes and values confusing, both as law students and as practising lawyers, their presence may also contribute to marked changes in the culture of the profession. They have certainly inspired professional bodies to consider the potential for friction when professional duties intrude on family life, and, because their styles of practice may depart from established patterns, the search for justice may assume new forms. A sizeable body of literature has been devoted to these issues so a brief review serves as a preamble to my discussion of legal training. Law school is but one piece of the larger picture – one that has been mutating over the past century and will continue to do so as the image of the learned gentleman fades.

Legal Norms, Values, and Attitudes: Winds of Change?

The culture of the legal profession has a strong impact on attitudes and values conveyed in the law school classroom. Culture is a difficult concept to isolate, but the definition advanced by Sonja Sackmann, Margaret Phillips, Jill Kleinberg, and Nakiye Boyacigiller provides a fitting framework for a discussion of legal cultures:

> The core of culture is composed of explicit and tacit assumptions or understandings commonly held by a group of people ... these assumptions and understandings serve as guides to acceptable and unacceptable perceptions, thoughts, feelings, and behaviours; they are learned and passed on to new members of the group through social interaction; and *culture is dynamic – it changes over time, although the tacit assumptions that are the core of culture are most resistant to change.*[25]

The italicized section of this passage aptly describes the legal culture and the potential for change as the profession becomes more diversified. Established legal scholars express strong support for the status quo, protecting their turf against intrusions by doubters, who are principally proponents of critical legal studies.[26] Paul Kahn defends the traditional view of "the rule of law," arguing for a distinct differentiation between legal theory and the practice of law. Kahn advocates a cultural study of law through the lens of Enlightenment philosophy rather than the wholesale reform of law by modern critics.[27] He is particularly critical of feminist scholars who seek, as he says, "to replace a false science of law with a true science."[28] Catharine MacKinnon is probably the most well known of these feminists. MacKinnon draws parallels between the law and the state, observing that male power prevails in both spheres but is masked by an apparent commitment to impartiality and objectivity.[29] Over the years, she has gathered a following of supporters who welcome a chance to apply her principles to the practice of law. Ann Scales, for example, makes a strong case for feminist jurisprudence, rejecting the "myth" of objective reality in favour of a radical feminist approach to legal practice.[30]

Kahn acknowledges the relevance of MacKinnon's charge of gender inequity in the patriarchal roots of the law, but he decries the reformer's habit of blurring the lines between scholarship and legal practice.[31] Richard Posner is even more explicit in his dismissal of MacKinnon as a "moral entrepreneur" whose passion for the feminist cause far outweighs the strength of her argument.[32] Feminists counter these claims with the assertion that an awareness and appreciation of women's lived experience is fundamental if institutions such as the law are to change. In MacKinnon's words, "grasping women's reality from the inside" in the face of entrenched male power is a necessary step.[33] MacKinnon's concerns were justified in the 1980s when the male presence in the legal system posed an identifiable target for women entering the profession, but her critics now call for an expanded vision, moving beyond gender essentialism to a consideration of the differences among women. For example, Joanne St. Lewis demonstrates the need to attend to the particular problems faced by racialized women.[34]

In spite of valid concerns about racialization and other competing statuses, the debate about equality in the profession has centred on gendered practices. Women's experience may, over the long term, change the culture of law and the dynamic body of knowledge that shapes legal doctrine but their entry to law school is only the beginning of a protracted process of feminization within the profession.[35] The real effects will emerge only if substantive law shifts its focus to incorporate areas such as employment equity or family law, and the practice of law is reshaped to accommodate family needs.[36] Women's patterns of practice will determine the speed with which these changes occur, but key questions remain unanswered. Will women follow the track set by their male predecessors or will they carve out unique viewpoints and styles of practice? Will they conform to a "man standard" or a "lady standard?"[37] Will they be expected, like Clara Brett Martin, to tread a fine line between professional masculinity and personal femininity or will the feminization process affect the profession radically?

Sheer numbers of women have changed the face of law, but have they altered accepted practices appreciably over the past twenty years? Apparently not. Some feminists have suggested that women entering the profession, like all outsiders, possess enhanced vision simply because they stand outside the charmed circle. Their critical faculties may be heightened, providing them with the power to effectively reshape existing practices. Carrie Menkel-Meadow advanced these optimistic views early in the feminist years, but she later reported widespread gender discrimination in American law firms throughout the 1980s. She found that women were less likely to practise corporate law and more likely to be found in legal aid clinics than their male counterparts. Their salaries were consistently lower and their status was undermined. The outsider's vantage point apparently provided no privilege because women's opinions continued to escape notice unless they adopted conventional masculine approaches. As Menkel-Meadow observes, "given the continuing barriers and disadvantageous working conditions, the more interesting question to ask is why women continue to seek entrance to the legal profession."[38]

In 1994, Mary Jane Mossman urged her legal colleagues to address "hidden" assumptions about gender roles, suggesting that the profession was undergoing a protracted period of transition that would mark women's advancement from pioneering status to effective advocacy for reform.[39] Women's numbers have continued to climb in the intervening years, but their progress within the profession has not kept pace. Mossman was referring to problems with the balance between legal duties and family life, but other, less obvious practices often prevent women from taking part in professional activities. For example, reports of sexual harassment by colleagues surface often enough to suggest serious underlying problems.[40] American researchers have found that women employed in public institutions are, to some extent, shielded from harassment, but women practising law in private firms often hesitate to acknowledge inappropriate behaviours because, by doing so, they might jeopardize their chances for career advancement.[41]

Similar patterns have been documented in the Canadian Bar Association's task force report on gender equity in the profession, from the "poisoned" learning environment of law school to the unfair practices that were commonplace in many law firms. They received widespread reports of sexual harassment, differential access to legal positions, a decided lack of interest in work-family balance, and career blocks at the most senior levels.[42] These patterns prevailed in the highest levels of the profession. When Justice Bertha Wilson surveyed women in the judiciary, she found extensive evidence of professional and personal discrimination, at times compounded by sexual harassment. Like the women in large law firms, women in the judiciary were routinely denied access to complex trials and were left instead to manage the "women's work" of family law.[43]

In spite of these persistent inequities, some feminists remain confident that women themselves may effect subtle changes in legal structures and practices. Carrie Menkel-Meadow suggests that women might reject the hierarchical structure of large law firms in favour of more egalitarian approaches, but her optimism appears to be misguided.[44] More recent works have documented the increasing centralization of legal services and the continuing expansion of mega-firms structured along hierarchical lines.[45] These trends have been particularly punitive for women because occupational segregation persists in the profession, and, as a result, the gender gap in earnings remains strong.[46] At every step of their legal careers, from the search for articles to the partners' boardroom, women face barriers to advancement that are uniquely theirs. Even when they attain positions of seniority, their levels of autonomy remain lower than those of their male counterparts. These patterns are evident across Canada, the United States, in many European countries, and in Australia.[47]

Why do women continue to lag behind their male counterparts in almost every aspect of legal practice? Fiona Kay and John Hagan invoke Pierre Bourdieu's theories of social and cultural capital to provide an explanation.[48] Bourdieu sees these less tangible forms of capital as critically important components of capital in general, supplementing the more obvious human capital – the knowledge and skills that workers are expected to bring to their jobs.[49] Social capital is evident in the connections and client networks that lawyers tap in the process of building their practices. The time needed to foster these connections is readily available to men because they are released from household duties after hours. Women in the profession are rarely so fortunate because they almost always add domestic duties to their legal responsibilities. Time itself becomes social capital – a gendered resource that favours men.[50] Kay and Hagan argue that social capital is also a critical component in the generation of trust within law firms. Successful lawyers develop collegial relationships, but they must also establish loyalty to the firm, participating at the highest levels and enjoying fair rewards for their work. Women lawyers are less likely to acquire this kind of trust. They often deal with the most routine files, receive lower salaries than men, and remain stalled in their careers.[51]

Cultural capital is an essential partner to social capital, and it is even more elusive because it incorporates a subtle awareness of the social niceties and appropriate behaviours that distinguish members of elite groups.[52] It also colours expectations for performance. Men who marry and have children are often perceived as reliable and trustworthy, but, for women, the arrival of children is a definite liability, signalling reduced career ambitions and lowering their status in the eyes of senior partners.[53] Large law firms draw on a pool of bright, committed candidates who are expected to be familiar with the culture of the firm and to understand both the explicit and tacit assumptions established by generations of conservative, well-connected lawyers. In this respect, successful applicants are like the most promising nineteenth-century legal apprentices, armed with the confidence that comes from membership in an exclusive class. However, women are often disadvantaged in this setting because the cues are unfamiliar and they are not rescued, as Menkel-Meadow has suggested, by their outsider status. They remain, like Portia, on the margins of the real legal culture, metaphorically sporting the costume but missing less visible signals that shape expectations for performance.

In fact, Kay and Hagan argue that women feel compelled to display their professional resources more obviously than men. If they are serious contenders for partnership, they must be able to attract clients and build strong stores of billable hours. If they take time out for pregnancy, they are expected to work until birth is imminent and return promptly to their practices, forgoing extended maternity leaves. Other forms of cultural capital are less obvious and more insidious. Women are pressured even more than men to support and advance their firms' policies, demonstrating that they possess a sense of objectivity rather than the stereotypically feminine emotional qualities that might better equip them for careers in legal education or law reform.[54] Cultural capital is the key to power in large firms, and, as long as women are underrepresented at senior levels, decisions about issues bearing on lawyers' family lives will rest, in large measure, in the hands of those least qualified to deal with family concerns, namely men with supportive wives or women without children.[55]

The foregoing discussion provides convincing evidence of inertia within the legal profession in response to women's requests for inclusion. The general body of legal knowledge remains intact and the power structure within law schools and large firms continues to favour men's interests. However, the debate about gender issues is a mark of guarded success. It would not have occurred without the influx of women to the profession. While there is much room for progress in this regard, women in Canada have continued to pressure their bar associations and law societies to develop equitable policies.[56] The 1993 Canadian Bar Association task force report played a key role in alerting the profession to discriminatory practices, and a follow-up manual provides an excellent educational source for addressing issues of inequality.[57] However, the task force members struggled with inadequate funding, and the final document raised a storm of disapproval in the conservative ranks of the profession. Justice Bertha Wilson defended the most unpalatable recommendations by insisting that law firms should adjust billable hour requirements to accommodate women with child care responsibilities without hindering their progress towards partnership status.[58] Law societies have responded since then by generating volumes of model policies.[59] Large law firms have commissioned more studies and prepared detailed policies, but, without addressing systemic inequities, the profession will continue to ignore the needs of more than half of its members and the culture will remain intact.[60]

Women's Styles of Practice: The Differences Debate

> The quality of mercy is not strained;
> It droppeth as the gentle rain from heaven
> Upon the place beneath. It is twice blest;
> It blesseth him who gives and him who takes.[61]

When Portia used this reasoning to resolve the dispute between Antonio and Shylock, she was demonstrating her commitment to an ethic of care. Shylock could exercise his entitlement to a pound of Antonio's flesh as long as he removed exactly a pound – no less and no more – shedding no blood in the process. Masculine values within the legal profession do not lean towards this kind of compassion. Anchored in a vision of the law as rational, objective, and distanced from moral concerns, they allow litigators to engage in adversarial tactics under the gaze of a learned judge schooled in the same traditions. Presumably, Antonio would have paid with his life if a male judge had held sway.[62]

Feminist scholars have turned to Portia as a model, suggesting that women in general bring unique styles to the practice of law, giving them the potential to effect a radical transformation of the professional culture. One of the most vehemently debated issues in this literature has centred on Carol Gilligan's hypothesis that women reason in a "different voice," valuing connections and relationships rather than the commitment to autonomy and independence that characterizes men's approaches to moral reasoning. Gilligan concluded that women lawyers, like Portia, tend to reject abstract universal principles in favour of an ethic of care, both in respect to their clients and in the interests of the opposing party.[63]

Proponents of Gilligan's work predicted changes in styles of lawyering with growing numbers of women in the profession, particularly in cases involving dispute resolution. Given their commitment to harmony, they argued, women might employ more conciliatory methods, preferring negotiation and mediation ahead of the aggressive, adversarial approach that has often characterized pre-trial and courtroom debates.[64] Studies have demonstrated some support for Gilligan's thesis, but most researchers conclude that women adopt a variety of styles. Some of them avoid the adversarial approach, others take a middle road, depending on the circumstances of the case in question, and a few are committed to the so-called male model.[65] Joan Brockman expands Gilligan's either/or approach, using a "conciliatory-adversarial continuum" to frame her findings, and concludes that most lawyers, male or female, are at best "reluctant adversaries."[66]

Gilligan's work provides a convenient explanation for the disjunction between women's experiences and the traditional masculine values of the legal profession, but it is more than a template designed to explain inequities in various professional practices.[67] Indeed, some studies find that professional women are more empathetic than their male counterparts, but the evidence is scant and the danger lies in generalizing these patterns to include all women.[68] As Deborah Rhode has stressed, "women's voice speaks in more than one register: its expression depends heavily on the social circumstances and cross-cutting affiliations of the speaker, including not only gender but class, race, ethnicity, age, and sexual orientation."[69]

Critics of the "differences" thesis argue that systemic gender inequality shapes attitudes. Women have been excluded from power so they have learned to be submissive in order to maintain smooth relationships with powerful men. The resulting gender differences have become solidified as socially constructed normative patterns that confine women and men to separate spheres. Catharine MacKinnon carries the metaphor of women's voice one step farther, arguing that women have been silenced completely because they have been rendered powerless. This pattern of male dominance and female submission, she argues, is so deeply embedded in the power structure that it is impervious to change.[70]

In her early writing, MacKinnon suggests that women could resolve some of the inequities by engaging in a process of consciousness raising and taking remedial action, but her analysis fell into the essentialist trap of casting all women as submissive and powerless.[71] As Sharyn Roach Anleu argues, this approach does a disservice to both women and men: "The 'difference' and 'domination' perspectives suffer from opposite limitations: the former assigns women practitioners too much agency; while the latter assigns too little. Both approaches offer a somewhat one-dimensional view of women as demonstrating greater sensitivity to clients and adopting a nurturant approach to legal dealings or as passive victims of male dominance."[72]

Naomi Cahn contends that the "differences" thesis, to some extent, misses the point. Women may be more attuned to the needs of others than men are, but perhaps the value lies in recognizing these tendencies and making use of them. The legal community could benefit by using this knowledge to advocate a more caring approach to clients in general, regardless of the gender of the practitioner.[73] However, Ann Shalleck argues in response that Cahn's work is incomplete because, by offering an ethic of care to round out the existing repertoire of legal styles, it conveniently skirts the issue of domination and subordination inherent in the old ways. Shalleck also challenges the whole idea of "style" as the framework for a feminist critique of professional norms and practices.[74]

In spite of these debates, some researchers argue that gender differences in performance become apparent in law school when entrenched professional norms set the tone for classroom performance. Students arrive at the law school door with roughly equivalent stores of human capital, but their access to social and cultural capital varies widely, leaving many novices in a state of confusion. In the classrooms of large schools, professors often take charge of the discussion, rewarding students who volunteer to participate. Students with a collaborative bent and empathetic listening skills are ignored or, worse still, singled out for comment and embarrassed when they have nothing to add to the debate. The aggressive tactics are foreign to them, but they are expected to hone their skills in preparation for the competitive culture of legal practice.[75] These patterns have been widely documented in American law schools, but legal education in Ontario has evolved in unique ways, responding to a number of competing forces over the past century, including the entry of women, the changing racial composition of Ontario's population, constitutional reform, enhanced awareness of basic human rights, and debates about legal education in general.

In the context of these overarching patterns, it is important to consider the ways in which law schools have failed to accommodate the needs of some students as well as the problems these failures have posed for their legal careers. What kind of knowledge is prized in professional circles? Should it be practical and utilitarian or theoretical and abstract? What is the most appropriate method of transmitting this knowledge? Is the apprenticeship model effective or does a formal academic setting provide better preparation for legal practice? How is the content of legal knowledge related to the culture of the law school and do some accepted pedagogical practices have negative effects on students who are cast as outsiders in the classroom? These questions provide a focus for discussion in the following pages, preparing the way for an examination of law school experiences reported by the women in this study.

Legal Education in Ontario

The history of legal education in Ontario is scarred by conflict between advocates of practical legal training and proponents of theoretical, black-letter law.[76] The latter is reflected in the Langdellian method, a pedagogical device that requires students to use their interpretation of case law as the basis for dialogue. Commonly known as the "Socratic method," the Langdellian approach allows experienced professors to demonstrate their skills with logic as they guide the discussion. Unlike the true Socratic method, where neither teacher nor student knows the answer in advance, the Langdellian method places the professor in an advantageous position.[77] Given the implicit power of the professor and the opportunities for student embarrassment, it is not surprising that feminists have mounted challenges to these methods and the doctrines that informed them. These challenges are an important part of the historical record because women and students from other disadvantaged groups have found them puzzling and, at times, offensive.

As in all legitimate professions, the architects of legal scholarship have claimed access to a specialized body of knowledge that was both abstract and utilitarian. This "credentialed" knowledge is central to the debate about legal education because it provides the key to professional status.[78] It has served as a powerful exclusionary tool, ensuring professional monopoly over valued expertise, and it has gradually assumed prominence as the

cornerstone of learning in the modern law school. Apprenticeship practices have faded and entry to the profession is possible through a single
route – graduation from an accredited institution and the acquisition of
the imprimatur of the professional body.[79]

In Ontario, the Law Society of Upper Canada, which was established
in 1797, continues to act as the guardian of legal knowledge by setting
law school curricula, administering bar admission courses, and designating articles as prerequisites to professional certification.[80] Early members
of the Law Society of Upper Canada assumed responsibility for legal education in the province, but they were also intent on preserving the patriarchal power of the entrenched Tory legal elite.[81] Although they tried to
establish Osgoode Hall Law School as a centre for legal education, advocates of the prevailing apprenticeship model thwarted their attempts to
formalize the process for a number of years, expressing concern about
centralization when many small town lawyers provided effective on-the-
job training. At the core of the debate, however, lay a deep distrust of
law as a scientific exercise. According to R.D. Gidney and W.P.J. Millar,
"the gap between the science of the law and the art of practice was simply too wide to be bridged."[82] As a result, the academic model did not
gain credence until the latter half of the nineteenth century when the
science of law was finally established as the foundation of legal training,
taking precedence over the view that the law was a craft to be learned in
the workplace.[83]

Osgoode Hall Law School was founded in 1889, with a divided mission: it would provide practical training, but the principles of jurisprudence would strengthen the knowledge base. Although the benchers
remained committed to this approach, some influential members of the
Law Society of Upper Canada favoured a more theoretical route to professional excellence, so the debate between these two factions simmered
for many years. In 1927, Cecil Wright joined the faculty of Osgoode Hall,
advocating the casebook method and Socratic debate as the most effective teaching tools.[84] Wright was a spirited critic of the system, but the
benchers remained committed to their founding principles, declaring supervised articles and lectures to be the best preparation for legal practice. He
continued to press for change during his tenure as dean of the law school,
and the controversy endured into the post-Second World War years, reach-
ing a resolution in 1949 when Wright resigned his position at Osgoode
to become the first dean of the new law school at the University of
Toronto.[85] The benchers had finally lost some of their control over legal
education with the advent of university-based law programs across the
province. In these new institutions, practising lawyers would be recruited
to give students a grounding in legal skills and, in a more subtle way, to
provide models of proper professional behaviour. The new curricula would

contain theoretical courses in academic law, incorporating the abstract principles designed to launch the profession as a learned enterprise with both scientific sophistication and practical value.[86]

In 1957, Osgoode Hall officials reached an agreement with the Ontario universities to initiate a province-wide program for legal education, authorizing them to develop a three-year, full-time LL.B. program contingent on two undergraduate years in the liberal arts. The agreement also established postgraduate requirements ensuring that students would serve under articles in law offices and attend Osgoode Hall for their bar admission courses. On the successful completion of the bar admission examinations they would be called to the Ontario bar. It seemed that the balance between the teaching of black-letter law and practical training had finally been achieved.

In spite of lofty ideals about academic law, some scholars argue that practical training remains the primary focus of legal education in university law schools across Canada. A core offering of first-year courses in property, tort, contract, criminal, and constitutional law is compulsory, leaving little time for optional courses such as social welfare, poverty law, minority problems, or women's issues, which are defined by many faculty members as part of a "fringe" area.[87] Although courses of study purport to provide both technical training and academic knowledge, students do not graduate from law school with the technical skills needed to practise law.[88] The profession is two hundred years old, but the debate about reform of legal education continues and many of the traditions remain firmly in place as it follows the elitist path established at its inception.

Law school admission appears to be more meritocratic with the adoption of grade point averages and law school admission test (LSAT) scores as keys to entry.[89] However, standardized tests may discriminate against members of minority groups and students from working-class backgrounds.[90] Costly tuition fees and delayed earning potential also keep some students out of the program, and this pattern is becoming more pronounced with recent decisions to increase fees.[91] Gender barriers have been eased with the widespread entry of women into law schools, but, until recently, the majority of law students have come from relatively affluent backgrounds.[92] Recent US findings indicate a modest gender gap in LSAT scores. On average, women's scores are slightly lower than men's scores, and women of colour are at a greater disadvantage than white women. These differences are not statistically significant, but excessive reliance on LSAT scores in the selection of law students could work to the disadvantage of these groups.[93]

The debate about Canadian legal education was sharpened by the publication of the Arthurs Report in 1983, calling for a series of alternative curricula to reflect professional specialties and provide courses dealing with the legal interests of disadvantaged groups. The authors also emphasized the need to develop law as a scholarly discipline, establishing a strong theoretical focus as a counterweight to the narrow professional training provided by law schools.[94] The Arthurs Report has been widely praised for its insight, but legal education in Canada has changed very little in the intervening years. The twentieth anniversary of its publication generated some excellent retrospective works lamenting the ongoing lack of scholarship dealing with legal education in the face of an increasingly complex body of legal specialties.[95] Recent works also stress the need for additional first-year courses in Canadian law schools covering ethics, the history of the judicial system, and the practice of law.[96]

Concerns about the narrow focus of legal education have surfaced in other jurisdictions as well. In 1992, the so-called MacCrate Report, commissioned by the American Bar Association, recommended that law schools emphasize practical skills instruction to prepare students for day-to-day life in law firms.[97] These measures were to be supplemented by mentoring programs within the firms, but, by the early 1990s, many firms claimed that the economic recession had impaired their ability to provide adequate mentoring for new lawyers. These developments have led some legal scholars to recommend a law school program of clinical training that parallels medical intern programs.[98] Margaret Thornton argues that technical reasoning or "technocentrism" has also become a guiding principle in most Australian law schools, largely because competition for scarce positions in law firms has impelled law school faculties to turn out skilled technocrats rather than thoughtful, analytical lawyers. These new graduates are well schooled in conservative subjects – commercial, taxation, and constitutional law – but they have no appreciation of social justice issues in areas such as family or poverty law. Their law is rules-oriented and practical, but it is devoid of social context.[99]

Graduates of Canadian law schools do not necessarily support the recommendations proposed by the authors of the Arthurs Report. Annual surveys conducted by *Canadian Lawyer* magazine suggest that many regard their legal education as unnecessarily theoretical. Opinions such as these shape the profiles of law schools on a national rating scale so, in an indirect way, they have an impact on the content of legal education. As Dawna Tong and Wesley Pue conclude, "[i]t should be observed that the heightened sense of insecurity and fear that pervades Canadian legal education at this time has produced an almost paranoid concern that any information about individual faculties might be construed negatively, might hurt their place in 'national rankings,' and, hence, might damage institutions irreparably."[100]

Biased surveys can also affect the normative goals and values of legal education. Margot Young provides an excellent assessment of Canadian law school surveys, suggesting that they have the potential to shape law school culture, often in damaging ways. Citing recommendations from the Arthurs Report, she sees aspects of the *Canadian Lawyer* survey as a threat to "human professionalism" embodied in an appreciation of law as an intellectual discipline.[101] According to Young, "they confirm, through the mouths of select law school graduates – who the magazine implies are the best judges of legal education – that law schools, in their emphasis on critical legal studies and interdisciplinary intellectual work, are failing to meet the needs of the profession they are supposed to serve."[102]

Until recently, the lowest *Canadian Lawyer* ratings were reserved for the University of Western Ontario, Osgoode Hall, and Queen's University law schools, often on the grounds that they had allowed feminist issues to intrude on classroom time at the expense of essential course material. The feminist debate seems to have subsided, but ratings continue to fluctuate. In the 2005 survey, Osgoode had moved into fourth place, Western was fifth, and Queen's ranked in eighth place.[103] By 2006, Osgoode had climbed to first place, followed closely by the University of Toronto. Respondents to the survey indicated that they liked Osgoode's upgraded facilities and the range of employment opportunities available to Toronto law students. Western and Queen's law schools had dropped to ninth and eleventh place, respectively, in spite of positive comments from former students. In general, graduates' concerns centred on escalating tuition fees and the need for more practical legal training.[104] Some disgruntled respondents also complained that special concessions for minority students, critical race theory courses, and political correctness in general undermine attempts to broaden the scope of legal education.[105]

The *Canadian Lawyer* survey does not rest on statistical excellence, but it does identify common themes. Graduates' objections focus on inexperienced, indifferent, or politically motivated faculty members, unfair testing practices, large classes, a failure to impart practical legal skills, and, more recently, inadequate physical facilities. In the 2005 survey, the University of Victoria had moved to first place because of its caring faculty, its mooting program, and its legal research and writing course.[106] In the previous survey, Calgary was favoured for its small classes, access to campus resources, and its balance of theoretical material with practical instruction.[107]

Law school curricula reflect a legal environment that has changed markedly from the professional culture that prevailed in nineteenth-century Upper Canada when a typical lawyer might have done some litigation but was more likely to be found drawing up mortgages, probating estates, collecting debts, or managing property for absentee landowners.[108] The practice of law in this provincial setting was very much a clerical exercise. In contrast, large law firms now operate in a world of international mergers and acquisitions facilitated by the lightning quick speed of Internet communications.[109] Many of these firms look for the skilled technocrats described by Margaret Thornton so they pressure law schools and law societies to help them meet their needs.[110]

However, law schools cannot ignore the concerns of other interest groups. Increasingly, some women and members of minority groups demand an educational experience that is relevant to the kind of law they want to practise. They are no longer satisfied with the standard curriculum, and, as we shall see in the next section, they have strong reservations about the hidden curriculum that shapes traditional law school culture and pedagogy.[111] Constitutional and human rights issues, feminist legal theory, race and gender studies, and socio-legal history all compete with the traditional core subjects for space in the calendar. Since these core courses are too important to be dropped, the task of designing a relevant law school program becomes increasingly complex, particularly in an environment where students demand value for their educational money.[112]

Law School Culture and Pedagogy

The law school is a model of hierarchical and patriarchal organization within which students not only are required to subordinate themselves to existing structures and practices but also are taught that subordination and conformity are the natural and inevitable incidents of legal knowledge and practice. The arrangement of power in the law school replicates that of the workplace and the wider society, and the subordination of students is openly defended on the basis that it is good preparation for the "real world."[113]

Critics of legal education in its present form see the law school environment as an invitation to conformity, preparing students for a lifetime of commitment to professional norms. They cite national rankings of law schools by media surveys, LSAT scores as an entry requirement, and hierarchically organized classrooms with the professor in a commanding position at the front as evidence of this approach to legal education. Even though students have some nominal representation on faculty councils and committees, their access to power in the larger hierarchy is limited. As transients in the law school setting, perceptive students realize that the hierarchy is designed to prepare them for life in large law firms, but many of them accept the prevailing system. They want to get on with their education as expediently as possible, so they hunker down and conform to the expectations of their professors and advisors.

Toni Pickard acknowledged these organizational patterns in her orientation address to law students at Queen's University in the mid-1980s, a time when faculty members were strongly divided over feminist issues.[114]

She described the law school classroom as a reflection of legal life generally, comparing the professor's role with that of a Supreme Court of Canada judge, noting that this was a reasonable arrangement if the professor or judge had been chosen wisely. However, she talked about misunderstandings that could arise under this system, citing the feelings of disengagement experienced by students who try too hard to conform to the professor's views. (Many first-year students assume that there is a right answer to every question, and they become frustrated when the professor repeatedly dismisses their answers as part of a Socratic exercise.) Beginning law students faced with this kind of confusion often conclude that their previous educational experience is irrelevant in the law school setting. In their struggle to make sense of the law school culture, they become emotionally upset and are unable to adopt the objective, rational approach that appears to be expected in class. If the situation becomes extreme, they are eventually so intimidated that they are afraid to speak out. The most vulnerable students are those confined to the margins – women or members of racialized communities or students from working-class backgrounds who do not share the values of those in power.

This arrangement suggests that those at the top of the hierarchy promote a vision of the law as objective and detached from emotion. If learned gentlemen or benchmark men fill these positions then they hold the keys to reasoned thinking, often addressing their students as "gentlemen"[115] and admonishing them to learn to "think like a lawyer."[116] Although this phrase has become a cliché in law school classrooms, the process of acquiring this skill is rarely made clear to students. Do lawyers really have unique thought processes or is this simply an attempt to promote a professional mystique? Kurt Saunders and Linda Levine summarize the voluminous literature devoted to this theme and suggest that successful lawyers learn to think rhetorically as they solve problems. They are trained to use fact, case, and statutory analysis to develop an argument and provide a critical evaluation of legal issues. They are then able to invoke these analytical skills when they turn to practical problem-solving tasks. Accordingly, they must learn to think like lawyers before they can act like lawyers.[117]

Views on the process of legal education have become polarized. Some scholars have argued that "thinking like a lawyer" involves a commitment to detached legal reasoning, which eliminates any concern for the moral significance of a given case. According to this school of thought, successful students learn the technique of legal practice – the identification of material facts and the selection of appropriate precedents and obedience to procedural rules – but, in doing so, they forfeit any awareness of social justice.[118] Certainly, this view confirms earlier practices in traditional law schools, evident in the routine message delivered by a well-known Harvard law professor to his first-year classes: "The hardest job of the first

year is to lop off your common sense, to knock your ethics into temporary amnesia. Your view of social policy, your sense of justice – to knock
these out of you along with woozy thinking, along with ideas all fuzzed
along their edges. You are to acquire ability to think precisely, to analyze
coldly, to work within a body of materials that is given, to see, and see
only, and manipulate, the machinery of the law."[119]

Increasingly, law students come from a range of backgrounds, and their
reasons for choosing law as a profession are varied. While some people
arrive at law school seeking only intellectual challenge, prestige, or the
independence that a legal degree can offer, others exhibit a strong sense
of idealism. Women students in particular often bring a liberal approach
to law school,[120] and women lawyers frequently report that they wanted
their law degree to enable them to help others in need of legal aid.[121] For
these people, law is more than a science reduced to a set of logical statements. Their reactions to legal knowledge and the law school culture in
general are unique, and they have found their way into a large body of
feminist literature.

The Feminist Challenge to Legal Knowledge

> Like childbirth, nothing had really prepared me for it [law school]. I
> stepped from the equivalent of a comprehensive school in no mean city
> into the pages of an Evelyn Waugh novel. Like a foreigner abroad, I smiled
> a lot to cover my bewilderment, and my benevolence was totally mis-
> read by hoards [sic] of public-school boys who did not know what it
> meant to have a girl as a friend.[122]

Helena Kennedy was the first member of her Scottish working-class family to attend university. Entry to the Inns of Court was a confusing experience for her because the distinctively masculine culture was built on a
body of solidly entrenched legal knowledge. This kind of knowledge, evident in the doctrinal coverage of precedents and procedural rules, springs
from a long tradition of patriarchal leadership. Successive generations of
women in law have shared Helena Kennedy's feelings of marginalization.
In response, feminist legal scholars have invoked Simone de Beauvoir's
characterization of woman as "Other" as an appropriate metaphor for the
law school classroom, replete with images of "the reasonable man" and
a cast of legal actors – professors, judges, shareholders, and citizens – who
are assumed to be male.[123] Women are largely invisible in this environment, receiving only occasional mention in cases dealing with domestic
violence or marriage break-up.

Other feminists have observed that law schools tend to describe their
courses in phallic terms, designating core courses such as property, contracts,

torts, and trusts as "hard" law in contrast to "soft" ancillary courses such as tax, family, or labour law. Courses in environmental law, Aboriginal rights, or women and the law are often dismissed as peripheral and unnecessary.[124] Occasionally, creative professors offer courses that provide a critical examination of traditional legal knowledge.[125] Critics of the established curriculum see this approach as essential for the reform of legal education, but many law school deans view it cautiously because it strikes at the heart of the discipline by challenging the accepted body of legal knowledge and calling for fundamental change in the way law is conceived and taught.[126]

The feminist debate was initiated in the 1980s when women began to tell their personal stories about life in the large American law schools.[127] Previous accounts of legal education had endorsed the status quo, documenting accepted practices without concern for women's experiences,[128] but these women had encountered a culture in which they felt silenced.[129] In their first-year classes, many professors used the Socratic method of instruction to sharpen students' analytical skills, seemingly unaware that it could become a ruthless attack on the intellectual ability of students.[130] Mona Harrington describes the process in Harvard classes where randomly selected students were exposed to relentless questions posed by the professor who prodded and pushed them through a reasoning process designed to clarify legal principles.[131] Harrington believes that women feel threatened and alienated by this process, especially in classrooms where they are routinely trivialized.[132] Catherine Weiss and Louise Melling suggest that women in this situation experience a sense of alienation from the material presented in the classroom that distances them from the law school community. The ensuing powerlessness in a setting where the professor seems to have all the right answers ultimately destroys their self-identity.[133] This loss of confidence can affect their success as articling students and haunt them throughout their legal careers.[134]

Loss of voice is an interesting phenomenon, especially for women who intend to make their living by communicating with clients, opposing counsel, judges, and courtroom officials. In fact, some women have suggested that their voices were "stolen" from them in first year, and others say that they lost their former "selves."[135] Since students are encouraged to isolate their analytical reasoning from their moral concerns, Carol Gilligan's views on women's "different voice" are attractive to critics of the law school environment.[136] However, with respect to law school as well as legal practice, Gilligan's thesis may be limited by her commitment to essential feminism – a one-dimensional view that ignores differences among women. If this is the case, then it is important to ask how many women are alienated and silenced, how many women resolve moral conflict in the ways suggested by Gilligan, and how these women may differ from their fellow law students. Anecdotal evidence from a few interviews does not provide convincing evidence in support of Gilligan's thesis.[137]

Feminist debates in Canadian law schools erupted as findings from American studies began to filter across the border. Sheila McIntyre's memo detailing sexist practices at Queen's University Law School was leaked to the media in 1986 and when, in the following year, Mary Jane Mossman was bypassed as dean of Osgoode Hall Law School in favour of a male candidate, many women believed that her strong feminist views had cost her the job. Her colleagues and students filed a complaint with the Ontario Human Rights Commission, and the battle lines were drawn. At the University of Western Ontario Law School, the gender wars raged on for a number of years, pitting students against faculty members and faculty members against each other.[138] These debates have done little to change the law school culture, but they have reinforced the view that women's experience in law school is different from that of their male counterparts. Critics contend that sexism, discrimination, and sexual harassment are endemic to the system, sometimes working in such subtle ways that they go unnoticed.

Feminist views are routinely dismissed in conservative law schools where masculine perceptions of reality hold sway. When a group of law students requested an institutional response to sexism within the University of Western Ontario Law School in 1989, conservative professors denied the existence of sexist practices, claiming the "right not to know."[139] The battle continued but the students were ultimately thwarted in their attempts to effect change. Commenting on this chain of events, Bruce Feldthusen suggested that the institution's response was typical, arguing that men who have not experienced discrimination adopt the only means of resolution that they know – a formal complaints procedure, adversarial adjudication (parallel to a trial), and the sanctioning of offenders.[140]

Women in law schools may also fail to recognize inequities in the system once their numbers have swelled to match those of men, but biases are still evident in the language of the law.[141] Intrigued by gendered patterns in the classroom, Christine Boyle asked her colleagues at Dalhousie University Law School to examine their teaching practices for evidence that they were treating their women students fairly. She also considered some radical ways of changing her own classes and discovered that she was hampered by the fear of negative student evaluations and the possibility that she might jeopardize her own position in the law school. At the height of the feminist movement, she was aware of a threatening environment: "My objective in listing these factors is to illustrate that the backlash against women and feminism is very real and extremely ugly, but also to demonstrate that such events have an impact far beyond any individual law school. The message is obvious – keep quiet and try to make the fact that you are a woman as inconspicuous as possible. I think more than twice about raising feminist values in a classroom when there is a danger that I will be accused of incompetence."[142]

Within the past ten years, academic research in the United States has shifted the focus from simple gender differences, introducing members of racialized communities, gays and lesbians, and disabled people as groups who are likely to suffer the effects of discrimination in law school as in other settings.[143] A similar watershed was reached in Canadian work in the early 1990s when the Canadian Bar Association's task force report on gender equality incorporated findings on women lawyers who fell into these three categories.[144] The essentialist argument has given way to a consideration of multiple sources of discrimination because scholars have expanded Carol Gilligan's vision of "voice," having realized that women's voices are a mixed chorus.[145]

Differences in the Different Voice

Essential feminism has frequently informed analyses of women's reactions to legal education. Building on this perspective, some have suggested that women bring a distinctive voice into their classroom experiences, but it is subordinated by a dominant male voice.[146]

Much of the earlier work on women in law school is limited in two ways: it ignores differences among women and it relies on women's anecdotal accounts of life in large American law schools. Cries of alienation and silencing are repeated like mantras throughout this literature, and they have been picked up, often uncritically, by new generations of researchers.[147] Women may well have been treated unfairly in law school, but the gender argument alone is an insufficient critique of legal education.

Most recent research incorporates a range of background variables, and the best works provide varied methods, random sampling techniques, and longitudinal data collection. Robert Granfield's study of Harvard University Law School exemplifies this approach. His use of both survey data and interview transcripts ensures that women from visible minority and working-class backgrounds will be included, making his analysis more rigorous methodologically than many previous works.[148] Granfield found some interesting interactions between gender and occupational goals. "Altruistic" women, as expected, were committed to social justice but the "individualistic" women in his sample resembled the men in their preference for financial security and prestige. Women from minority groups tended to be individualistic, avoiding poverty law and becoming more pro-business as they advanced through law school. Many of the altruistic women came from working-class backgrounds and were more likely to identify faculty biases against women, but their individualistic counterparts dismissed them as "their own worst enemies" who "bring these problems on themselves."[149] Granfield's research is enlightening because although he acknowledges potential gender differences in the law school experience, he also introduces factors that can separate women and, at times, turn them against each other. He suggests that women at Harvard, from time to time, may hold common views but that Harvard is an elite law school and social class can operate to divide women into different camps. The potential for a feminist backlash is clear from the comments of individualistic women in his study.

Lani Guinier and her colleagues also incorporated quantitative and qualitative data sources in their longitudinal study of law students at the University of Pennsylvania Law School.[150] Their analysis focuses on gender comparisons with only a brief mention of race effects, but they confirm earlier reports that women are alienated by their exposure to the Socratic method. First-year women are more critical of legal education than their male counterparts, but their critical sense fades during law school and they tend to abandon social justice interests in favour of corporate law. On a disturbing note, Guinier's group reports uniform entry qualifications but notes that men consistently achieve higher grades and are more likely to graduate near the top of the class than the women in their cohort.[151] The career implications are clear from these findings. Women win fewer honours than men and they are less likely to attract the attention of recruiters from the most prestigious law firms. Law school performance can imprint a complete career pattern.

These studies overcome many of the limitations of earlier research efforts, but, like most previous works, they focus on the culture and pedagogy that prevail in Ivy League law schools. My study provides a Canadian perspective and extends the sample to include women from all the Ontario law schools.[152] This broad sample is important because individual law schools attract different pools of students, and their methods of instruction depart in varying degrees from the Socratic model. The women in this study were asked to indicate why they went to law school and how they recalled their experience there. Their answers ranged from "terrifying" to "boring" to "exciting," and they reflect the views of women from widely differing backgrounds. This project demonstrates clearly that women law students are not a homogenous group of people.

Is the professional gentleman still the model for successful law students? If so, many women will have a difficult time with the law school culture. A woman's social class helps to shape her law school experience, but its effects are compounded by other factors. The law school itself bears consideration. Does it have an elitist reputation or does it encourage diversity and collegiality among students and faculty? Does it have a history of feminist debate? Is the pedagogy modeled on the Socratic approach adopted almost universally in first-year American law classes? Law students also bring different resources with them. Mature students typically experience law school in unique ways, and students from middle-class backgrounds often have an advantage over their working-class counterparts. Finally, the overall intent of legal education is an important consideration. Many nineteenth-century lawyers learned their craft by apprenticing to a legal master, but law students now spend three years in university before they advance to their articles in search of a mentor. Is their education designed to provide practical skills or does it concentrate exclusively on the abstract principles of legal reasoning? If they are equipped only with theory, have they been adequately socialized for life in the profession? These questions provide the focus for a discussion of the material gleaned from interviews with the women who took part in this study.

The Ontario Sample: "What Were Your Impressions of Law School?"

> Law school is three years and it's three very different years. The first year is "Oh my god! What have I done?" It's a completely new way of being taught and there is a heck of a lot of reading and a completely new way of thinking that you have to learn ... Definitely for the first semester you just feel overwhelmed. You feel like you're an idiot and you wonder how you ever got in and then you start to feel a bit more comfortable. Second year is the hardest year, I think, because your articling job and everything thereafter depends on your marks in that year. That is the most important year. And third year is a total party. (Family lawyer, small firm, called to the bar 1991)

Law school is probably never "a total party," but this woman identified reactions shared by many other women in the study. When they entered law school, they were unsure about their abilities and their aptitude for law, but most of them recalled that their courses became more manageable in second year. By third year, they had narrowed their interests, gaining the confidence needed to move on to their articles and begin practice. One woman said that she hated first-year law school, especially the courses where marks were determined entirely by performance on the final exam. However, her comments indicate that she gradually learned to overcome any early difficulties as she developed familiarity with the process of legal reasoning. She said:

> I had been out in the working world. When there were difficult issues,

you thought about them – and to try to answer something in an hour – for a 100 percent mark ... But the subject matter I found very interesting and in my second and third years when we had more flexibility in terms of courses we took ... I enjoyed some of my courses a lot, in fact, probably more than I did during my previous degrees. (Administrative lawyer, medium-size firm, called to the bar 1994)

Almost a quarter of the women recalled that law school was generally a positive experience, providing a comfortable learning environment, relevant course material, and access to supportive faculty members. One very successful lawyer described her law school years thoughtfully, identifying the importance of adapting to the new culture and learning the logic of legal reasoning:

Law school was a very interesting experience. I had always, throughout any level of education, achieved a very high level of marks and it was a standard that I set for myself and tried to maintain for myself. So my undergraduate marks were all extremely good. I mean, I don't think I ever had anything lower than an A-minus and the same thing prior to that – and going to law school was an entirely different experience. While my marks were good, they weren't all consistently A's and A-pluses, which was a difficult thing to adjust to. I also found the process quite different. The whole thrust of a legal education was very much different from what I had been used to in undergrad ... And I think it probably took me until third year to really get my stride on that, to really understand what the idea was behind legal analysis, legal thought, interpretation, all that sort of thing. So, while I worked every bit as hard and probably harder than I ever had, I didn't quite get it until probably third year. (Corporate lawyer, large firm, called to the bar 1988)

Other women were less enthusiastic about their legal education and, in fact, suggested that their ideals about legal ethics and social justice had been misconceived. One of them said:

My first impression of law school and most lasting one was that most of the people who were attending didn't want to be there. That was a deep disappointment to me because, for me, it was the culmination of a lot of effort and the fulfillment of a dream – and other people were there because they didn't know where else to be. There was a saying when I went to law school that they scared you to death the first year, worked you to death the second year, and bored you to death the third year, and I would say that's an accurate reflection of how law school was. (Family lawyer, large firm, called to the bar 1985)

A second woman recalled being even more disillusioned by the process when she said:

> Maybe I was foolish to think that justice and law were connected – and maybe many young law students feel this way. I expected everything to relate back to something ethical or something that would represent right. And I also expected, I *really* expected to find crusaders. I expected people in law school to go there with the same intent, which was to learn how to apply the law to accomplish something in the world. And it was so disappointing to realize that law school was simply a very rigid teaching of certain areas of the law. (Family lawyer, medium-size firm, called to the bar 1987)

This theme of social justice runs through many of the studies concerned with gender differences in law school experience. Women who enter law school with interests in human rights and poverty law are often disappointed by the lack of concern for ethics, both in the lectures and in the minds of their fellow students. The divide between altruistic feminist interests and the Langdellian approach has been particularly pronounced at Osgoode Hall Law School. Graduates were aware that their school offered academic excellence and an entrée to established Toronto firms, but some of them resisted the lure of money and fame. One woman talked about her professors' efforts to channel her into prestigious positions and her overriding determination to practice poverty law. She said:

> They start grooming you ... the contracts professor ... wanted me to do what he had done and study contracts and go and clerk at the Supremes ... so I get interviewed at the Court of Appeal and I realize I don't want to do any of the things that they want me to do. I'm not interested. I'm not a wannabe. I don't want to earn a lot of money. I don't want any of these things. I don't want lots of fancy names. (Social welfare lawyer, clinic, called to the bar 1990)

Another Osgoode graduate echoed the words of women in large American law schools when she recalled the large classes and intimidating professors:

> It was terrifying. It became clear to me and, I think some other people, that we weren't going to have our egos built but we were going to have our egos completely smashed – told that we weren't very smart, that we probably wouldn't last past the first three months ... And then I think, secondly, I found it just really disappointing. I guess I shouldn't have watched *The Paper Chase*. And it definitely wasn't that but maybe I thought it would be more fun. (Criminal lawyer, sole practice, called to the bar 1991)

The other women in this study expressed widely ranging views about their law school experience, but their overall impressions can be reduced to several key themes drawn from their recollections of the course material, their professors, and their fellow students.[153] Some of them were aware of the impact of their gender in the law school setting, while others noted that their social class impinged on their law school experience. Age also played a part. The mature students in particular talked about some of the impediments posed by financial constraints and family responsibilities during their years at law school. The interviews also reveal tensions in the law school environment that heighten the effects of gender and social class. The climate in many Canadian law schools was inherently masculine and conservative until the 1980s when groups of feminist students and faculty members began to challenge every aspect of legal education. Given the retrospective nature of my interviews, these themes emerged more strongly in this study than in the recent US works. In some respects, my work provides a bridge between earlier personal accounts of law school experience and the large sample surveys of the 1990s.

The law schools at both Queen's and Western endured tumultuous times in the 1980s and early 1990s when a number of feminist law professors openly questioned the attitudes and teaching practices of their male colleagues. The hostilities have faded, leaving in their wake a corps of conservative students intent on erasing the feminist chapter from law school histories.[154] The women in this study who attended Western's law school at the height of the feminist debate registered mixed reactions. One committed feminist said:

> I had many sexist experiences there, starting from the first day we walked into the classrooms and the professors clearly favoured the men over the women in terms of answering questions. They streamlined the men into business and corporate and taxation law and gave very little encouragement to the women as to those types of law ... It was very right wing, very conservative. There were very few professors who were doing really interesting radical work ... I think there are some law schools where there is a larger contingent of feminist professors – at Queen's, at Osgoode, at UBC ... But, you know, Western is still very bad for lack of support for feminists and so is U of T. Windsor is a different kind of law school. (Family lawyer, sole practice, called to the bar 1986)

Feminist students and professors at Western established the Women in the Law group in the mid-1980s, but many women students either regarded it with suspicion or chose to ignore it.[155] Women who said that they had not experienced sexist treatment often qualified their comments, suggesting that they had not been familiar with feminist ideas when they were in law school or that they had had a feminist awakening after graduation. Most women were too intent on getting through the process to focus on gender inequities. For example, one Western graduate expressed some regret that she had not been more sensitive to the issues:

> There wasn't the obvious sexual discrimination that a lot of people think about but ... I believe there is all kinds of systemic discrimination ... In the end, most of the female professors were either forced to leave or quieted in some fashion. One of the female professors had conducted a study on sexual discrimination in professional workplaces and had used the faculty as part of her study. And there was a huge backlash, *huge* backlash to the point where her work was discredited publicly. It was awful! Because I lived outside of the campus and had so many other time constraints, I couldn't fully participate in that. But I was on the edge of it and got to know what was going on ... [I] *just knew enough to bide my time, get my degree, get the hell out of there, and go someplace else* [italics added]. (Family lawyer, sole practice, called to the bar 1993)

Several of the women in this study expressed their feminist views hesitantly, assuring me that they had never experienced discrimination at a personal level. One of these women talked about the appearance of equality fostered by the University of British Columbia Law School but suggested that inequality was still present. However, her concluding comments were mixed when she recalled:

> But certainly to this day, I would have to say I don't think my life or career has been affected by discrimination. So I guess my point is that at law school they certainly made an attempt to at least verbally say we were equal but it was subtle things that still made us feel that the men who were there were going to go farther and be greater and we were all going to drop out and have babies and, you know, that kind of thing which wasn't said every day but was certainly felt, I think. (Criminal lawyer, small firm, called to the bar 1993)

Another woman talked about the insults directed at women who spoke out in class or challenged conventional views, relating a personal story about her attempt to deal with sexist material:

> It's the subtle kinds of remarks that you can't ever really identify. I remember one incident that is humorous really but it reflects that sort of thing going on. We had an exam that was worded in a way that, you know, a lot of us found very offensive and we were trapped reading this exam for three hours ... There were a number of us who were very upset and my

two friends and I complained about it. We made an appointment with the associate dean ... His secretary let us into his office. He wasn't there yet. We sat down and she closed the door and on the back of the door there was a poster of Loni Anderson in a bikini with a pair of [the university] underwear thumbtacked onto her body. We just looked at each other and said: "We are barking up the wrong tree." (Family lawyer, medium-size firm, called to the bar 1988)

Women who came to law school with a strong sense of their feminism sought out feminist professors, often in classes with a focus on law and social issues. Some of them talked about the importance of successful women in law faculties as mentors, role models, and, occasionally, as advocates. Two of the Osgoode Hall graduates who attended law school as mature students voiced strong praise for one of their most committed professors, recalling that they relied on her for information, access to teaching assistantships, or advice about dealing with problems. One of these women talked about her encouragement during a period of great anxiety:

She was absolutely excellent ... I remember going and speaking with her and she said to me that getting into law school was the toughest part. She said that basically people who don't make it out are people who have other issues in their lives ... because I was feeling very: "I don't know if I can do this. This is really overwhelming." [This was first year?] Yes, and she said: "No, you can do it. It's the rest of your life – when it falls apart – that you can't do it." (Civil litigation lawyer, small firm, called to the bar 1991)

Several of the lawyers in this study also talked about their admiration for a professor whose views epitomized a liberal feminist approach. She had chosen to avoid the activist route, electing instead to advance her career by adapting to the masculine culture. One of these women said:

She's just a phenomenal professor and she's probably the main reason that I really loved law school ... she was always telling us that we had to make our own definitions of success and this was one thing that I took very strongly away from knowing her, that you decide what you call a successful life. And at the time she had two children and of course she's very devoted to her family so that was really interesting for me to watch and see how she was doing that. (Corporate lawyer, medium-size firm, called to the bar 1987)

A second woman praised the same professor for skilfully blending family obligations with her academic career, concluding that "she just sort of did it all!" For these women, it was better to adapt to the norms of the profession, turning a blind eye to discriminatory practices in law school, legal practice, or the judicial system in general. Many women seem to approach their legal careers in this way. A few of them succeed, but others realize eventually that they have chosen an impossibly competent role model. Women who take this route usually begin and end law school with the individualistic occupational goals evident among some groups of women in Granfield's work.[156] They will serve them well in corporate law.

Although very few of the women in my study had well-defined goals when they entered law school, their family backgrounds influenced both their choice of law school and the type of practice they eventually entered. Some of the women came from middle-class families and a handful were from privileged backgrounds, but many of the women were from working-class backgrounds. These women, often the first members of their families to attend a post-secondary institution, were keenly aware of class differences in the law school setting. Fear of being unable to keep up in a pool of very bright people was one of the most common emotions expressed by the women in this study, and, in fact, a number of them thought that they had been admitted to law school erroneously or because the gender quota had been altered to include more women. One woman said that she entered law school during International Women's Year and was convinced for a long time that she was part of an expanded cohort for this reason. Several other women said that for months they thought there had been a clerical error and that someone would find out that they should not have been accepted. One woman was very clear about her insecurities during her first year of law school:

> I didn't enjoy it – and partly, I think, because of the individuals I was there with, and their different expectations from my own and, you know, a lot of them coming from a privileged background and really having an idea, perhaps, of where they were going in law. And I was doing it knowing I could have a career out of it but even when I was at law school I wasn't sure that that was for me ... And fear, fear, fear. All I could remember from September to the first set of exams was whether I was getting it, which in hindsight is ridiculous but it is such an important thing at the time when you spend so much money on it.[157] (In-house lawyer, called to the bar 1997)

Feelings of marginalization appeared to be most pronounced among University of Toronto graduates. They tended to defend the scholarship that had secured the school's prestigious reputation, but, like the woman cited in the next quotation, many of them recalled that the culture had been excessively competitive and exclusionary. This lawyer did not come from a working-class family, but she felt distanced from her fellow students because she had grown up in another region of the country where values were different:

> It was absolutely not what I expected. I particularly hated U of T Law School. The people there weren't my kind of people. I shouldn't have gone there ... I found they were very competitive. They didn't know how to have fun ... I found that they were a bunch of snobby little rich kids who wanted to be lawyers because they liked the idea of being a Bay Street lawyer whereas I had come from a very different background and wanted to be a lawyer and didn't want the money part of it. That's not what I was there for ... It was a great degree but it also wasn't the type of law school that I should have gone to for what I was interested in. (Criminal lawyer, large firm, called to the bar 1988)

Social class is a powerful influence in the formation of student networks that often reflect family backgrounds.[158] Some mature students in this study were painfully aware of their marginal position in this respect. Many of them had minimal educational credentials, and they did not realize that social capital was a precious resource. Some of them found it easy to make friends with the professors, but others were overwhelmed by the law school environment. Many of them were married or divorced with dependent children so they did not have time to engage in the social banter that helps to fill gaps in understanding and pave the way to a promising career in a prestigious firm. These women were often shocked by the contrasts between themselves and their fellow students. One of them expressed deep gratitude for the opportunity to attend law school, but she had struggled financially and was critical of her younger privileged classmates:

> The thing about law school that grated me a lot was that there were so many rich kids ... a lot of the students were just so bummed out, so turned off, and I think that that just had everything to do with the fact that they'd never been out there and seen what's out there ... it really bothered me when, come Christmas time, they would fly off with their families to the Caribbean or Europe and they lived in apartments that their parents paid for and they drove cars ... I felt very, very impoverished and overwhelmed with debt burden and that just got worse every year I stayed in school. (Government lawyer, called to the bar 1989)

Another woman had made major sacrifices to attend law school when her child was an infant. She, too, recalled the class differences that set her apart from many of the younger students:

Okay, I'll be frank with you. I was working-class. I'm the exception. Most of the kids in my class – they know what trust funds are. I had one kid next to me say: "Well, doesn't everyone live on a trust fund?" Well why wouldn't they? I mean they truly believe that and that's a good three-quarters of the class at Osgoode. There's a lot of money. It's very elitist. (Civil litigation lawyer, small firm, called to the bar 1991)

Age and experience can also bring deeper levels of awareness. One of the so-called privileged women in this study had chosen a relatively modest practice, but she demonstrated a remarkable sensitivity to class issues when she said:

It wasn't until I grew up I guess that I realized that being white and being a daughter and granddaughter of fairly prestigious people really did give you equal status to being a male. I was one of those women that probably thought that women that didn't get to law school just weren't as smart as I was. You know it took me a longer time to come to the realization that there were privileges that I had that a lot of people don't have. (Family lawyer, small firm, called to the bar 1984)

Race is a key variable in many American studies, but its effects are less apparent in my study. Certainly the population of law students in Canada includes people from a range of racial and ethnic backgrounds, but records kept by the Law Society of Upper Canada have not reflected this diversity until recently so it has been difficult to draw representative samples. Law Society statistics indicate that 15 percent of students in the 2005 bar admission course were members of visible minorities and 1.5 percent of students were Aboriginal.[159] Several women from racialized communities were present in my sample but very few of them reported problems related to their racial background.[160] However, one of these women described an incident of blatant racial stereotyping in a law school classroom. She said: "I was so embarrassed. I was just mortified! And I went to see the professor after. Actually it took me a few days. I talked to a friend about it and he thought I should go and say something to the professor, and I did. But I was very – I wasn't expressive or articulate at all. I was just a scared little law student, you know." The professor in question was also extremely embarrassed by the incident and posted a public apology. However, the most disturbing aspect of this story was the reaction of other students. The woman in my interview said that she overheard some students reading the apology and saying: "I wonder who complained about that. It's such a stupid thing to complain about!" The fact that these students were blind to the discrimination behind the comments suggests that the culture of the law school still leaves little room for diversity.

A student's sexual orientation may also affect her legal education, but, like race, it does not play a major role in a study of this size. I interviewed several lesbians but only one of them discussed her law school experience in light of her sexual orientation. Her comments do, however, provide a view of a very conservative culture:

> I became involved with a woman for the first time in law school and so I was in the process of coming out. It was an extremely hostile environment. In fact, I didn't come out until much later. I was very closeted in law school because there was absolutely no place for gays and lesbians in law school. There were some of us and we knew each other but we were terrified to be out. So it was not a good place to be a woman. It was definitely a bad place to be a feminist and a bad place to be a lesbian.

Although not commonly perceived as disabilities, other aspects of women's lives can hinder their progress through law school. Pregnancies and miscarriages, childbirth, postpartum fatigue, family responsibilities, and stress-induced illnesses are events that many women experience. None of the other studies considered these unique phases of women's lives, but, given the proportion of mature students in my sample, they merit some consideration.[161] Six of the women in this study talked about the problems they encountered with pregnancies during law school. While some of them laughed as they invoked memories of fatigue and frustration, others had been deeply affected by these burdens and their recollections demonstrated the extent of the sacrifices they had been forced to make. One of them said:

> I remember being in law school and, just the couple of times that I was actually pregnant at law school, and getting larger and larger as time wore on, and I stopped really paying any attention to what I looked like ... So I remember showing up in jeans and basically the uniform was jeans and a great big, extra, extra large sweatshirt and I'm sure I looked like an absolute slob through most of law school but it was just – it was an interesting experience. (Corporate lawyer, sole practice, called to the bar 1989)

These women talked about their strategies for dealing with fatigue. They cut classes, skipped readings, and somehow survived the process. One woman who had her baby just before the beginning of her third year described the way in which she and her student husband balanced their busy lives:

> I missed the first week of law school – of third-year law school but I still went back and we did this juggling act with my mother in the middle ... it was quite hellish. I've got all of these photographs of me lying on

the couch with the baby lying on my chest and a law book in my arms. But I made it through. I basically didn't read anything at all in third-year law school. I just got by. I made sure I attended every single lecture and got through the exams based on what I learned in lectures. I didn't do too badly. I still graduated *magna cum laude*. (Family lawyer, sole practice, called to the bar 1994)

Some of the women juggled family responsibilities with long-distance commuting throughout their law school years. In some cases, the effects were devastating but they were amazed by the support that they received from professors and classmates. One woman described her harrowing life:

I went to law school when I was thirty-nine. Going to law school was very difficult for me because I used to drive up to Western on a Monday morning after I had taken my children to school. I used to stay overnight. I used to usually be the last one in the Law Library Monday night and then I'd be there Tuesday and then I would race home on Tuesday so that I could be home for dinner at six o'clock ... Then Wednesday morning I used to do the same thing again. I used to take them to school and race up to – along the 401 with my foot to the floor, so I could find a parking place, get into class, and be sitting down ready to go again. (Contracts lawyer, sole practice, called to the bar 1995)

She repeated this process on Thursday, allowing herself to work at home on Friday. Her account was fascinating but disturbing. In the end, she became completely exhausted in her attempt to struggle with competing loyalties. However, she was impressed by the support she received from the two law schools she attended. She said: "I think both Windsor and Western were incredibly – I mean – they actually – at Western at one point in time came to me and said: 'You know, you look exhausted. Are you okay?' They couldn't have been nicer. They were both, like – I can't speak highly enough of either law school."[162]

As we fanned out across Ontario, we discovered that many of the women in small communities had attended the University of Windsor Law School, often as mature students.[163] They all recalled their law school years fondly, in spite of the demands of the program. One of these women talked about the initial stress of returning to school as a single parent with a part-time job. She also commuted a long distance to law school so it was not surprising to hear that she developed a severe viral infection in the middle of her first year. The illness forced her to miss several months of classes, but the response of her professors and fellow students when she regained her health was overwhelming. She said: "What happened at the school, not only the people I went to school with, but the school said: 'You can start all over again the next year or we'll take a whack at tutoring you' ... So, for the latter part of my first year I literally had profs tutoring me on my subjects and I had the people that I went to school with – you know – your little group, alphabetically of course ... I was just astounded by the amount of support!"

Clearly, the women who attend law school are not a homogenous group. Some of them come from wealthy families while others are single mothers struggling to get through school in search of a secure income. Some of them are very young and inexperienced but others are looking for a second or third career. A student's gender can affect her law school experience but other factors can work to heighten negative effects. Consideration of these additional variables is important because they can determine a woman's choice of law school, and they can shape her entire legal career.

Conclusion

In spite of Clara Brett Martin's early success in gaining admission to the legal profession, women in most jurisdictions are relative newcomers, and they have entered a world where the customs and beliefs have been mapped out by men of a certain class. These men built a culture that reflected elitist values, and they learned to speak a common language based on a masculine version of reality. The Ontario bar is no exception. The image of the nineteenth-century professional gentleman lingered in the corridors of large firms and law school classrooms until the final decades of the twentieth century. Many writers and activists point to continuing gender differences in earning power and levels of autonomy as evidence that the hidden assumptions of the profession still favour men. Until these patterns change, they argue, women with family obligations will be unable to build up the precious stores of social and cultural capital that foster professional success. At their most optimistic, they see hope for feminist inspired reforms at all levels, suggesting, in some cases, that women's unique styles of practice will alter traditional approaches to the administration of justice.

The potential for change took root when women began streaming into law schools in the 1980s. Perplexed by some of the practices, a few women sought out feminist professors, and, together, they began to challenge the customs, the pedagogy, and the language of the law. Conservative faculty members reacted immediately, generating conflict that was especially sharp at the Osgoode Hall, Queen's, and Western law schools. The University of Toronto Law School remained relatively unscathed, while newer schools such as Windsor and Ottawa appeared to escape most of the feminist debate.

Many of the women in this study attended law school during this critical stage of legal history. A few of them formed strong alliances with other feminist students and faculty members, but most of them remained on the fringes of the debate, intent on getting through their courses without additional stress. Some scholars have suggested that the law school culture posed serious problems for women, particularly by relying on the so-called Socratic method to generate debate. They reported that women experienced a sense of alienation, a loss of self-confidence, and a general silencing when faced with the demands of the first-year law class. These themes are particularly evident in the accounts of women who graduated from large American law schools in the 1980s. Written by the first wave of women in classrooms characterized by a strong masculine presence, they reflect the rise of essential feminism as a way of addressing gender inequities.

Recent works look more closely at the background characteristics of law students, examining the effects of their social class, their occupational goals, and their race on their performance in law school. The substantial body of literature in this area is concentrated on prestigious American law schools, and many of the studies have been done at Harvard, the birthplace of the Langdellian method of instruction.[164] My study deals with women educated primarily in Ontario law schools where they were far less likely to encounter the Socratic method. Osgoode Hall was one of the few Canadian law schools to use large classes and Socratic techniques in its first-year courses. Consequently, the choice of law school is influential in shaping a woman's response to her legal education.

Osgoode and University of Toronto graduates in this study expressed mixed feelings about their legal education. Although many of them cited academic excellence as an advantage, women from Osgoode tended to feel overwhelmed by the large classes, and Toronto graduates recalled an elite, competitive environment. Graduates of Queen's and Western were more likely to comment favourably on their law school experience, in spite of the feminist conflict that marked the 1980s. Ottawa graduates were generally pleased with their legal education, but the University of Windsor Law School was the clear winner in the minds of its graduates. They all talked about their appreciation for accessible faculty members and cooperative classmates. Many of them commuted to Windsor together weekly, and they said they acquired a circle of lifelong friends during their law school years. Without the divisive effects of feminist debate, they seemed free to concentrate on the study of the law in a very supportive environment.

The unique character of Windsor's law school suggests that it would make an interesting case study. Are the faculty members less conservative than their counterparts at elite law schools? Does Windsor attract a student body less likely to challenge the old ways? Is the environment particularly appealing to women students? These questions remain to be answered in future studies. We can say with certainty, however, that Windsor has aimed for a diverse student population from its inception in 1967, sometimes bypassing academic credentials and LSAT scores in favour of life experiences when considering potential students. As a result, a large proportion of mature students have been channelled into Windsor's law school.

Mature students emerged as a very perceptive group in this study, demonstrating a keen awareness of the class differences between themselves and younger students, who are often armed with generous funding from their parents. Mature students are typically over the age of twenty-five and often lack an undergraduate degree when they enter law school, but the women in this study were a very diverse group. Their pre-law education levels ranged from Grade 10 to doctoral degrees. For some women, law was an escape from a bad marriage or a low-level job, but several women also chose law after pursuing academic careers. Their only common characteristic was the fact that they were older than the students who had come straight out of undergraduate programs.

A woman's race or her sexual orientation may have an impact on her law school experience, but my findings in these areas are limited to some brief anecdotal material. A random sample drawn from a large population of law students would undoubtedly provide a broader spectrum.[165] The same criteria would apply to a study of women law students with disabilities. This study did, however, reveal potential sources of stress that have not been emphasized in previous works. Once again, an examination of the lives of mature students is a useful tool, demonstrating that pregnancies, childbirth, and family demands can complicate the lives of women attending law school. These factors help us to place women's lives in a larger context, both as a measure of their law school experience and as a predictor of their career paths.

Reports from the women in this study do not confirm the widely held view that theoretical legal knowledge is intimidating and exclusionary because it represents a detached, masculine approach to learning. Theoretical law has been seen as a partner to the Langdellian method, but the Socratic approach has not been used widely in Canadian law schools. First-year classes at Osgoode Hall were, until recently, the exception, but very few women identified problems with the pedagogical methods employed. Other schools use a small group approach to foster debate and build mutual support networks among students.

Several studies emphasize women's preferences for law that deals with social issues, concluding that the prescribed law school curriculum leaves little room for courses focusing on poverty or welfare law. The women in this study did not register strong levels of disappointment about the failure of the system to accommodate their interests. Some of them indicated that they would have liked more course options in their first year, but most of them found that they could expand their course selections in subsequent years.

It seems that the shadow of the professional gentleman is fading somewhat with the arrival of a new century, but women have yet to establish
themselves as respected authorities on legal matters. Like Portia, they are
still seen by some as temporary actors in a profession committed to traditional practices. With larger cohorts of women students, the population
of Canadian law schools has changed dramatically over the past thirty years,
and it will change even more profoundly during the next thirty years. Available evidence suggests that Canadian law students are increasingly drawn
from low socioeconomic backgrounds and law schools have encouraged
diversity by including quotas for groups such as First Nations students
who would otherwise be underrepresented.[166] As immigration patterns
alter the demographic face of Canada, future generations of law students
will undoubtedly reflect the multicultural complexion of the country.[167]

The larger question centres on differences among law schools – the candidates they attract, the fees they charge, and the career paths open to
their graduates. This study suggests that gender alone is an insufficient
measure of these differences but that women with limited financial resources are doubly disadvantaged. Traditional law schools such as Toronto,
Queen's, and Western will continue to recruit students with strong academic credentials and, increasingly, generous financial backing.[168] However, other law schools will probably attract a broader range of students,
often bound for modest practices far from Bay Street in Toronto.[169] Once
again, the effects apparent in this study will, in all likelihood, be magni-
fied in future. Class differences are bound to persist, both in the classroom
and at the entry gate, but other factors such as gender, age, and racial
background will interact with social class to favour some students and
leave others in second-class positions.[170]

4
Caught in the Time Crunch

Each of us knows disillusioned young lawyers who are
terribly worried about the pressures on practitioners today.
Some of them are strong enough to say no – and they get out.
Others stay in, often unhappily, because there is no realistic
alternative. The degree of stress is often unmanageable and the
effects on family life can be horrendous – and all of this is
without considering the special problems of women trying to
balance the demands of practice and a family.[1]

In 1990, Morris Gross, a retired Toronto lawyer, offered these words to
an audience of classmates from his Osgoode Hall Law School graduating
class, celebrating their fortieth anniversary in legal practice. His wisdom
was profound in light of the attitudes towards women in law that prevailed throughout most of his career. He would have had a handful of
women as classmates in 1950, but the changes in gender representation
over his legal lifetime were marked. By 1990, women had become a visible presence in the profession, but the demands on their time exerted
pressures that Morris Gross and his contemporaries would not have
dreamed possible at the beginning of their careers.

These kinds of pressures have led commentators to adopt terms such as
"famine," "squeeze," "crunch," and "bind" to describe the temporal constraints experienced by busy families. Accounts of their harried lives appear
regularly in print and on television, but, in spite of their media appeal,
these terms require empirical backing to justify their reliability.[2] One of
the most effective measures in current use is the quantitative index of "time
crunch," which was developed by testing responses to a battery of statements about the impact of temporal stress in respondents' lives.[3] Researchers in this field confirm clear patterns of time-induced stress that
are most pronounced for families with young children and intensified for
those who add elder care responsibilities to their daily schedules.[4]

Scheduling problems are now so widespread that family time management has become a dominant theme throughout the social science literature. International awareness of work-family time conflicts has generated
numerous interdisciplinary conferences, policy initiatives, generous private and public funding, research centres, and copious banks of data.[5]
The process began with the flood of women into the labour force during
the 1960s, and the first scholarly works began to appear early in the 1980s.[6]
Working families became the focus of research produced over the next

twenty years, and the findings were indisputable. Throughout the literature, women were identified as the single group most likely to suffer from time-triggered stress because of the widespread expectation that they should continue to manage home and family activities along with their labour force commitments.[7]

Interest in the topic has continued to gain momentum, giving rise to a steady stream of publications since the beginning of the new millennium.[8] These works have covered a broad range of issues around time, perhaps best summarized as a "time divide" that separates the overworked from the underemployed, women from men, and parents from non-parents.[9] These divisions are important because simple averages reveal scant change over time.[10] However, the proportion of Canadians working more than fifty hours a week rose from 10 percent in 1991 to 25 percent in 2001.[11] Men still work longer hours than women, but dual-earner couples spend more time in the labour force than the male breadwinners of the 1950s.[12] Some studies report that increased working hours disrupt the work-family balance for men, but the effects are less pronounced for women.[13] Managerial and professional people work the longest hours, and women in these occupations experience heavy stress because the model of the two-person career still prevails.[14] The arrival of children compounds these time pressures. Even though families are smaller than in the past, middle-class parents spend more time with each child and the responsibility for ferrying them around to music lessons and soccer games often falls on working mothers.[15]

These patterns have been documented in the lives of many women practising law, but, once again, it is important to look beyond the number of hours spent at work. Jean Wallace reports that the *perception* of excessive work demands rather than the number of hours worked per week has contributed to "work-to-nonwork" conflict among the lawyers in her study, and subjective feelings of work overload have been particularly problematic for women.[16] Since these kinds of attitudinal variables add depth in studies of working hours, a quantitative analysis of time crunch levels for the women in this study forms the backbone for this chapter. Their scores on the time crunch index are examined in relation to the scores reported by women working in other sectors of the Canadian economy. By isolating specific items in the index that are relevant to the lives of the lawyers, I have also established links with the qualitative material gleaned from their interviews, confirming the presence of time crunch stress from various sources. The lawyers are part of a profession that has been male-dominated until very recently, so their time crunch levels are higher than those of most other employed women. Moreover, the women who practise law in large urban centres report higher stress levels than their colleagues in outlying areas of the province. My aim in this chapter is to advance our understanding of the scheduling problems that professional women face in everyday life and, as preparation for Chapter 6, to shed some light on the ways in which these patterns influence their career paths.

Women, Time Crunch, and Stress

North American culture is characterized by a view of time that reflects the workings of industrial society generally. Theorists have used various terms to contrast the times of these societies with those that prevail in less developed societies.[17] In fact, life in contemporary industrial societies reflects a complex blend of times, so employed women move across many temporal boundaries, both physically and mentally, as they navigate the course of a working day.[18] If they have young children, they may have to deal with sleep disturbances, erratic feeding patterns, and annoying interruptions. If they have aging parents, they are often called upon without warning to deal with their special needs. Their time at home expands to embrace daily duties, weekly events, and annual rituals – mealtimes, bedtimes, weekend plans, birthdays, and vacations.

These patterns are most pronounced among women working full-time in managerial and professional occupations. For example, women who practise law often balance the unpredictable time of family life with the highly regimented commitments demanded by their practices. Their appointment books are full, hearings are scheduled months in advance, and many of their clients expect immediate feedback. Most lawyers use the ten-segment billable hour to keep records, which leaves them at the mercy of clock time.[19] This system imposes long days and frequent weekend work on lawyers who are forced to meet their quota of hours, based either on their employers' expectations or on their own economic circumstances. The working day has been lengthened further with the widespread use of voice-mail, e-mail, and cell phone technology, stretching the limits of the workplace and intruding on private time. Conflict between these competing spheres can lead to time crunch and a host of potential stresses.

Current research on the legal profession attests to the problems posed by long working hours, especially among women practitioners.[20] Although none of the works cited deal specifically with the issue of time crunch, women's general vulnerability has been demonstrated repeatedly. For example, results from John Robinson's 1991 national US study confirm well-known gender differences in time crunch, pinpointing women between the ages of thirty and forty-nine as the group at greatest risk, particularly if they are single mothers.[21] These findings are corroborated by studies based on Canadian General Social Survey data, identifying the mid-life years as the most heavily time-stressed period for women, especially if they live in dual-earner households and work full-time outside the home.[22] Although the range of explanatory variables differs slightly from study to study, the most commonly cited stressor is the length of the working week.[23] Findings from the 1998 General Social Survey on Time Use indicate that these trends have grown more pronounced over time.[24] The working day is longer than it was when the previous survey was conducted in 1992, and time crunch stress continues to escalate in response to the increase in hours on the job.[25] The gendered division of labour also persists. On average, women spend more time on unpaid work than their male counterparts, while men continue to work longer hours in the paid labour force.[26]

Occupational demands and personality characteristics leave some groups of people open to these kinds of stresses. Anna Kemeny demonstrates these patterns by using a single item from the time crunch index as a measure of workaholic tendencies. By analyzing respondents' responses (agree/disagree) to the statement "I consider myself a workaholic," she concludes that 27 percent of Canadian men and women see themselves as workaholics and that the patterns are most pronounced for people employed in high-income occupations. Making use of other items in the index, Kemeny reports that workaholics experience stress trying to accomplish more than they can handle, feel trapped in a daily routine, have no time for fun, and worry about insufficient time for family and friends.[27] While it is risky to apply a label such as "workaholic" based on a single item, Kemeny's findings have some bearing on my work. Workaholism may be a feature of legal life because many women in my study agreed with three of the four items singled out by Kemeny as symptomatic of workaholic tendencies.

Catherine Lee and her colleagues used similar indicators, but they drew conceptual lines between time and stress. In interviews with women employed in the public sector in the national capital region, they asked: "Do you feel that there are enough hours in the day to accomplish everything you have to do?"[28] Eighty-seven percent of the women responded negatively to this question, and two-thirds of the women indicated that they had considered quitting their jobs because of time pressures.[29] The women in their study reported a preference for jobs with flexible work times and locations, leading the authors to conclude that women in managerial and professional positions ("career" women) had an advantage over women in administrative or clerical jobs ("earners").[30] In response to questions about their time constraints, career women said that they forfeited individual leisure, while earners said that they cut back on housecleaning and child care. These patterns may reflect income differentials that have allowed the career women to hire domestic and child care workers.[31] The presence of young children has also compounded scheduling problems for women in general in this study. Not surprisingly, the burden was heaviest for women with children under fourteen. However, many women reported that life became easier as their children grew older and they developed routines to deal with their work and family demands.[32]

One noteworthy aspect of this study is the disjunction between women's responses to the time management questions and their scores on a stress scale. Where time management questions dealt with daily time commitments and priorities, the stress scale tapped issues of control and organization in the face of mounting responsibilities. In spite of their reports of time management problems, career women reported lower levels of stress than did earners. In summary, the career women appear to have more flexible schedules, more resources for dealing with household and family needs, and lower levels of stress than their counterparts in clerical and administrative positions. Does this mean that their lives are more manageable or that their time crunch levels are lower? Not necessarily. It may be a reflection of the sample chosen for analysis: professional women in the public service may enjoy scheduling advantages that are not generally available. In addition, the authors of this study relied on four separate measures of time management that were treated as discrete variables in a set of cross tabulations. A more comprehensive measure of time crunch would have allowed them to use regression analysis to gain a clearer picture of the women's perceptions of time conflicts.

Lee's work is valuable because she differentiates between professional women and those in clerical positions. My study narrows the focus further by centring on women in the legal profession. An examination of time crunch stress in their daily lives provides a snapshot of their temporal constraints and allows comparisons with other women. Using a standard measure of time crunch, I compare their scores with those of women working in other occupations, identifying aspects of the time crunch index that are particularly relevant in the lives of the lawyers. I also compare time crunch scores for women practising law in three different types of settings – Toronto, London, and a number of other communities throughout the province. Finally, because the women in this study are a diverse group, I look closely at their scores across time, identifying the sources of pressure in their lives. Does the presence of children increase levels of temporal stress? Do other family obligations lead women to reduce their commitments? Does the type of practice affect a woman's time crunch levels? In short, who are the women with the highest levels of stress and how is this stress manifested? Since some of the women have managed to control or reduce time-related stress in their lives, I conclude with a brief discussion of their experiences and compare their lives with those of the busiest women in the study.

Measuring Time Crunch

Questions included in the ten-item time crunch index are shown in Figure 4.1. This index is a copy of the one used by Statistics Canada in the 1992 and the 1998 General Social Survey on Time Use. Analysts with Statistics Canada adopted this index after consultation with John Robinson at the University of Maryland.[33] Canadian researchers modified the index for use in the General Social Survey, retaining eight of the original items and developing two new ones.[34] They also conducted factor analyses to confirm the strength of the index as a measure of time crunch.[35] When the items are added to produce a ten-item measure of time crunch, the resulting index provides a reliable measure of time crunch.[36] Statistics Canada analysts classified respondents as "severely time crunched" if they agreed with seven or more items, "moderately time crunched" if they agreed with four to six questions, and "not time crunched" if they agreed with less than four items.[37]

In this study, we conducted an SPSS analysis of data derived from a set of structured questionnaires administered at the time of each interview.[38] Table 4.1 shows levels of time crunch for the women lawyers, contrasting their scores with those for a national sample of women aged twenty-five to sixty-four who were employed full-time in the paid labour force.[39] Levels

Figure 4.1

Ten-item time crunch index, Statistics Canada General Social Survey on Time Use, 1992 and 1998

	Agree	Disagree	
1.	❏	❏	I plan to slow down in the coming year.
2.	❏	❏	I consider myself a workaholic.
3.	❏	❏	When I need more time, I tend to cut back on my sleep.
4.	❏	❏	At the end of the day, I often feel that I have not accomplished what I had set out to do.
5.	❏	❏	I worry that I do not spend enough time with my family and friends.
6.	❏	❏	I feel that I'm constantly under stress trying to accomplish more than I can handle.
7.	❏	❏	I feel trapped in a daily routine.
8.	❏	❏	I feel that I just do not have time for fun anymore.
9.	❏	❏	I often feel under stress when I do not have enough time.
10.	❏	❏	I would like to spend more time alone.

of time crunch increased for women in the general population during the 1990s, and these patterns are particularly pronounced for employed women: in 1992, 41.8 percent of these women reported little or no time crunch, but, by 1998, this figure had dropped to 33.1 percent. The women lawyers in this study are still more likely to experience moderate levels of time crunch than their counterparts in other occupations, but the gap is narrowing. Sixty-nine percent of the lawyers reported moderate or high levels of time crunch, but they were less likely to report severe time crunch than women in the 1998 General Social Survey. Perhaps their stress is alleviated by their access to paid domestic help and some measure of control over the scheduling of their work hours, but their responses to individual items in the time crunch index may also help to explain some of these differences.

The most pronounced differences between the women lawyers and their counterparts in other occupations are apparent when we compare their responses to individual items. As indicated in Table 4.2, the lawyers were more likely to agree with four specific items than Canadian women in general. These items tap feelings of frustration about their inability to deal with an unending round of obligations and their resultant lack of time for family and friends. Time crunch and time famine are relentless partners in the lives of these women. The lawyers also differed markedly from women in the general population on some other questions in the ten-item index. In spite of their positive responses to questions that Anna Kemeny links to workaholism, they were less likely to report that they considered themselves workaholics. They also were unlikely to report that they felt trapped in a daily routine or that they did not have time for fun anymore.

The findings in Table 4.3 reveal some regional differences among the lawyers. Toronto women reported the highest levels of time stress, followed by the women in London and the remaining centres respectively.

Table 4.1

Levels of time crunch for employed women in Canada aged 25-64 and women lawyers in this study

	Employed women aged 25-64, General Social Surveys (%)		Women lawyers in this study (%)
Level of time crunch	1992 (N = 1,462)	1998 (N = 1,957)	1994, 1996, 1999 (N = 110)
Severe (7 or more)	24.7	27.9	25.4
Moderate (4 to 6)	33.6	38.9	43.6
None (3 or less)	41.8	33.1	30.9
Total	100.0	100.0	100.0

Note: Due to rounding, columns may not add up to 100.

These findings suggest that life is slightly more relaxed for lawyers living outside large urban centres. Their counterparts in Toronto typically deal with longer commuting times and are less likely to enjoy back-up support from family members. The faster pace of urban life is reflected in their practices as well. Overhead costs necessitate high billings and longer hours on the job.

Since the four items in Tables 4.2 and 4.3 have particular relevance for the women in this study, they were used to construct a second index designated "time crunch stress."[40] In contrast with the other items in the Statistics Canada ten-item index of time crunch, this index incorporates a measure of women's feelings and worries about their work and family loads. Where the other items focus on coping strategies, self image, and personal needs, each of the four items in this index reflects their feelings of stress as they attempt to manage their daily schedules and still make time for family members and friends. These qualities make it a more focused measure of time crunch stress for the women in this study than either the ten-item index from the Statistics Canada Time Use Surveys or the single-item measures of time management used by Catherine Lee and her colleagues.[41]

Table 4.2

Four measures of time crunch for employed women in Canada aged 25-64 (1992 and 1998) and women lawyers

Time crunch items	Respondents agreeing with statement (%)		
	General Social Survey 1992 (N = 1,462)	General Social Survey 1998 (N = 1,957)	Lawyers in this study 1994, 1996, 1999 (N = 110)
At the end of the day, I often feel that I have not accomplished what I had set out to do.	52.9	53.6	59.1
I worry that I do not spend enough time with my family and friends.	47.2	54.3	65.5
I feel that I'm constantly under stress trying to accomplish more than I can handle.	44.9	48.9	60.0
I often feel under stress when I do not have enough time.	62.1	72.1	80.0

"I Worry That I Don't Spend Enough Time with Family and Friends"

An examination of changes in the lawyers' time crunch scores on the four-item index over time revealed some interesting patterns. Almost two-thirds of the 110 women had mid-range scores on the index that were consistent across the three- to four-year time span between interviews, but the experiences of the remaining thirty-nine women suggest that time pressures present major problems.[42] Twenty-one of these women had scores of four, making them an appropriate group for further scrutiny. In some cases, their high scores remained constant over time, while, in others, levels of stress were higher when we returned for the second interview. Five other women had increased their scores from one to three over time, and thirteen women either had consistently low levels (zero or one) or had decreased their scores to zero or one over time. These low-stress women serve as a comparative group, providing some clues about the successful balancing of professional life with family and community obligations.

Many of the women with high time crunch scores are caught between competing professional goals and family ideals.[43] Having committed themselves to their legal careers, they are haunted by images of the "good mother" as they assume responsibility for the perfect family.[44] They blend their professional and family duties skilfully, priding themselves on their faithful attendance at their children's activities. Since many of them were

Table 4.3

Four-item time crunch index scores for initial interviews: Toronto 1994, London 1996, and Ontario 1999

Time crunch	Lawyers agreeing with statement (%)			
	Toronto 1994 (N = 30)	London 1996 (N = 30)	Ontario 1999 (N = 50)	Total sample (N = 110)
At the end of day, I feel that I have not accomplished what I had set out to do.	63.3	63.3	54.0	59.1
I worry that I do not spend enough time with my family and friends.	80.0	70.0	54.0	65.5
I feel that I'm constantly under stress trying to accomplish more than I can handle.	66.7	60.0	56.0	60.0
I often feel under stress when I do not have enough time.	83.3	80.0	78.0	80.0
Mean score (out of a total of four)	2.93	2.73	2.42	2.65

raised in traditional middle-class families, they often carry an image of their own stay-at-home mothers and express guilt about not measuring up to their levels of family involvement.[45] One of the lawyers demonstrated mixed feelings about her divided roles when she said:

> I generally try not to leave [the office] much past four-thirty or five because now I have to pick M up from daycare. I think ever since she's been born I've always tried to get home at a reasonable hour, because I just feel so guilty about, you know, leaving her all day and then she's in daycare, she's at school, then she goes back to daycare and, I mean it's just like a little mini-institution for this poor little thing. But she's quite content and happy. At least that's what I see ... I'm finding myself a little more stressed with work and M, only because of the various activities that she's involved in and I just – I feel it's unfair because both of us work outside the home – that she gets ripped off and doesn't get to do the things that she might do if there were a parent at home – whether it be me or my husband or whatever. And I know when I was growing up I – my mom was always at home and we did the swimming and this and that and – I guess because that was such a big part of my life and extra-curricular activities that I want her to at least experience ... I try not to push her but try to just get her exposed to various things and then she'll get to decide if she likes sports or music or if she hates it all and wants to do art or read or whatever. Who knows! ... So I find that is hard because she wanted to take a ballet class but I just couldn't fit it, for me to get her there, and I couldn't get anyone else to do it so, you know, I find that really breaks my heart. (Criminal lawyer, sole practice, called to the bar 1987)

Two other women emphasized their commitment to parental roles and their record of nearly perfect attendance at school and music performances in the face of very demanding work schedules. The first woman, a judge, described the rigid scheduling of courtroom time and the frustration of responding to her children's everyday needs. The second woman had an equally demanding position, but she assumed a large share of family responsibilities because she believed that mothers were more drawn to their child care commitments than fathers:

> It's extremely demanding time-wise. You have no control over your own time, which is odd. You'd think – you know – they can't do it unless the judge is there so you get to control your own pace but you just don't ... you're in court all of the time, and any time you're not, you're writing or you're just extremely pressed for time. And so the simple things in life become almost impossible obstacles, like doctor's appointments or getting

your hair done. A kid comes home and says: "I need a white turtleneck for the concert on Thursday," and it's already Tuesday. It's a crisis. There's no possible way I can do that ... Now I have actually done things like shut down court and go to things ... But, you know, there are things that I miss. I didn't make it to N's choir in the Kiwanis music festival. I tore in the door just as the choir finished – which was so disappointing. But – you know – there are things like that that I just can't make it to. (Judge, called to the bar 1980)

And then the arrangement was that he [her husband] would come home. He'd leave the office at six ... so that he would be there to relieve our nanny ... and I would then, if need be, stay late. But I found that I really didn't want to stay late. I wanted to go home and so typically what happens is I try and leave at six ... And it's funny because people say: "Oh well, you know, this is a reflection of men not wanting to do their share" or whatever, but I look upon it quite differently. I look upon it more as this is really what I'd like to do. I'd like to be spending the time with my children ... It's a terrible pull, just a terrible pull ... There's only been one thing that I've missed for either of my children, although they're both still pretty young. But still, I've gone to everything – like all of their presentations, all of their special things. There was only one thing that I missed and, in the overall scheme of things, it wasn't like a school concert or anything like that. It was something much more modest in scale but I've always been really very rigorous about that. But none the less I do feel that society has engaged a bit in sort of an experiment if you will in terms of child care – who looks after the children – you know – women working, et cetera. I question what the outcome of it all will be. (Civil litigation lawyer, large firm, called to the bar 1978)

The model of the good mother is evident in the comments of two other women who lamented the lack of time simply to "be" with their children, free from the round of scheduled activities. Time for them was clearly a commodity to be spent judiciously on lessons and sporting events or earmarked for bath time and the ritual bedtime story. The first woman expressed resentment at the expectations surrounding her parental obligations, invoking the image of her own "good mother" as an unattainable model. The second woman was devoted to her children, but she was aware that her time with her husband had suffered:

I work usually till six – till seven a couple of nights a week. It's summer time, so we have soccer on Mondays and Wednesdays and I'm the mother that prays for lightning because I don't like going to soccer ... My husband's out of town all night Tuesday night, so on Tuesday night I do everything – and sometimes Wednesday night as well. And we've got violin on Thursdays at five so I have to leave at five to go to violin class, and I'm always late. And I *hate* it. I *hate* violin class. It's not fun. What I really find is missing is that quality time with your kids. Not that I'm not there. It's just that I'm not focused on them. I'm just always running from one activity to another or stuff that I have to do. And I find that I feel – my mom was way younger when she had us, but she was down there and dirty with us and we were always doing stuff with her. And I'm not doing that with my kids. My nanny does, but I don't. And I don't just hang out and do stuff – just play. There's not even playtime in there. Not that I think I would be very good at it if I was there, but I feel like there's just – it's all activity based or it's – we've got to do this, got to do this, got to do this, rather than just sort of: "So, how are you and what do you want to do? Do you want to go for a walk or something like that?" ... Everything, everything is activity-based. It's either dinner, bath time, bedtime, story time, go time. You know? It's not just playing time. (Real estate lawyer, small firm, called to the bar 1984)

I feel stretched between my work and my family. I mean – I feel that I need to spend more time with my children, teaching them things, doing their homework with them, reading with them, playing tennis with them, talking to them, doing whatever with them. And I don't get to do that nearly as much as I want to do. And then in terms of my family, I think because clearly my children come first in my family, my husband and I don't get to spend enough time together as a couple ... If I had thirty-six hours a day, I could probably feel that maybe I could get done what I needed to get done. But there are only twenty-four hours in a day, so I think I end up feeling that I don't get to spend enough time with my children, my husband, and my immediate family, let alone my friends ... I guess I'm spending time with friends when we're at children's activities, for example, at soccer. I mean the boys on my kids' soccer team – some of their parents have become friends over the years ... But I don't necessarily call that spending time with friends. I call that a child's activity where the sort of friends are peripheral to what is being done. And the same thing – my children both play Suzuki violin which takes three hours every Saturday morning and so I will see parents who are friends there. But again, it's in the regime of watching our children or helping our children play violin. (Family lawyer, medium-size firm, called to the bar 1981)

Rituals are also important in middle-class life: the organization of daily, weekly, and annual family occasions is often seen as integral to women's roles.[46] Since food is an important part of ritual, many of the lawyers in this study expressed regret that their mealtimes were rarely family-centred events. In most cases, family members scattered after a quick breakfast and returned home at the end of the day, too tired and hungry to endure elaborate dinner preparations. Nannies often made dinner for small children or mothers arrived in time to feed their children, but many fathers returned home after their children had been fed and bathed. Parents' dinner was often a quick bite after the children had been put to bed. One woman told me proudly at her second interview that they no longer ate bagels for dinner because they had tried to make time for "real" dinner. However, her comments indicate that her attempts to provide a family meal remained thwarted:

> My kids really get the worst of me during the week. The morning is a – it's just a schmozzle. To add to our life, we got a dog in September because we don't have enough to keep ourselves busy with. So the morning now includes the hassle of which kid is going to walk the dog ... Now we have real dinner. We don't eat it together. The kids still eat before we come home. On the weekends we always sit down together but [during the week] they'll eat before I come in, depending on the time of year. If it's winter they're still in the house so one of them may sit down with me. Even my son will sit down and have some chat. This time of year they're gone. They're out and [my husband] will eat whenever he gets in and often I'll sit and talk to him. But we keep stupid hours. (Government lawyer, called to the bar 1982)

A second woman indicated that her life had become slightly less stressful since she had eliminated an hour of commuting time from her daily schedule. However, her practice had grown, many of her clients booked appointments late in the day, and she still had difficulty getting home for dinner with her husband and teenaged children. The ticking of the clock was evident in her description of an average working day:

> If anything, I've been able to spend more time with them than during the last four years, partly because I'm ... commuting a half an hour less each way ... I still don't make it home as early as I should – or at least not this last year. I don't get home. Oftentimes I'm not there for supper. Everyone else will have eaten and I'll be picking up the leftovers ... Now, my husband tells me the average is seven to seven-thirty even though I say: "Oh yeah I'll be home, I'll be home." It's seven to seven-thirty before I get there. There aren't too many days that I leave the office before six or six-thirty. (Family lawyer, sole practice, called to the bar 1993)

Children are aware of the time pressures in their mothers' lives and often demonstrate a remarkable level of maturity as they attempt to fit in their own activities. One woman recounted a telephone conversation with her daughter, amazed and yet saddened by her daughter's readiness to accommodate her schedule:

They're terrific kids. But – you know – I feel really bad when things happen like – E called me one day at work and she said: "Are you busy?" And I said: "No honey, what is it?" She said: "I just want to know whether or not you had motions court next week." And motions court is a really heavy, heavy week because you're in court all day and you have these files that get delivered, like sometimes two box loads, at four or five one day for the next day and then, you know, you have to do all – it's just an enormous workload. So that week it's deadly and the kids have just come to know that, you know. That's just a horrible week ... So, instead of calling to say: "Can you help me with my whatever project next week?" she said – the first thing she said was: "Are you in motions court?" And, you know, she was fine when I – It's just I find that kind of difficult. (Judge, called to the bar 1980)

A second woman told me that she had had many conversations about her legal career with her children and, even though they knew her profession was important to her, they still wished for a mother who could take part in more of their activities:

They would like me to be more available to do pizza days at school. The school fair was last week for example and my son was – you know – "Aren't you volunteering? You did the arts and crafts table last year. Aren't you going to volunteer?" And I said: "No, I think I missed the sheet because I don't think I signed up." And that night somebody called: "Can you do blah, blah for us?" So I said: "Oh, you know, your timing is perfect because my son wants me to volunteer" ... It was really interesting because it was really important to him that I be a mother involved ... So he was really pleased that I was. I'm going to face paint and he thought that was great and he got all of the girls that he knows to hang around. (Government lawyer, called to the bar 1982)

All the women with children told us that they had established strict priorities in their lives. Their social lives had been reduced dramatically, and, barring a critical situation, many of them spent little time with their relatives. Their focus was definitely on the needs of their children. One woman viewed her commitment to her children in the context of her entire lifetime:

We both work full-time and we both work long hours and we decided when we had children that there would be a period where all – most – I won't say all – but most of our spare time would be spent with our children and with their activities. I mean – already my twelve-year-old is – well, he's twelve, but I can't believe that he's been here for twelve years ... already more than half of my time of him being with me is gone. And it's absolutely amazing that that could have occurred. So, we both made a decision that they're only in your life on a full-time basis for a relatively short period of your lifetime, and you might as well spend all the time you can with them. We didn't have kids for six years or seven years, so we had six or seven years as a married couple where, you know, we had lots of time and then presumably ... we'll have a bunch of years after that as well. So we made it a joint decision that we wouldn't take holidays and go away without our kids. So we just don't. (Family lawyer, medium-size firm, called to the bar 1981)

A second lawyer demonstrated her complete commitment to her preschool son and her inability to include extended family members in her busy life:

I try to use pretty much all of my off-work time for my husband and my son. But I don't see my family. They are all busy with – I have two brothers and one sister. I don't see one of my brothers a whole lot ... His life moves in a different direction than mine but my sister has four kids and B being an only child, these are the only cousins that he has. You know they are sort of similar but they are a little bit older than he is but still at the age that he can play, so I would like to see more of them ... My mom and dad, they just live in [a nearby city] and yet I don't get through there very often at all – you know. And just because on a weekend, which is really the only time I could ... There is so much else that needs to be accomplished – you know – tasks around the home, what have you ... I don't spend enough time. (Child protection lawyer, community agency, called to the bar 1987)

A third lawyer talked about her exclusive focus on family activities, expressing regret that she no longer had access to friends from law school or university. Her feelings of marginality were similar to those that surfaced in discussions with other women who, like her, had chosen to practise in small communities:

My mom is still alive and so she is in the area, so we get together with her a fair amount. But really, in my life I'm more focused on my husband and my two kids. I enjoy their company so if I had my preference as opposed to expanding it to an extended family, that's where I would spend my time ... Probably in one area I am noticing I lack – partly because a lot of the friends I had – career, university, work – that I had a common interest in – they've moved on to Toronto or they've migrated more in that direction, where I've kind of gone in the other direction, so there's not a lot of opportunity to get together, plus you get on and get busy with your own lives, either in their own practices, or many of them were single during university so now they've settled down and are just having families, so I'm at a different stage of life than they are. I grew up in an area where I live now, so that a lot of people that I know from – say high school – most of them I don't have a lot of things in common with anymore. Our lives have just taken different paths. (Family lawyer, sole practice, called to the bar 1993)

Women often mentioned their desire to have more time with their husbands and, in response to one of the time crunch questions, their need for time alone. One woman said that she and her husband used their front porch for serious conversation in the summer time but that their children were never far away. Other women in the study told us that they set aside one night a week for a "date," but most women were too busy to work this kind of organization into their days. Some of them alluded to marital problems, and, for most of them, time alone was squeezed into the weekend schedule. Two of the time-crunched women talked about their need for more discussion with their partners or simply time to be alone:

I've even recognized the two areas where I think I don't have enough time. I'm content with the amount of time I spend on work and I'm happy with the amount of time I spend with my daughter but it's my husband and myself. And they're totally different. But I was thinking that it's not just that I would like more time to myself so I could spend it with my husband. It's that I'd like time with him and I would like time alone. (Criminal lawyer, small firm, called to the bar 1986)

[How much time do you spend alone?] Saturday morning and then maybe an hour. Maybe I'll read for an hour. I mean, [her husband] is always about but I don't know if I'd count it as alone time. I don't know, a couple of hours a weekend. I guess a couple of hours a week ... I kind of feel guilty about that sometimes and think I should be – you know – spending more time enjoying my kids because you know, they're not going to be kids forever. And there will be a day when I'm yearning for them. So, I should be spending more time. So, I want to spend more time. I feel guilty about ... spending the time alone. (Family lawyer, sole practice, called to the bar 1988)

A few of the women talked about the added responsibility of parents who became seriously ill. One of these women struggled to keep her legal work up to date as she sat at her mother's bedside. She told me that her firm set such high performance levels that she did not feel she could take a break, even though her mother lived at a distant location. Her comments highlight the overpowering effects of the quantitative time of the office to the detriment of body time, first her mother's and then her own when she finally succumbed to pneumonia:

> This past year for me was quite extraordinary in that my mother was very ill. And my mom and I are very close and she lives in another city and she had a very aggressive form of cancer and I learned firsthand about the health care system in Canada and some of its ways. But she's a real fighter and I was out there many times and spent at least three weeks camped out in a hospital, acting as some kind of nurse's aide in the process ... I was basically expected to maintain my production so, while she was sleeping, I would sit in the cafeteria and work. Before I went to the hospital in the morning I'd check in with the office ... I kept working like a maniac and trying to do what I had to do and wanted to do for my mom. And in March my body finally said: "That's it!" And I got pneumonia for the first time in my life. But again, you know the whole time when you have incidents like that where you have personal family crises or you're sick yourself, all you do is worry about your billable hours ... It's insidious. I don't want to be like that, but the way law firms are managed, you have to be like that ... It's every big law firm. We are not unique, not at all. What I am saying, I truly believe, applies to them all because I've talked to my friends at other firms and – you know – the people I've talked to are all moaning the same. (Corporate commercial lawyer, large firm, called to the bar 1978)

"When I Need More Time I Tend to Cut Back on My Sleep"
The pressures of work take their toll in other ways as well; women with high time crunch scores were more likely to report that they cut back on their sleep when they had heavy workloads. Even the women who did not consciously reduce their sleeping time said that they would often waken in the night thinking about their legal work. Two women described their strategies for dealing with these disruptions caused by periodic increases in their workload:

> On a good night when I can get back to sleep, I will average maybe seven hours, sometimes a bit longer. But that's rare. That's really rare so I function probably at anywhere between four to five hours a night ... but it

depends on if I can get back to sleep when I wake up or if the kids wake up and they want – because I hear everything. And I sleep with ear plugs too ... If I have something that needs to be done or a trial coming up ... It's hard to shut that off, especially when you're preparing at night. Because I may prepare starting at nine o'clock at night after the kids have gone down, and I'll stay till twelve, twelve-thirty. And you can't just shut it off ... Some of my best cross-examinations have been at three o'clock in the morning because you start thinking about it ... I have called into the office and left myself a voice-mail message at three o'clock in the morning: "Don't forget about this. You've got to do this," because sometimes I find it's all in my head as I'm driving and as I get closer, it goes somewhere else because something else will have come up. (Family lawyer, medium-size firm, called to the bar 1986)

I have to get *x* number of things done during the day and, if I don't get it done and have to get it done, I'll go to bed at two in the morning or get up at five in the morning to get it done ... there may be times when I do it one or two nights a week for several weeks in a row, and there may be times when I don't do it at all for five or six weeks in a row. And sometimes when I'm really busy in court or really busy, like on a trial, I'll do it for – you know – I just go on adrenalin ... I normally would sleep from eleven-thirty to six-thirty. That's what I function best on. If I get that – and you can do it for – I expect anyone can function on a little amount of sleep for maybe four, five, six days. But after that, it probably starts showing ... So I mean, if I go for, say, more than a week with three or four hours a night, I find that I'm getting pretty tired. (Family lawyer, medium-size firm, called to the bar 1981)

Children's needs can compound sleeping problems and trigger stress in the middle of the night. Several women talked about the effects of these interruptions and then went on to describe the kinds of night-time worries that could take shape in their minds:

For a young child it's a matter of course, that your sleep does get cut back based on the mere fact that the child will get up in the middle of the night. You know – I think it's – now he's three and a half – especially when he was younger – you know – children do tend to get up a lot. Also, previously, I had evenings. If I didn't have a spillover of work I could do it in the evening after supper. Now it's left until after he's been bathed and put to bed and so on, so everything kind of gets moved back. So the only time that is left to do this is the time before I go to bed. That affects my sleep and I think also that the job itself has become – the volume has increased, the stress has increased so that has also impacted on my sleeping patterns ... I'm pretty tired if I only have six hours, you know. An eight-hour night would be much better for me ... What happens is, during the week I don't get eight hours but on the weekend I tend to overcompensate and sleep late, too long – as long as my son lets me. Ultimately, he's my alarm clock on the weekends. (Child protection lawyer, community agency, called to the bar 1987)

For many of the women, sleep deprivation was part of an ongoing pattern. They were regularly haunted by the work that they could not leave behind, and they were simply resigned to lives marked by inadequate sleep. One of them said:

Oh I need a lot of sleep – a good seven and a half to eight hours and I don't cut back on my sleep. If I do, I pay for it. Probably the worst thing would be being stressed and waking up in the middle of the night when it's been a particularly busy stretch, and if I get overtired, then I'm more apt to be lying there wide awake at two o'clock and can't go back to sleep. (Family lawyer, sole practice, called to the bar 1993)

A second woman said:

If I'm stressed out, I wake up at three or four in the morning and don't get back to sleep ... I'm not very good at night but I'm pretty okay in the morning and I find that, if I wake up at four, it means I've got stuff to do and I just go and do it usually. It's way easier to do it than to toss and turn ... My doctor calls it a lifestyle choice ... It's the only way you can get it done ... I probably do it for about a month at a time every three months. And then you sort of get caught up and go back to normal ... Having a computer at home has helped. Having voice-mail has helped, so you can call. I mean, sometimes it's just that you wake up thinking about the fourteen things, and you just get on the voice-mail and you plug into your secretary's phone line and go: "Do this, do this, do this, do this, do this." "Oh, I can go back to sleep now. I just dumped it all on somebody else and it will be done when I come in, in the morning." But usually, you just get up and just sort of work through what it is. And it's also the only quiet time. I mean that's the big problem with what I've got going on in life right now. There's a lot of noise time. There have been like forty phone calls already this morning and – you know – it's hard to find time where there are no interruptions. And at four in the morning, there are no interruptions. (Real estate lawyer, small firm, called to the bar 1984)

"I Feel That I'm Constantly under Stress Trying to Accomplish More Than I Can Handle"

Finally, the women with the highest time crunch scores seemed to be perpetually stressed, searching for the spare moments that represent small change in a world of commodified time. Their comments suggest visions of women on the run, always struggling to get things done as they race against the clock:

> There's just too much to do and not enough time. And there's always that sense that – you know – if I just had that extra fifteen or twenty minutes on that particular file I could make sure I had all the loose ends. (Family lawyer, sole practice, called to the bar 1993)

> You know, [I'd love] to be able to spend some playtime with my son ... I don't accomplish that as much as I would like because you're home at five-thirty. Six o'clock you have supper and then it's bath time, and before you know it, it's bedtime ... at work too it's just that the volume has really picked up so you may have a sense of: "I will get *xy* instead accomplished today at the office" ... I'll find I'll get to the end of the day and I've spent the whole day putting out fires ... I'm always running to catch up on everything I do it seems. I'm running to get stuff done for my kids, I'm running to get stuff done for my mother, for my sisters, for my husband, for me, for my friends, for my clients. I just – you know – never ever get done. It's an endless list of stuff that needs to be done, and I'm never caught up. But that's simply the way it is ... I don't know when I'll get caught up. (Child protection lawyer, community agency, called to the bar 1987)

> I always feel like I'm running to try and catch up. There's just never *not* a relatively long list. I could always do more violin practice with my children. We could always sit down and read more of Harry Potter. I could always be organizing their drawers of winter and summer clothing. We could always be – you know – I can go on – playing tennis. We could always be golfing. I could always be in here working. I could always be cleaning ... There's always laundry to be done. There is always just a big long list of things that need to be done ... if I finish working on ten files, there are always ten more ... there is always stuff that needs to be done. (Family lawyer, medium-size firm, called to the bar 1981)

Some of the women had gained a new perspective by taking time away from work. Two of them had reduced their stress during maternity leaves, but, with the return to work, their time crunch scores shot up again. The first woman registered mounting levels of stress, but she seemed exhilarated by the challenge of dealing with her busy life. At one point in the interview, she told us that her husband was so busy with his work that she felt like a single parent, adding: "Now I'm busier than I've been probably in the last five years. I'm doing a little more speaking out of the office, those sorts of things ... It's just hard to keep schedules straight and who's going where – and between swimming lessons and ball hockey ... I can't really add anything more."

The second woman was very thoughtful about her attempts to find balance in her life:

> Well, I can really identify with that ad on television where the mother is getting ready in the morning and she's talking about something at work and the kids want to go to the beach and she says: "I can't. I have to meet with a client today." And the little girl says: "When can I be a client?" It's true. You do feel sometimes that you're not giving them all that you should be. But – you know – I know that I like – I want to work – so that's not – I'm not constantly struggling with that conflict. I know that it's better for me to work. And whether it's four days a week or three days a week or right now, temporarily – you know – I'm quite busy with these other files that I have because I'm covering my colleague's practice. I know that at another point in time I'm going to be able to give them more – my kids – more time and – you know – I just know that I have to juggle the things as they come up and I think I can work that out. (Family lawyer, small firm, called to the bar 1988)

"I Plan to Slow Down in the Coming Year"
Not surprisingly, the women in this study were almost universally subjected to severe time stress. However, a few of them had reduced their time crunch markedly over the four-year interval between interviews, largely because they had gone through professional or personal transitions. One woman was in the process of leaving law, and a second one was taking time to consider a major career change as she recovered from the trauma of government cutbacks. Two other women had moved from very stressful urban practices to legal positions in more relaxed settings. One of these women had gone through a remarkable transition. At the first interview, she was polite but very guarded in her comments. The interview was short because she tended to give one-word answers to my questions, apparently concerned about getting back to more pressing duties. I found her four years later in a very different environment and could not believe that this was the same woman. She was relaxed and happy, chatting openly about her new life and declaring that she would never go back to the

pressured environment she had left behind.[47] The other woman had re-assessed her time with her children and chosen an environment where she could provide a more balanced approach to parenthood and her profession:

> You know, it's never perfect and you never – you know – I still feel guilty about the daycare and the after school program and the summer, saying: "What camp can I send you to because I can't take the summer off" ... And I find some days it's funny. On the weekends we'll say: "Let's go do something." And all they want to do is just be home. And I thought: "Yes, that's right. If they just want to lie in front of the TV for a day, I don't care." (Social welfare lawyer, community agency, called to the bar 1986)

A fifth woman had dealt with the pain of an unexpected death within her family. After years of professional commitment, she had taken stock of her life and reduced her work time in favour of a fuller range of leisure activities. She was determined not to let her practice interfere with the rest of her life, and, in fact, she was questioning the very underpinnings of the profession that she had respected deeply:

> I know that [partnership in a large firm] is supposed to be the pinnacle of achievement in the profession but it just doesn't have any attraction for me anymore ... There was an event in my life that changed how I felt about everything ... it was as if it crystallized everything that was stu-pid and useless and awful about what lawyers do. And I thought life really is truly short and fragile and precious and I will not have that stuff wreck up any other part of my life ... There's an enormous pressure to bill hours and to be here and to do that stuff and to be on call for people all the time and to live and breathe this stuff. And so it's really, really hard to keep it away and there was a point where I thought: "I am really tired of having to fight. I would rather have a life where I don't have to fight so hard for my personal life, where it's just taken for granted that of course you'll have a personal life." (Family lawyer, large firm, called to the bar 1985)

The most balanced women in this study were the ones who had man-aged to maintain time crunch scores of one or less. One of them had come to terms with her own frustrations with legal practice, and, when we talked to her, she was turning an extended period of sick leave into a less stress-ful life outside the profession. A second woman had appeared to handle her work without stress, but, when she developed pneumonia, she real-ized that her work was a contributing factor and decided to reduce her hours. The five remaining women had achieved an enviable balance be-tween family time and work time. They were very thoughtful in their

efforts to accommodate time pressures in the context of a complete lifetime. One of them was engaged in an ongoing assessment of her priorities. She had experienced a work disruption because of illness early in her
career, and, when we interviewed her the second time, she was faced with
a parent's serious illness. She was trying to picture her own life on a large
screen:

> There are many things in my life that are important to me. Yes, my pro-
> fession is important to me but so is my family. I mentioned to you last
> time that, when I got married, just spending time with my husband was
> important to me – certainly spending time with my daughter [is impor-
> tant] ... So things are kind of smooth. There are always little problems
> but I try to make sure that work has the right kind of place ... my hus-
> band will say: "Don't worry about it. Just sit down." And – you know –
> it's great that sometimes he's teaching me but there comes a point when
> you say: "Well, I don't want to build it all up for tomorrow because there
> are just things you have to get done" ... Women are busier. All the women
> I know are much busier. We're just different ... I have a sense now that
> I'll figure it out. (Civil litigation lawyer, large firm, called to the bar 1982)

A second woman described her busy practice, but she also looked at her
life on a broad canvas, suggesting that levels of time crunch varied widely
across the life course. It was much more than an immediate problem:

> I've cut back dramatically. For example, one time a couple of years ago
> when I was writing a couple of papers, I had a due date that I was work-
> ing towards and that was reminiscent of university days when you basi-
> cally pulled the all-nighters ... I'm a firm believer that when you look
> back over a period of time, your life should be in balance ... The reason
> I think I've got two check marks out of ten [on the time crunch index]
> as opposed to eight out of ten is because, although it would be nice, I
> look at balance not only kind of on a daily basis, not only one day a
> week or on a monthly basis, but I also think, in terms of your life, there
> are times when maybe your work takes up more of your life and your
> family takes up more of your life and then later you kind of get it back ...
> It's a wonderful coping mechanism – you know – with denial or what-
> ever but I guess I sort of say to myself and hopefully I'm not kidding
> myself: "I will have lots of time to spend with myself and on my own,
> and probably pretty soon if my son is grown and out of the house" ...
> it's manageable when you can see that it's a certain time frame ... I'd
> rather my son said: "Do you want to go to the show with me, Mom?"
> You know? Or shall I read a book on my own if I'm consciously choos-
> ing to spend the time with my son? Because a day will come very quickly

when he won't want to hang around with me anymore. (Family lawyer, large firm, called to the bar 1986)

Conclusion

In recent decades, the pace of life has increased markedly in Canada, as in other industrialized countries. Families with young children experience the highest levels of time crunch and women, in particular, report that their loads are often unbearably heavy. These patterns have attracted the attention of researchers and policy advisors around the world, generating a vast multidisciplinary literature that reflects increased concern about the consequences of time famine. Studies provide clear evidence of a "time divide" separating women from men and parents from non-parents.[48] When working time is tallied, the divide goes even deeper, singling out managerial and professional workers as the ones most likely to work extended hours. Within these occupations, women experience the heaviest stress, and some professions are exceptionally demanding.

Women who practise law are among the most stressed groups, and, as this study demonstrates, they have higher than average levels of time crunch, especially with respect to their daily accomplishments, their time-related stress, and their lack of time for family and friends. Although women lawyers in large urban centres report higher levels of time crunch stress than their counterparts in smaller communities, their type of practice does not appear to affect their levels of stress. Whether they work in government offices, large firms, or sole practices, many of the women in this study reported elevated levels of time-triggered stress.

The women with the highest time crunch scores typically had young children at home and were determined to devote time to their children's activities. Many of these women were struggling to fulfil the role of the good mother, often in the shadow of their own stay-at-home mothers. Some women expressed resentment as they considered society's expectations about mothering roles, and they all mentioned the ongoing pull between family needs and work demands. Many of them lamented the lack of unstructured time with their children, and several women expressed sadness that their children were painfully aware of their mothers' work schedules. All of the women in the high stress category talked about their efforts to prioritize their lives, placing their immediate families first and eliminating time with friends from their busy lives. They frequently mentioned the lack of time with their husbands and expressed guilt at taking small fragments of weekly time for themselves. Many of them also experienced interrupted sleep patterns, either because they worked late in the evening or because they wakened in the night thinking about their clients. During the day, they ran from one obligation to the next, forever trying to catch up with the growing list of demands.

A few women had either lowered their time crunch scores over time or managed to maintain low levels of stress, in spite of their multiple demands. Several women had cut back their activities after experiencing personal or family illnesses, while some women were in transitional phases. Some of them recognized that they were not committed to careers in law, while others were recovering from major upheavals at work. The women who appeared to manage their time most effectively tended to view their competing obligations from a lifetime perspective. They recognized that their time with their children was all too brief so they tried to reduce stress by focusing on the years ahead.

What have we learned from the experiences of the women in this study? It seems that we continue to hold out impossible ideals to women. In spite of the fact that their working hours are longer than average, they still shoulder much of the responsibility for their children's lives. Scheduling extends into every corner of family time. When women are fatigued from work, they are still expected to attend soccer games and violin lessons or organize family celebrations. Until these pressures are removed, women such as the ones in this study will continue their race against the clock.

Pressure to handle professional and family demands is a recurring theme in this book, but some of the women have taken steps to overcome the harried lives that marked their early years in practice. One of these women appeared happy and relaxed in her 1994 interview as she sat nursing her child at home, but, four years later, she was stretched to her limit, having given up time with her husband and left her children with nannies for long days at work. When I talked to her recently, she told me that she had left the high-pressure firm and moved into a less demanding area of law that allowed her to work part of the time at home. She recently sent me a brochure for her new enterprise, and the picture on the front shows a relaxed, confident woman. Her experience suggests that the most successful women in this profession are the ones who are not afraid to take stock of their lives and reduce the time crunch stress, even if it means making a dramatic change. Her comments about identity confusion are quoted in Chapter 2, and, in Chapter 5, we see some of the pain that she endured as she struggled to hold on to her professional identity. Her life is now much more balanced, but her story raises larger questions.

Why is the practice of law so demanding that people are forced to make choices about their careers or their lives with family and friends? Women are often the ones who make the greatest sacrifices, but many men may also question the performance expectations in this most demanding of professions. Morris Gross sounded a warning in his 1990 speech, urging his retired colleagues to help re-humanize the profession by putting pressure on their colleagues and their professional associations – the Canadian Bar Association and the various provincial law societies. He was not asking for a dramatic shift in professional attitudes: "Some lawyers will, of course, still want to work round-the-clock and that's fine, as a matter of choice. But I'm talking about a sense of values where lawyers who don't earn $200,000 by their tenth year, are somehow made to feel second rate. In fact they may be the smart ones ... I've never known a first-class lawyer who wasn't a hard worker. But I am thinking of career gratification. I am thinking of fine lawyers who are strong practitioners, but who are unwilling to be caught up in the spiral."[49]

One of the major sticking points centres on compensation when lawyers (almost exclusively women) take parental leaves or reduce their hours in the office. Morris Gross was quite clear about this issue: lawyers who choose to work fewer hours should have their compensation reduced accordingly. Three years later, Justice Bertha Wilson and her colleagues formalized some of these concerns in their comprehensive report on gender equality in the profession. Although they stopped short of recommending equal compensation for lawyers who take extended leaves of absence, they made a number of creative recommendations designed to ease financial burdens on individual lawyers and protect their careers. For example, they suggested an extension of federal government parental leave benefits for self-employed individuals, the provision of a family benefit program under the auspices of the Canadian Bar Association and other professional associations, and government support for a tax deductible "birth and child care fund."[50] They also recommended alternative work arrangements and flexible models of career advancement for lawyers who choose to reduce their working hours.[51] However, law firms continue to commission studies and lawyers still complain about the backbreaking loads. It seems that little has changed in the past decade.

5
Choreographing Daily Life: Clocks, Calendars, and Cycles

In some ways things work out. But what a *time* it's been. It's been a *time*. It's been a *time*, I must say. From the *time* I met you last until, I'd say, a year ago, I've just been working constantly. I really, really – through that period of *time* when I started working again, I had to work so hard to build up again. When I came here, for the first while, you know, I worked very, very hard and I really didn't see much of my kids for those – I'd say for the first three years of J's life, I wasn't around. And so it's so nice for me now to have a little bit more *time* ... What I do long for is more of a life. We went out to the top of the CN Tower for our wedding anniversary and we go out about twice a year and that's not good and I long for more *time*. If only there were enough *time* [italics added]. (Civil litigation lawyer, medium-size firm, called to the bar 1987)

The lawyer quoted above was describing her struggle to build business when she moved to a new firm after her maternity leave.[1] I was struck by her repetitive use of the word "time." She called it "a time" initially as if it were a single concept, but it quickly became clear that her time was multidimensional. In this brief statement, time appears as a definable period in her life, as a memory summoned up from her previous interview, as a broad, life course sense of temporality surrounding the birth of her son and marking her wedding anniversary, and as a priceless but scarce resource in her daily round of activities.[2] She makes no mention of clocks or calendars, but her words invoke a linear image of time passing all too quickly. A second woman described a schedule that is typical of life in large Bay Street law firms, saying: "I get up at five. I get to the office usually at six-thirty. I'm here before anybody. I don't eat lunch. I usually go and work out at lunch. That's really the only break I get. I finish off most days between six-thirty and seven." Her standard workweek was sixty hours long, and she talked about the panic she felt if she was unable to be at her desk by six-thirty in the morning. When we interviewed her first, she had been in practice for six years, and she said that she had finally eliminated weekend work from her schedule but that she was still haunted by the unopened briefcase that she always carried to her cottage. She had achieved partnership without the added responsibility of children but was hoping to have a family.

It is not uncommon for women in her position to work seventy-five hours a week. The discussion in Chapter 4 confirms that many of them turn to their legal files after tucking their children into bed or cut back on their sleep when they are pressured to meet workplace deadlines. Several of the women in this study said that they sometimes got up in the middle of the night to work, and slept again for an hour before dawn. When they were under this kind of stress, their personal, private time was invaded by work that most people leave at the office. These women were reacting to the pressures inflicted by the linear time of clocks and calendars that has become commonplace in all industrialized countries. Linear time is ordered and sequential, but it is only one of many kinds of time, often presented as polar opposites – linear versus cyclical, quantitative versus qualitative, or historical versus traditional.[3]

Clocks and calendars mark the passage of time, providing a precise accounting of events and making possible the synchronization of varied schedules, but they are only part of the picture. Recent writings present expanded visions of time, portraying women's time in particular as uniquely rich and multifaceted. Theories of time have evolved from simple dichotomies through a series of feminist revisions designed to reflect women's increasingly complex roles. Researchers studying the gendered nature of time have identified a range of other "times" that characterize life in industrial societies. "Feminine" time is commonly differentiated from "masculine" time, while time devoted to family and leisure interests differs from "work" time. These are the times of public and private life, but women's time also covers the territory between these spheres, mediating and "weaving" time into new symbolic forms.[4]

Time is a critically important resource in the pursuit of professional excellence. Freedom from private obligations centring on family activities represents a valuable form of social capital.[5] As indicated in Chapter 2, diplomas and certificates, prestigious office space, and professional dress all contribute to a lawyer's reputation, but these trappings provide the most obvious signs of success. At a deeper level, it is access to free time and the ability to be available on short notice that often sets men apart from women in a professional sense. Time becomes part of the metaphor suggested by the robing process. Since law firms often fail to take account of women's other roles, women are hampered in their struggles to succeed, never quite measuring up to established expectations. On the surface, they appear to be successful professionals and, in most respects, they are, but closer examination reveals that their lives are radically different from those of their male colleagues. These patterns are perpetuated because professional demands still rest on the perception that law is a "two-person" career, leaving married male lawyers free to expand their working hours at will, while women are almost always committed to tight schedules at work and at home.[6]

These changing images provide the framework for a discussion of temporal pressures in the lives of the women interviewed for this study. Their stories are disclosed in the following pages, illustrating the complicated daily schedules that they manage as they move from home to their law practices and back again. Time devoted to family activities is often unpredictable, but the clock ticks constantly as they docket the time they spend on legal files. Some of them have succeeded in balancing their lives, but others have rejected the punishing pace and, after years in practice, have decided to either modify their work patterns or move into different careers.

Conceptualizing Time

Absolute, true and mathematical time, of itself, and from its own nature, flows equably without relation to anything external.[7]

Isaac Newton's vision of time was groundbreaking in the seventeenth century. Divorced from any social context, time moved steadily forward to the beat of an invisible metronome. Many social scientists have adopted the Newtonian vision of time, using terms such as *mathematical, quantitative,* or *linear* to describe historical events or the schedules and appointments that structure people's working lives in modern societies. This vision of time is the polar opposite of the *traditional, qualitative, cyclical* time that reflects biological rhythms, daily patterns of life, and seasonal fluctuations. Barbara Adam mounts a strong argument against these dualistic approaches, suggesting that anthropologists, historians, and sociologists have attempted to view "other" time through the lens of Western time.[8] One variation on this theme is Edward T. Hall's view of pre-industrial time as *polychronic* or simultaneous in contrast to the *monochronic* or sequential time that prevails in industrial societies.[9] In fact, time is much more than an abstract dualism. It is a complex pattern of awareness underlying the tempo of our daily lives, best described in Adam's words:

Time is implicated in the attention to instructions and the headlines in the newspaper ... It is fundamental to the sequences, durations and simultaneities of thoughts and actions, to knowledge of traffic rhythms and routines on aeroplanes, in colleges and hospitals. It is part of seasons and our relationship to them ... time has something to do not only with clocks or timing but also with sequential ordering according to priorities. It further relates to irreversible changes, records and identity, to both cyclical and linear processes, and last but not least, it is used and controlled as a resource ... All these aspects of time are equally important.[10]

In this brief passage, Adam identifies layers of meaning that are missing from conventional views of time. She acknowledges the presence of linear and cyclical patterns, but she reminds us that time embraces thoughts as well as actions, forcing us to consider the duration of sequential activities and overlapping duties. Above all, she stresses the economic character of time in modern industrial societies where it is a jealously guarded resource, especially in the hands of powerful people.

Visions of time as polarized ideal types cannot be translated into neat packages of everyday activity. Although the modern work schedule typifies quantitative time, daily work patterns frequently incorporate pockets of qualitative time that transcend simple calculation. For example, the woman quoted earlier in this chapter described the problems she encountered when she docketed her time. Since she worked on fifteen or sixteen different files a day, she was constantly switching from file to file, recording the time spent on each one. Her comments on clock time were instructive – "I have my clocks here. They tell me the time but I don't look at them. Besides, I'll start writing a letter and the phone rings so I'm not going to write down the time ... the real kicker is the time and it's just astronomical. Such an overwhelming amount of time has to be devoted to this." She was pressured to meet the demands of clock time, but she was also engaged in a service to her clients. When they called for advice or reassurance, the time she spent with them was not accountable but she regarded it as an important informal part of her practice. If she stopped to talk to a colleague or check her e-mail, she was no longer operating according to linear time. Like many other women in the study, she was trapped between unstructured qualitative time and the tightly monitored time that determined her quota of billable hours.

Since many of these women work in pressured environments, they keep track of their time in quantitative terms, but, clearly, most of them feel the stress of moving from one temporal domain to another. Are they atypical in this respect? Academic researchers and government policy-makers have generated huge databases confirming the seriousness of time stress in all industrial societies and repeatedly demonstrating that women carry the heaviest burdens.[11] Lawyers, like women in many other professions, are expected to work long hours, and, in addition, they are encouraged to map out career paths.[12] Time constraints are apparent at this level as well. Many of them postpone pregnancies or limit their family size in favour of career development, while others accept truncated career paths interrupted by childbearing and rearing. Are pregnancy and parenthood the only impediments to their career advancement? I deal with these questions in more detail in Chapter 6, but, because men and women often have different temporal experiences, a discussion of gendered aspects of time provides an appropriate starting point.

Feminist Theories of Women's Time

Women's *status* knowledge once served them well in agrarian societies where traditional gender roles prevailed, but, as the demand for scientific knowledge rose, their domestic statuses lost value and they were relegated to the margins of industrial economies.[13] However, a generalized commitment to traditional gender roles has lingered, both in dualistic theories of time and in the realities of the workplace.[14] Quantitative, linear, or clock time is prized in industrial societies and its influence is far-reaching.

Life in the modern law office reflects this kind of time, evident in the long hours culture that dictates lawyers' performance goals and often dominates their lives.[15] Women in the profession experience elevated levels of stress because cyclical time often takes over when they attempt to organize their lives beyond the office. It is evident in their reproductive cycles, in the unpredictable cries of newborns, and in the uneven pace of family life in general. Since women have traditionally assumed responsibility for domestic organization, theorists have tended to view the quantitative time of the workplace as masculine, contrasting it with a vision of cyclical time as feminine. However, these easy stereotypes have sparked an ongoing debate among feminist theorists intent on challenging accepted theories of time.

Even within the feminist community, members have contested the nature of women's roles and their attendant experience of time. Some have elevated the status of motherhood to Madonna-like proportions, while others have seen women's experience in a broader light, challenging the norms that perpetuate views of time as "masculine" or "feminine." Julia Kristeva glorified motherhood in her portrayal of "women's time" as *cyclical*, anchored in reproduction and cast against the backdrop of historical, *linear*, masculine time. Linking these divergent visions of time to the rise of the women's movement in twentieth-century Europe, Kristeva contrasted the turn-of-the-century, first-generation feminists favouring political activism over maternal feminism with second-generation, post-1968 feminists searching for a vision of women's distinctive identity in psychological and religious symbolism.[16] Kristeva's third-generation feminism was visionary, acknowledging the reconciliation of cyclical and linear time as a major challenge.[17]

Kristeva saw cyclical time as primeval, following the cadence of women's cycles as they moved in harmony with the rhythms of nature. Women's time, like Nietszche's *monumental* time, was infinite, transcending the bounds of linear time. It was the time of *reproduction* rather than *production* and was concerned with larger issues than a simple chronicling of events. It reflected life itself, the miracle of birth, and the survival of the species.[18] Her decision to polarize time along gender lines provoked charges of anti-feminism, but her representation of motherhood lent new respect to a role that had previously been accorded secondary status: "The desire to be a mother, considered alienating and even reactionary by the preceding generation of feminists, has obviously not become a standard for the present generation. But we have seen in the past few years an increasing number of women who not only consider their maternity compatible with their professional life or their feminist involvement ... but also find it indispensable to their discovery ... of the complexity of the female experience, with all that this complexity comprises in joy and pain."[19]

Motherhood is a powerful stage in the lives of many women, but it is only part of a much larger picture. Carol Watts contends that Kristeva's vision of the mother is intrinsically "double-coded" because it embraces both a woman's independence and her profound sense of unity with her child, but, by ignoring a woman's life prior to the conception and birth of her child, it fails to identify conflicting times in the life of a mother – her need to answer to the time of production along with the time of reproduction. In Watts' view, Kristeva has divorced the figure of the mother from the socio-political sphere, positioning her squarely in the realm of the symbolic.[20] By assigning women a place outside the linear time of history, Kristeva's work disregards the most critical aspects of women's time in contemporary societies: "Crucially, Kristeva's essay is unable to acknowledge 'women's time' as an index of the experience of the contradictions of capitalist modernity: specifically, the demands made upon women, and increasingly men, by domestic work and the necessities of the wider division of labour. If the figure of the mother – central to Kristeva's ethics – continues to be the locus of a great deal of ideological work today, it is because women's labour in the home and in the workplace articulates contradictions that reach to the heart of the experience of modernity."[21]

Watts also argues that Kristeva's emphasis on motherhood is an incomplete portrayal of the lives of mothers and of women's experience in general. The childbearing years are very important in the lives of many women but they usually constitute a small part of a woman's lifetime. By emphasizing women's reproductive roles, Kristeva overlooks their labour force involvement outside the childbearing years and she ignores the experience of women without children.

In spite of its limitations, Kristeva's work serves as a foundation for renewed discussions of feminism and temporality, allowing a new generation of scholars to refine the language of gender and soften the boundaries between male and female time that serve to reinforce rigid patriarchal ideologies.[22] Many of these writers focus on normative aspects of women's time and examine the effects of societal expectations on women's patterns of behaviour. For example, Karen Davies identifies "male" time as the dominant temporal framework in patriarchal societies, arguing that it is manifested in the pervasiveness of linear, clock time.[23] Karin Jurczyk differentiates between "masculine" and "feminine" time, seeing feminine time as a distorted representation of women's temporal reality because femininity, like masculinity, is a social construct grounded in historical and socio-political processes. Thus, feminine time is only one of the many dimensions of femininity, reflecting widely accepted beliefs that women should care for others, no matter what additional responsibilities they shoulder.[24] "Women's" time lacks the normative character of "feminine" time, but it is, nevertheless, shaped by expectations of appropriate feminine behaviour. It is the real time of women's lives, splintered and cross-hatched with the competing temporal obligations that mark their daily routines.[25] When women challenge the norms imposed by feminine time, they experience conflict because they are seen to be stepping outside their traditional nurturing roles. They have failed to measure up to the ideals of feminine behaviour that help to provide the bedrock for our culture.

Pamela Odih also challenges the dualistic approach, citing the power of masculinity and femininity as multidimensional constructs, shifting in response to the winds of time. Selecting a single strand of "femininity," she examines the ways in which women tailor their personal and social relationships to the demands of linear time. She sees the social representation of the "feminine ideal" as a powerful agent in women's lives: "For many women and some men, the culmination of the feminine ideal finds expression in the subordination of self to the 'needs,' demands and desires of significant others, be they family members, friends, super-ordinates, etc. ... In this sense, the feminine ideal is expressive of a 'relational' mode of engaging with the world."[26]

Drawing empirical support from her interviews with employed women, Odih describes expressions of this ideal femininity as sensuality and an emphasis on embodied social relations. Women who embrace this ideal carry a sense of immediacy into their personal relationships and their workplace duties as they struggle to harmonize interpersonal relationships at the expense of their personal time. Since they become preoccupied with the present, they often focus on day-to-day tasks instead of mapping out elaborate career strategies with clear objectives.[27] This ideal can have more profound effects as well. The "fictive feminine" can shape women's visions of themselves, mirroring widely held views that men are their intellectual superiors and thus worthy of more powerful positions.[28] The contrasting ideal is often characterized as masculine, disembodied, and focused on long-term goals. Its obvious temporal expression is found in linear, historical time, and, according to Odih, it provides the dominant organizing principle for the capitalist economy. People who see time in these terms are willing to bypass some personal relationships in favour of broader personal objectives.[29]

How are these conceptualizations of time relevant to the experience of contemporary women? Odih maintains that entrenched views of women as mothers rob them of power over their time by according their temporal needs a lower priority than those of other family members. However, she injects a note of optimism, suggesting that women can exercise resistance to dominant temporal conceptions by supporting feminist movements and employing negotiation tactics. As an example, she argues that extended coffee or lunch breaks allow women to gain some measure of control over their time.[30] Strategies such as these may allow women to steal a few moments of time from more powerful people, but, in spite of Odih's optimism, they do not represent an improvement in women's control over linear time. In fact, they may serve to reinforce the view that women are not committed employees.

Jurczyk also sees women's ability to negotiate as crucial to their welfare in the public sphere. Since linear time is prized in this domain, they can enhance their power by laying claim to a portion of it. She argues that professional women occupy a particularly strong bargaining position because their time away from the home is viewed as their "own" time, granting it priority over time devoted to domestic responsibilities.[31] Consequently, it becomes valuable currency in family debates about time allocation because men no longer have exclusive claims that their professional duties free them from domestic chores.[32] She is, however, less optimistic about women's long-term gains than Odih when she observes that control over time is critical in societies obsessed with effective time management in response to dramatic increases in the tempo of daily life.[33] Citing the erosion of rigid work schedules in a "round-the-clock society," changes in family structures, the expansion of city space, and the rapid rise of new communication technologies, she argues that time has become a key indicator of social inequality and that a new discourse has developed around the issue of power as a reflection of temporal control. Women in the labour force, particularly those in professional occupations, have entered an arena where debates about time are contested and they have made dubious gains. Jurczyk concludes, sadly, that "in many respects, women today are located 'in-between times.' They have neither revolutionized professional and family-related time structures ... nor quite adjusted to them. They move between the two without ever really being able to control either."[34]

Other feminists paint a brighter picture of women's time. Karen Davies suggests that women weave time into a tapestry made richer by their contribution.[35] Carmen Leccardi expands this image, emphasizing the creative, innovative character of women's time:

Feminist analyses have emphasized, in particular, the capacity of adult women to construct symbolic (and creative) mediations between different family times and the times of social institutions, between times of paid work, times of care and time for oneself. This mediation, it should be emphasized, generates and creates time. It thus transcends the mere use of time as a resource ... It is a time necessarily rationalized but it also has a high affective content; it conforms to the logic of clock time but it is also rich in shared meanings because it is built around significant relationship structures. It is a time able to make a significant contribution to the social temporal order and, at the same time, it produces a greater sense of identity.[36]

Although this discussion of feminist theories ends on a positive note, it reveals underlying patterns of temporal conflict in the lives of women. In a world where the majority of women work outside the home, the old norms still hang heavily over women of all ages. The woman cited in the opening pages of this chapter touched on these pressures when she talked about her guilt over a work-free weekend at the cottage. Women's time is expected to embody outdated ideals of femininity – a subordination of self in the service of others and a denial of personal needs in the name of efficiency and harmony. These expectations are unrealistic in contemporary industrial societies where the struggle for gender equality continues, but, in spite of our best efforts, many women still try to coordinate their overloaded schedules, both at work and at home.

Kristeva's vision of motherhood is a welcome affirmation of women's nurturing capabilities, but it does not deal adequately with the pressures of linear time in their lives. Leccardi suggests that women exercise a unique kind of wizardry as they blend linear and cyclical time into an appealing new temporal mix, promoting harmony between the family and other social institutions. Her contention that they build this order around significant relationship structures is laudable, but it suggests a stereotypical commitment to the relational time that Odih sees as a reflection of the feminine ideal. Watts is more realistic when she argues that the time of capital is a much stronger force than women's mediating powers. Both Jurczyk and Odih acknowledge that the times of production and reproduction are inherently at odds with each other in societies where linear, masculine time sets the pace and women's time is seen through the lens of idealized feminine behaviour.

Adam's rejection of time as an "either-or" concept is particularly relevant to the lives of busy women. As they struggle to balance cyclical and linear time, their minds are often racing with plans for tomorrow and memories of yesterday or last week. Their working lives are controlled by clocks and calendars, but their private time is often unpredictable. It becomes clear from a reading of the literature that time is prized as a resource to be controlled and bartered or forfeited to those who exercise the greatest power. If the linear time of the capitalist economy is as pervasive as Watts and others suggest, how then do employed women deal with their competing schedules? If they have professional commitments, they can bargain or buy their way out of some mundane family duties, but most of them continue to organize family calendars as they struggle to retain some autonomy over their time at work. Of necessity, work time is often tightly scheduled and closely monitored because productivity and accountability are valued in many workplace settings. Women lack the power to guard their time against intrusion, so it is often fragmented and spread thinly across a range of social networks. Without marked changes in the organization of work and family time, they continue to face frustration as they coordinate their own time around the schedules of other people in their lives.

This brief review highlights overlapping visions of women's time. Borrowing from Leccardi and Davies, we can examine motherhood, family life, and women's constructions of time as creative enterprises, enriched by their unique organizational talents. However, the tempo of family life is unavoidably affected by clock time. The women in this study talked about children who dawdle in the morning, unaware of their mothers' impending court appearances, or the "witching hour" when everyone returns home at the end of the day. Recognition of these patterns overshadows rose-tinted visions of mothers' time, laying the groundwork for a discussion of the power of linear time in the legal profession. We also need to acknowledge women's lack of control over time in general. Timing is central to the lives of women with young children, but temporal realities for women without families at home deserve a hearing as well. Perhaps women at every stage of life are haunted by an unattainable feminine ideal.

Lawyers as Mothers: Creative Mediators or Slaves to Linear Time?

If you go down the hall you will find the male partners my age with little kids who are feeling a lot of the same pressures that I am, maybe not to the same extent, but they're still feeling them ... that they have to work too hard, that they're not spending enough time with their children ... I do think that women feel it more and maybe they are more willing to verbalize it ... Every so often we have these little chats ... and that's how I know that they feel it as well. But there's always the recognition to me that: "Well, you're the mom and you therefore have a lot more pressure placed upon you than we do, because you have all the expectations." ... Even in my own household, although we're both lawyers and we both probably work about the same number of hours and we're both very involved at home and with the kids ... the person they call for in the night when they're sick, is Mom ... In terms of the truly nurturing stuff, I do so much more of that and so I'm the one they cling to and whine to – they're getting better – but the "holding on to Mom on the leg issue at the door" – "Don't go Mom, don't go!" That didn't happen to Dad. (Family lawyer, medium-size firm, called to the bar 1981)

This lawyer recognizes the clash between her duties at work and the demands made by her children, identifying a pattern that is common among women. In spite of the limitations of dualistic theories, Hall's differentiation between polychronic and monochronic time suggests a gender divide. Women's time is polychronic, a complicated bundle of overlapping activities, whereas men tend to adopt a monochronic approach, single-mindedly dealing with a sequence of discrete tasks, usually confined to the workplace.[37]

Many of the women in this study described the kinds of complex schedules that are typical of polychronic time. They often took complete responsibility for scheduling domestic chores and their children's activities. If they shared tasks with their husbands or partners, they almost always indicated that they did the overall planning and coordinating of routines. This pattern is not necessarily related to the number of hours worked: Carroll Seron found that the women in her study covered most of the household and child care duties, even when their practices demanded more than a full-time commitment.[38] In my study, understandably, single mothers were the most burdened, evident in the comments of one busy woman:

When I sit down at my desk, I start two lists – what I have to do today at work and, when I get home tonight, what is required. And if I can remember what I have to do tomorrow night when I get home, that's good too. So I've got down today: "Tuesday, store, snacks for [son's] workshop" ... I don't know too many men who have two lists. (Government lawyer, called to the bar 1992)

Other women with limited domestic responsibilities cited a wide range of friendship networks, community activities, and professional obligations as part of their repertoire. In spite of their freedom from family duties, their time incorporated all the layers of simultaneity identified by Barbara Adam. Women's time is, however, more multifaceted than gendered stereotypes would suggest. It is, in Leccardi's words, "lived" time – a balance of family time, cyclical time, body time, and personal time cast against the lengthening shadow of clock time.[39] This blend of "times" adds to the complexity of women's lives. If they are lawyers, they are repeatedly reminded that they are not men or, to use Simone de Beauvoir's well-known phrase, they are simply "Other," the negation of everything masculine and valued.[40] Invoking the metaphor of the robes, women in the legal profession are often viewed as impostors in masculine dress. One woman in my study described a scene that emphasized the clash between her divided roles, raising images of Superman in reverse. She was involved in a hearing, but, as soon as court was adjourned, she grabbed her coat, threw it on over her legal robes, and dashed from the court to the parking lot, driving across town to see her daughter perform in a school production.

Descriptions of women lawyers' daily patterns of time use confirm the complexity of women's time in general and demonstrate the level of creativity required to coordinate competing times in their work and family environments. Since summaries can sometimes clarify patterns of activity, Tables 5.1 and 5.2 encapsulate the daily routines reported by twelve of the women in this study, showing the increases in temporal pressure when small children are present. These women live in towns and cities across the province and their law practices vary widely, but they are more likely to be found in urban centres where time pressures are more extreme than in small communities. They are all married and have at least two young children. Their comments were presented in response to the question: "Will you take me through an average working day, from waking in the morning to falling asleep at night?" These diagrams highlight the number of overlapping duties that take place as women prepare for work in the morning and after they leave the office in the afternoon or evening.

Their descriptions of their daily schedules make it plain that they are almost always running against the clock. However, they are, without exception, superb organizers, so their lives sound like carefully orchestrated dances where they play the role of choreographer. On good days, the dance moves like clockwork, but, if anyone misses a beat, chaos can ensue, and it is the choreographer's job to restore order. The women have built these patterns through trial and error, but they are constantly adjusting the score – weekly routines often differ, seasons change, children move into new stages of development, and, sometimes, unexpected crises disrupt the flow of daily life. Their lives possess none of the predictability of pure linear time. These patterns are clear in the morning routine described by one energetic lawyer with four children:

> I get up at six-fifteen, six-thirty. Three days a week I try and run, or a fourth day. So [my husband] gives [the baby] the bottle ... Get home. If I can grab my shower then, that's critical, because otherwise – you know – I've lost my beat. And then I get the baby, change him, take him downstairs. The other ones come down as they will, but one of them has to go off to school on the school bus by ten to eight. So [my husband] makes his lunch and I get his breakfast ... And the other two – I feed them when they come down. But I have to get the house a little bit together for [the nanny] because she's their caregiver. She's not to be doing housework and I don't want her to be so distracted with that that

she's not attending to their needs ... And there are always a million things
– you know, money for school lunch, for school pizza day, or notes, or
something, and you attend to all those things. And so, somewhere in the
midst of it all I take two seconds to get changed ... [The nanny] comes
at about ten to nine and I have to tell her how things are – sort of the
verbal handoff. So-and-so has eaten, so-and-so hasn't, so-and-so is running fine today, or whatever. And then I get here by around nine-twenty
... And then by the time I hit the office sometimes it's already full energy
happening here. (Corporate commercial lawyer, small firm, called to the
bar 1987; "Laura" in Tables 5.1 and 5.2)

The overriding factor in this woman's account is her constant awareness of clock time. Her clipped sentences describe short, breathless bursts
of activity as she recounts her early morning schedule. Between six-fifteen
and nine-thirty, she knows exactly what she must accomplish, and, if any
of her family members require extra time, her personal time is crunched
to accommodate their needs. For example, she says she tries to "grab"
her shower and manages to get "two seconds to change." She is fortunate because her partner shares duties. She told me that he arrives home
ahead of her at the end of the day and gets dinner ready while she finishes
up at the office. She returns home sometime after six-thirty, and they
spend the rest of the evening dealing with their children and their household tasks. Although she said that they had been trying to get to bed earlier, it is usually midnight or after before they have finished their work.
Her legal practice was very busy when I spoke to her and, at one point,
she lowered her voice and said: "It's just so intense! And it's been even
more so having had the fourth [child]!" In spite of the pressures, she continues to take responsibility for the organization of family needs. She said
that she either works through lunch or tackles an ongoing list of family
duties. When I asked her to elaborate, she said that she was busy setting
up registered educational savings plans for her children and that she
always shopped for clothes for the whole family, including her husband.
In some ways, her noon-hour shopping trips provided a welcome break
from the office routine, but, once again, she had overridden her body
time by passing up lunch to look after other family members.

Her story is not unusual. Like the women in Carroll Seron's sample of
lawyers, many women in this study assumed far more than their share
of domestic and child care responsibilities, leaving their partners free to
spend time at work. Seron found that, among lawyers who work "normal" hours, men use their free time for leisure or professional networking while women turn to the backlog of chores at home.[41] One woman
with two very small children confirmed this pattern in her description of
her afternoon and evening schedule:

I have to be home for the nanny by six but I also have to accomplish, not only all of my professional things, but all my personal things, between nine-thirty and five-thirty so I do my client phone calls and my preparation for things coming up, pre-trial meetings and stuff in the afternoon. And then I leave to go buy groceries or diapers or go to Toys "R" Us or whatever it is we need in order to get home between five-thirty and six. Then our nanny leaves and I feed the children from, usually six to seven, because it's a real chore getting them to eat. And then after that I clean up the kitchen and let them play a bit, take them up, and give them a bath. My husband usually comes home just before or just after the bath. And then we sit with them and read books for a while and they drink some milk and then we put them to bed ... we carry them to sleep every night. They don't fall asleep on their own so that usually takes between ten minutes and a half an hour. So we usually have them in bed somewhere between eight-thirty and nine. Then we clean up the rest of the house where they've played, and we do our laundry, and we wash the bottles and the nipples. And then we return our various phone calls that have to be done for business purposes. And then I make dinner. And I make dinner every night. And we usually eat around ten. By about ten-thirty or eleven, I'm ready to go to bed ... And then the children tend to wake up in the night and clients phone in the night ... this morning I had one child up at three-forty-five and the other one at four and then the other one got up at five. He came to bed with us and he woke up at twenty after five and he stayed up. And while I was trying to get him back to sleep at five-thirty, a client called. And then the other child got up at six. (Criminal lawyer, small firm, called to the bar 1983; "Patricia" in Tables 5.1 and 5.2)

In contrast to the previous lawyer, this woman's words flowed out in long run-on sentences as she described a string of simultaneous obligations, punctuated with "and then" eight times in her short account. She was obviously the one who straddled the gap between work and family time. Even though she and her partner had similar work duties, she always left the office early to shop on the way home. Like the previous woman, she organized things for the nanny and assumed many of the caring roles at home, feeding and bathing the children before her husband returned home, and cooking dinner for him late in the evening. When I interviewed her, she was very stressed by her schedule. She arrived half an hour late for the interview because she had been stuck in traffic on her way back from court, and she talked about the constant fatigue that she felt. Her comments confirm her obsession with clock time. She noted the time of various events eighteen times, even throughout the night, as she recalled the exact waking times of her children and the call from a client.

These women are undoubtedly skilled organizers and their talents could be called "creative," but they are robbing themselves of important personal time. A third woman talked about the necessity of relying on paid child care workers to ease some of these tensions:

> There are certainly days that it's a grind and yes there's stress ... Personal time is an issue. I don't have much time to myself but as I guess I organize, some of it is being done for a time when [my husband] and I get out. We have permanent babysitters on retainer. That's one of our little secrets. I have two girls in the neighbourhood that are fantastic. They've been with us since the kids were born and we know the parents very well and they literally come in every second Saturday without ever having to make the phone call. They're on permanent retainer. I have a wonderful nanny, an older woman ... she has never had a sick day. She's just very much a pivotal element in my existence and I would say we pay her very well and it's not a time in our lives where we should be cheap about having help. So this is a woman whose career is child care ... She's as career-oriented about child care as I am about law and I don't buy into any guilt that I can do it better because I can't. The amount of time I spend with my kids is optimal ... (Corporate commercial lawyer, medium-size firm, called to the bar 1987; "Sally" in Tables 5.1 and 5.2)

This woman acknowledged her lack of personal time, but she had taken steps to deal with the problem. She was one of the few women who set aside regular time to spend with her husband, and she was willing to hand over total responsibility for children and household to the nanny. She also relied on daily workouts and a jogging program to alleviate the stress of her job. In fact, she said that she usually stopped to do a workout on the way home, leaving her husband in charge of dinner with the children. She was quite clear in her belief that the children's needs could be worked around her law practice and her career.

Another woman described her strategies for avoiding stress on her return home at the end of the day by establishing the family dinner hour as an important ritual in the midst of their busy lives:

> [My husband] will start dinner. I usually plan the meals and my babysitter does my shopping too – my grocery shopping. So I'll plan the meals and he'll start them, or else I'll start them if I'm home by five-thirty, but I'm usually not home until six or six-thirty. Sometimes I'll run just before I go home so that's done. And then we have dinner. We usually sit and have our glass of wine every night and, while the kids are watching their TV, we touch base. Then we have dinner usually at seven or seven-thirty. (Estates lawyer, small firm, called to the bar 1986; "Megan" in Tables 5.1 and 5.2, and in Chapter 6)

Table 5.1

Morning schedules for twelve lawyers and their families

Family	6:00 am	6:30 am	7:00 am	7:30 am	8:00 am	8:30 am	9:00 am
Patricia 2 preschool	Toast, coffee, paper Both sit with children		He showers	She feeds children, cleans up, changes diapers	Nanny arrives	She showers	Both leave by 9:30 am
Rachel 2 preschool		Read paper	Both shower	He leaves She dresses and feeds children	Nanny arrives She drops off child	She leaves	
Caroline 1 preschool 1 school			Both shower He wakes children	She dresses children	Fast breakfast Leave by 8:10 am		
Janet 2 preschool	Wash and dress, pack bottles, feed	Shower and dress		At work			
Sally 3 preschool	She feeds, dresses children He leaves				Nanny arrives She leaves		
Samantha 1 preschool 1 school			She feeds children They watch cartoons	She eats, reads paper		She showers He gets up	Nanny arrives Both leave

Gillian 2 preschool	He wakens older child, changes, feeds baby, showers		She gets up	He leaves She feeds, dresses children	She takes children to babysitter		
Arianna 2 preschool				She feeds, dresses children He helps	She dresses, eats He leaves	She drops off children	
Sylvia 2 preschool		She gets up He leaves	She wakens and dresses children			She drops off children	
Tanya 1 preschool 1 school			Both shower	Both waken children, feed them, clean up	One leaves Nanny arrives Other leaves		
Laura 2 preschool 2 school	He feeds baby She runs	He runs She showers	Older children get up	She makes breakfast He makes lunch	He leaves		Nanny arrives She leaves
Megan 1 preschool 1 school	She makes beds, starts laundry	Nanny arrives	He makes lunches, tea She does dishes		Both leave		

Table 5.2

Late afternoon and evening schedules for twelve lawyers and their families

Family	5-5:30 pm	6-6:30 pm	7:00 pm	7:30 pm	8:00 pm	9:00 pm	10:00 am
Patricia 2 preschool	She leaves, office, goes shopping	She gets home Nanny leaves She feeds babies	She cleans up, bathes babies	He comes home They read stories, put babies to bed		They clean house, do laundry, wash bottles	She makes dinner They go to bed
Rachel 2 preschool		Both home, time with children	They put children to bed		They eat dinner	She does legal work	They watch news They go to bed
Caroline 1 preschool 1 school		She gets home, nanny has fed children	Homework, piano practice	She bathes and reads to children	Children go to bed They eat dinner	They wash up, work, or watch TV	They go to bed
Janet 2 preschool	She picks up children	She feeds children and dog	She bathes and reads to children		She does legal work, eats dinner	She gets ready for bed	If he is home, they share duties
Sally 3 preschool	He gets home Nanny leaves He feeds kids	She goes to gym for a workout	She gets home, spends time with children until 9:00 pm			They read to children In bed by 9:30 pm	
Samantha 1 preschool 1 school		She gets home, spends time with children, cooks dinner	Time with children	Baths	He puts baby to bed, she supervises homework	Adult time	She goes to bed Baby up in night

Gillian 2 preschool	She gets home He picks up children	They take turns with dinner and sports activities		She bathes children Video time	She puts children to bed	She does dishes, tidies up, watches TV	
Arianna 2 preschool	She gets home Nanny leaves	They eat dinner then play with children		Baths	Story time	Children to bed She cleans up, does a bit of work	"Collapses"
Sylvia 2 preschool	She picks up children	She makes dinner He washes up	Time with children			Children go to bed She sometimes works	
Tanya 1 preschool 1 school		She gets home Nanny leaves She cooks dinner	Play, musical practice, and homework with children		Baths, stories Children go to bed	She cleans up, does some work	To bed at 11:30 pm
Laura 2 preschool 2 school	He gets home	She tries to get home	They spend time with children	They do household organization			To bed at 11:30-12:30 pm
Megan 1 preschool 1 school	He gets home, supervises homework	He starts dinner (She plans meals)	She gets home They have a glass of wine Children play nearby	Dinner with children		Baths Children go to bed She goes to bed	

Like the previous woman, she had learned to rely on her husband for some of the daily child care and she had found ways to encourage family discussions. Her concern for formal meal times was a welcome change from many of the frenzied eating patterns described by other women. However, she still saw herself as the primary organizer of family time. She planned the weekly meals and drew up the shopping list for the nanny, referring to the task as "my shopping." She also told me that she made sure the beds were made and the kitchen was spotless before she left in the morning. Her relaxing evening dinner was the result of meticulous planning on her part.

In spite of efficient planning, family time often clashes with the linear time of institutions, leaving women feeling guilty about the amount of time they commit to their children. One woman recalled her daughter at age two saying that when she grew up she was going to be "just a mommy" because her babies would need her. Another woman described her mixed feelings on dropping her children at the daycare centre and the rush to pick them up after work:

> I'm running to the hearing and I'm running. Usually by then I'm stressed – like, has the drop-off gone okay? Are they crying? And I've got this hearing. And I still battle with that because some days I'm at the daycare and they want to show me things or they don't want me to go, and I'm saying to the teachers: "I'm sorry, I've got to go. I have to be at a hearing in ten minutes. I'm just dropping them off for you." On those mornings that I do have hearings in the morning, I try to get there a bit early, just to give them some time to get in there and get organized, but it doesn't work out always. Got to go and run out the door ... There are days at five o'clock, if I've got to pick up, I'm just dropping everything and just – you know, – I've got to run. And I am – like literally running out the door to get in the car to get there to pick them up. And many times I've got files under my arms to say, "Well, I couldn't finish this today so – you know – I'll get the kids to bed tonight and I'll have time to finish them then." (Criminal lawyer, Crown attorney's office, called to the bar 1991; "Gillian" in Tables 5.1 and 5.2)

Her language and sporadic sentences reveal her frustration as she runs from one place to another, worrying her way through the day and wondering whether she has treated her children fairly. The clock ticks off the seconds as she races from the daycare centre to the courtroom and on to her office before reversing the path at the end of the day. By then, she has the added burden of unfinished work, suggesting that the files under her arm somehow account for any delays in getting to the daycare centre.

Children unwittingly sabotage parental schedules and mothers are often the ones who deal with the results. One lawyer talked about the process of urging her children to get dressed in the morning, saying: "My daughter will be standing nude on the coldest winter day, reading a book, and completely forget that she needs clothes to go to school." Another woman referred to herself as the "sergeant-major" and said: "So that's my job. I'm the one who sort of marshals them down and makes sure that they get their breakfast and my husband is there backing me as necessary but, because of the way we organize things, I tend to be the one who gets the movement going."

Bedtime is often an occasion demanding flexibility and patience on the part of parents, but it is also one of the most rewarding times of the day. Many women referred to the joy of spending quiet time with their children, whether they were infants or older. One woman expressed mild frustration when she said: "[My husband] goes downstairs with [the baby] to get him to sleep. We haven't gotten bedtime done really well for him yet. I know there are people who can put their kids to bed. We can't. We're not good at it. [The baby] will only go to sleep in your arms. He's a very needy kid." Another woman talked about her older child's needs, saying: "My eldest son now is going through a stage, I guess for maybe about six months, where he really likes me to lie down with him in bed and just talk. You know, he wants to talk about things with me now." A third woman treasured the evening time with her son, saying: "From about seven to nine it's a really wonderful time that I have with my son. I give him his bath – and I always do – and I spend time reading to him and playing with him and cuddling and snuggling and kissing and rocking and then he goes to bed." This island of time was carved out of a very busy schedule: she sometimes began work at five in the morning, but her usual working day stretched from nine in the morning until one or two the following morning. Once again, linear time served as a framework for the day, with breaks for mealtimes and her son's bedtime. This woman had found a way to balance her nurturing roles with her legal work, but she told me that she would probably not have another child. There would not be enough hours in the day to contain everything.

Most of the women with families said that they reserved one day on the weekend for a combination of shopping and family activities. Saturday was usually family day, but many of them spent part of Sunday catching up on their legal work. Weekends also provided an opportunity for open-ended time with children. One woman recalled the stress of her "superwoman years" as partner in a large firm and told me that she was training herself to "work smarter." She described her weekend time, saying: "I'll just hang out in my terry bathrobe until – like noon – and read the paper or play with my daughter. And so, to me, that is real slowdown time and I'm learning to appreciate it."

One of the most obvious difficulties for these women was their lack of personal time. When I asked them if they made time for themselves, many of them said that they had almost no personal time. One woman summed it up in positive terms:

> I don't divide my time. I don't think of it in that way – in terms of – I don't categorize it as personal time versus family time, you know. My personal time is my family time because I don't think to myself: "If only I could have five minutes to myself." I don't really think of that because my children are what I like to do and I do other things too. I like to play tennis. I play as much tennis as I can but I don't have the sense that I need to get away from my family. (Constitutional lawyer, medium-size firm, called to the bar 1989)

Some women talked about the importance of workouts or regular jogging programs while others said that they enjoyed walking a dog early in the morning or in the evening. A few women used their lunch break as a social time, but women with small children talked about the luxury of a solitary lunch with a good book. However, I was shocked by the number of women who ate at their desks or simply passed up lunch altogether. This observation raises concerns about the importance of body time. The clock is so intrusive in the lives of these women that their biological rhythms are often interrupted or ignored. Most of them began by saying: "The alarm goes off at ..." and ended their descriptions of a working day by saying that they "collapsed" or "fell" into bed. One woman said that her children often tucked her in at nine o'clock. Only one woman in the study was willing to let her body determine her waking time in the morning, saying: "I sleep as long as I can. Usually [I get up] around seven but sometimes eight-thirty, which is a big surprise because I haven't had an alarm clock for eight years. I haven't needed one."

The mothers in this study are undoubtedly very good at organizing their multiple schedules, and their reports confirm many of Leccardi's visions of motherhood as a creative endeavour. However, women in this profession are still caught "in-between times" as they attempt to meet expectations for performance in the workplace while continuing to take full responsibility for household organization.[42] They are still haunted by norms that stress the importance of women's relational roles, both at work and at home. We have seen how measured their morning and evening schedules can be, but the time they spend at work also merits scrutiny. How is it monitored? Do they have control over their time? Is it fragmented or interrupted? How do they schedule the precious clock time that frames their working days? In the discussion that follows, it becomes clear that their working time is a commodity to be measured and weighed as evidence of their productivity.

The Power of Linear Time in Legal Practice

We docket our time in increments of six minutes so 0.1 is six minutes, 0.2 is twelve minutes, 0.3 is eighteen minutes. Throughout the entire day we keep dockets of various client files that we work on and they each have a number for accounting purposes so, at the end of the month, there will be a record in the computer system of exactly what I've done and how long it's taken. Then the machine knows my billing rates so it will multiply the time by the billing rate and come out with a suggested billing. Now it's only a suggested billing. You can either go more or less depending upon what you think the value is to the client. But, at the end of the year, you've got all of the work you've done as an aggregate number of the hours you've spent and the amount that was billed and collected. Those are your performance statistics. And those are what's driving the firm's assessment of your value to the firm. It's no longer a qualitative subjective assessment of your skills, the nature of the clients you serve, or any of that. It's really a statistical thing. And it's a five-year running average as well. They not only look at the year that you're in but they look at your performance over five years ... [and then she said] I was on the subway the other day and I saw an advertisement for a breakfast bar cereal and it made me stop in my tracks because it said: "Do you realize that it takes the average four-year-old fourteen minutes to tie her shoelaces?" You know, if it takes a little one fourteen minutes to tie her shoelaces and she has a lawyer as a mother, that's 0.2 of a docket. (Corporate commercial lawyer, large firm, called to the bar 1978)

The language of quantitative time is evident in this woman's comments. She is very aware of the power of technology to record and calculate her billings on a daily, monthly, yearly, and five-yearly basis. Her preference for a qualitative evaluation of client service is clear, and her observation that lawyers have been reduced to a set of statistics is unsettling. She makes a poignant observation when she relates the experience of a four-year-old child to the docketing practices of the modern law firm, capturing all the nuances of time lived according to the incessant beat of clock time.

Women who choose to practise law enter a culture where time is cast in linear terms, both in daily life and over the long term. Lawyers are expected to advance along a career path, often in an institutional setting where long-term financial goals determine the timing and organization of work. They are required to meet stringent billing targets, set up appointments, schedule hearings months in advance, and provide fast feedback for their clients. These patterns signify success in large elite law firms and these firms have, wittingly or otherwise, established punishing time norms for the entire profession. Part-time work is not an option for those who wish to be taken seriously. As Cynthia Fuchs Epstein and her colleagues conclude, "most of the lawyers we studied who work fewer hours than their peers (or their 'class') are *de facto* deviants from the established guidelines for work time ... because women's commitment to work has not been fully accepted, and because disproportionately they acquire part-time status, they face being defined as double deviants."[43]

In spite of pressure from clients to adopt fixed-fee or results-based billing, many lawyers still use the ten-segment billable hour to keep track of their time.[44] This strategy represents linear or quantitative time in the extreme. As the lawyer notes in the earlier quotation, she is required to record her time in six-minute intervals, stopping periodically to deal with voice-mail, e-mail, faxes and colleagues' conversations. Lawyers who log two thousand billable hours a year actually work three thousand hours or more than eight hours a day, seven days a week. Billable hours vary widely by the type of law practised, but one criminal lawyer estimated that they constitute 50 to 80 percent of a lawyer's working time. The average number of billable hours in US law firms has risen from seventeen hundred hours per year in the 1960s to a figure between twenty-three and twenty-five hundred, a target that requires lawyers to work twelve hours a day, six days a week.[45] Increasing acceptance of two thousand billable hours as a benchmark in large firms has raised concerns about the damaging effects of this practice. Conscientious lawyers cannot maintain this pace throughout their careers, and the potential for fraudulent billing is a matter of concern among professional associations.[46]

These kinds of demands have prompted increasing numbers of women to abandon their practices with large firms.[47] One of the women in this study who had moved to a very small firm said that she would not have had time to have a child if she had committed herself to the partnership track in her previous firm. She talked about the hectic pace of life in the large firm, contrasting it with her schedule in her current situation:

> There was pressure to work eight hours a day, which meant you worked ten to twelve [hours] so my first year there I billed twenty-three hundred hours ... No, I lied. That twenty-three hundred was articling. At [the large firm] my first year was twenty-one hundred and my second year was eighteen hundred, which was a big drop and they weren't happy. Eighteen hundred is – ask anybody – a hell of a lot of hours! Here, I usually get here

by eight-fifteen and sometimes by eight-thirty and I go to court at nine every day. I try to leave here by six o'clock every day. There have been a couple of times – there was one day when I got home and that was after seven and she [her infant daughter] was already in bed and I was – it killed me. Twenty minutes later I was up in her room. I got her up. I was not going to have a day when I did not see my daughter and that just offended me. (Criminal lawyer, small firm, called to the bar 1993)

Although most of the literature on billable hours focuses on practices within large urban firms, the docketing of time is routine in most law offices. Lawyers in small practices appear to have more control over their time because their hours are not set by an executive group, but they often have high overhead costs. They cannot afford to stay in business without careful attention to the hours that they bill their clients, so they rarely have access to part-time work or periodic extended breaks.[48]

All lawyers are vulnerable to fluctuations in the economy, but the pressure is particularly strong if they work in small firms or sole practices.[49] I began these interviews in the middle of a recession and was struck by the number of lawyers who were in financial difficulty. One of the criminal lawyers referred repeatedly to the economy, saying: "I'm still whining about the economy and it's sort of tough right now and I think it would have been great to have a salaried position and the benefits and everything else." The Ontario Legal Aid Program had cut its payments drastically, leaving many criminal lawyers without regular incomes. With the downturn in the real estate market, a number of real estate lawyers had turned to criminal law and, as a result, her field had become very competitive. Unlike some of her colleagues at the criminal bar, one lawyer had survived the economic crisis and, in her follow-up interview four years later, was cautiously optimistic:

I was a duty counsel first, before I started private practice. I never needed a line of credit. Everything was great. After I had the baby I took five months off. The Legal Aid crunch hit and then obviously I had to start looking at my business and getting into debt a little bit. I've found that over the last few years I'm – it's a lot better. I think I've settled down a bit – not so freaked out and panicked by it. I'm surviving making an okay living ... it's still stressful. I still worry and ... As a criminal practitioner, I do a majority of my work as Legal Aid. I don't have real white collar criminal types, although I've noticed with the change in Legal Aid I'm trying to be more aggressive about getting private retainers and cash clients as opposed to Legal Aid, but the way I've developed my practice it's difficult. (Criminal lawyer, sole practice, called to the bar 1987)

Lawyers employed in the public service face a different set of constraints. Although they avoid the stress of billable hours, they also forego any of the bonuses earned by productive lawyers in large law firms. This does not mean that they escape the temporal demands reported by lawyers in private practice. All the provincial government lawyers interviewed in this study talked about the increased workload resulting from severe cutbacks in Ontario's public service during the tenure of the Harris government in the 1990s. One woman had chosen a government position because she wanted to have a family, but she found that time pressures at work had escalated over the years:

> When I first came to it, it was a nine-to-five job which fitted in very well with my family life but, in the last few years, because of the cutbacks, the work environment and work ethic are pretty much like private practice. So I have the exciting, challenging work but I've got far more of it than I want to handle and the salaries are about 50 percent lower than I would earn out there. So, ultimately, it was a really lousy career decision, financially. (Civil litigation lawyer, government, called to the bar 1982)

Advances in cell phone technology have also increased lawyers' time pressures, allowing professional commitments to invade their personal time and space. The invisible seam between work time and home time increases efficiency in the short run, but it heightens time-related stress, especially for women who have demanding schedules when they leave the office. One busy mother explained:

> Some days I get so stressed because I've got thirty-five new voice-mail messages the next morning. And really, it's been so busy lately, and I'm thinking: "They all think now the ball is in my court because they've left me the detailed message." But how much of this can I really digest and get back to, within a reasonable period of time? ... I feel like I'm shoving it all into these timeslots to get home to have a good time with the family. (Corporate commercial lawyer, small firm, called to the bar 1987)

The pressure is equally intense for women working in large firms. One of them talked about the various ways in which clients could contact her and the expectation that she would respond immediately:

> In fact, technology makes more work. When I started practising law, making photocopies was a big deal, right? And you had electric typewriters and things. If they were typed wrong, unless you wanted to use the white stuff, they were retyped. It gave people breathing time. Now, with the phone-mail, they can leave a message ... All of these things put a lot of

pressure on us. We work harder. We do a lot. We are able, I think, to do more decision-making at a higher level because we probably have fewer clerical tasks but I wonder ... (Family lawyer, large firm, called to the bar 1987)

Technology can complicate lawyers' lives, but this stress is heightened when people get caught in the overlap between cyclical and linear time. Many women use their briefcases and their laptops as portable offices, available any time of the day or night:

I can start work at five in the morning sometimes. I like the early morning hours, or I did, at least before I got pregnant. I was just so driven. I would be here sometimes at four-thirty. It was crazy. I loved it though. There are times that I get home and I'm disappointed that I didn't get as much done during the day, but I make it up in the night. I have to do that or I'd feel too far behind. I do it until it's done. I don't stop. And I rarely will stop for sickness or anything ... [After the birth of her baby:] It was making my stay at home very stressful because I knew if I got a phone call from my partner it would be an emergency and I'd be freaking out, you know? And I was breastfeeding so it was really hard for me ... I learned a lot about myself during the pregnancy. I learned that I loved, loved, *loved* my career. And I learned that I couldn't give it up. I knew that I couldn't give it up, even for my son. And that was the most bizarre thing. When I say "not give it up," I couldn't be away from it for too long. I could give my son the couple of months that I needed to, but in order to make me a happy person, I needed to be here. And so that taught me a lot. (Civil litigation lawyer, small firm, called to the bar 1991)

Like many other lawyers in the study, this woman experienced strong conflict between the cyclical time of her body rhythms and her work demands shaped by linear time. This pattern is very common among lawyers in all kinds of practices. Another woman described the tension between her home life, her own needs, and the demands of the office:

I try to get up at seven and this morning I got up at five because I had to prepare. I didn't finish at court yesterday and it was my son's birthday. But I try to get up at seven and then the sort of panic starts and I do those morning things. I don't eat breakfast. I never have anything. It's just – you know – get your hair washed, get your clothes ironed, get down there, pull the messages off your machine, see who's gone ballistic overnight and what they need from you. And then my mornings always feel – if I'm not in court – they always feel very hectic. I always feel from about ten until noon I'm just juggling a hundred different things at a time – letters, phone calls, documents, decisions – and it just keeps coming at you. My secretary sort of catches the balls on the way out and we juggle them back and forth. (Family lawyer, large firm, called to the bar 1985)

Women's biorhythms are particularly vulnerable during pregnancy. One woman described the conflict between her physical needs and her work towards the end of her pregnancy, saying: "I was working seven days a week and I can remember sometimes thinking: 'Oh my gosh! I've been so busy. I mean, first of all I'm sitting here at a computer terminal and I don't even want to consider all the supposed hazards of VDTs when you're pregnant but I haven't even stopped in the past twelve hours to feel the baby's kicks.'" She worked twelve-hour days for the last month of her high-risk pregnancy. When she went into labour three days after starting her maternity leave, the ultrasound technician turned to her assistant and remarked that this woman had to be a lawyer because, in her experience, they were all the same. They did not know when to stop.

A similar pattern is evident in the comments of a woman caught between her personal needs and the demands of her clients:

My first son was born on a Monday at six-ten in the morning. And he was a little bit early, and I worked on the Friday ... So I phoned the office at nine o'clock [on Monday morning] and I told them that I wouldn't be coming in today because I'd had a baby. And they said: "Okay, fine." I hung up the phone and I was lying in the hospital bed, and at nine-fifteen the phone rang, and I answered it, and it was a client. They'd phoned the office and been told that I was in the hospital, so they called the hospital with their question. And I was so surprised that I just gave them their advice and hung up ... It wasn't until a lot later that I realized, my gosh, I was entitled to not have that happen. (Family lawyer, small firm, called to the bar 1984)

These comments confirm patterns indicating that many women in the legal profession are caught, in Karin Jurczyk's words, "in-between times."[50] All the women in this study were conscientious workers intent on doing their best for the firm or the institution that employed them. Very few of them had talked frankly with senior partners about the timing of pregnancies and the attendant need for family and personal time. The women who do try to build boundaries around their personal lives often come away disillusioned by the power of the job to control their time. Who or what controls their time at work? There is no easy answer to this question. It is tempting to assign all the blame to senior partners in large firms who raise the performance bar higher with each passing year. However, the problem appears to be a systemic one. Lawyers in private practice are business people and vulnerable to economic fluctuations. Many women seek government positions because of the economic security and regular hours, but, in recent years, they have experienced added tension because of massive cutbacks in the Ontario civil service. Finally, technological change has brought the dubious benefit of laptop computers, cell phones, and fax machines into the office and the home. In a competitive environment, the lawyer who responds most quickly to her clients' demands is the one who builds a successful practice.

Women's Attempts to Control Their Time: Shattered Illusions

My legal career is one aspect of my life ... Am I making time for travel? For my husband? To socialize with my friends? To read? Do I still have time to see my family and see my grandmother who never ceases to amaze me with the stories she tells me? ... I'm a very physical person and for me success is when I'm living a full, full passionate life. I would hate to live this life just based on my work. (Family lawyer, small firm, called to the bar 1987)

This woman was clear about her desire for a balanced life when we interviewed her in 1996. Her practice was small, she had no family responsibilities, and she enjoyed free time with her partner. When I talked to her again four years later, she had moved to a larger community, become a partner in a well-established firm, and had her first baby. In spite of these changes, her life still seemed full of promise: her legal partners were accommodating and parenthood was apparently not weighing heavily on her shoulders. However, this kind of optimism is rare among women with small children.

Childbirth is a particularly strong factor in the organization of women's professional lives. It forces them to reassess their career plans, it changes the division of labour at home, and it often casts women in a different light in the eyes of their colleagues.[51] Before they have children, many women believe that they will be able to manage busy law practices along with their family responsibilities. One successful young lawyer told us in her first interview that she planned to adopt a nine-to-five work schedule when her children were born. She was determined to set a new model of partnership participation, one that would accommodate both professional and family interests. When we returned four years later, after the births of her first two children, she expressed strong disillusionment with her firm and with the profession in general. In her earlier interview, she had talked about problems with the firm's maternity leave policy, but, on our second visit, she had become quite militant, repeatedly mentioning the failure of the profession to accommodate family needs:

It will never change. It will always be run by men and, as much as they'd like the perception to be out in the law schools and on the street that they support women and promote families, they do not! ... It's hugely disillusioning because I am a far better lawyer than 90 percent of them and ... it's just such a short-sighted attitude. They would be way better off supporting you throughout your pregnancy. (Civil litigation lawyer, large firm, called to the bar 1988)

She makes an interesting point when she says: "As much as they'd like the perception to be out in law schools and on the street that they support women and promote families, they do not!" Law students and beginning lawyers are rarely asked to consider the long-term implications of career development. In one publication aimed at law students, the author presents a very positive but decidedly one-sided picture of motherhood and career, citing the experiences of three women who, in their words, "have successful legal careers but remain devoted mothers and daughters. Here, the women share combined years of wisdom on how to 'have it all.'"[52] This woman had fulfilled her promise to work nine-to-five, but she had accomplished her goal at great personal cost. In spite of problems during her pregnancies, she had continued to travel and work long hours until just before the births of her children. When we contacted her the second time, she was so stressed that she agreed to a meeting and forgot to attend. In the rescheduled interview, she talked about her pattern of fitting in work time after her children were in bed. Neither the workplace nor the family had accommodated her need for more time so she was caught in the uncomfortable space "in-between times."[53]

Women in sole practice or small firms have more direct control over their hours of work than their counterparts in large firms where many of the policies are set by senior partners. Mandatory parental leave policies are widely available now, but the old attitudes towards motherhood are still very much in place. One of the women in this study was comfortable with her partnership role in a large firm when I interviewed her the first time, but, when I returned four years later, she was very concerned about proposed policy changes within the firm. She was guarded in her comments, but she showed me a document outlining guidelines for a "sustainable practice." Aspiring partners were expected to meet high billable hour quotas, do "timely billing" and "timely docketing," maintain their client base, cultivate new clients, and fulfill various community obligations. She explained the issues:

I think there's a sense that the people who are now managing my department and other departments in the firm feel that anything short of seventeen hundred and fifty billable hours is unacceptably low. And, for example, just to get sixteen hundred and fifty billable hours a year means that each and every day that you're working, you have to bill seven and a half hours, so to get seventeen hundred and fifty [hours] would be eight billable hours a day. That doesn't include any non-billable activities of which there are always – I put in an hour or two a day on non-billable activities – so you're, minimum, asking people to work, I think, ten hours of strong time and that doesn't account for doing anything in the way of chores or going to the washroom or meeting people for lunch or anything. (Corporate commercial lawyer, large firm, called to the bar 1978)

This woman had seen a generation of new lawyers come and go from her firm. She had had a very successful career but, in middle age, had begun to question the firm's increasing demands for time. Her final comment confirms the value of time as social capital, raising images of women too time-stressed to fit in the activities necessary to cement collegial ties and client contacts.[54] With such impossible demands, it is easy for senior partners to typecast women as appropriate candidates for the so-called "mommy track" – valued for their dogged commitment to day-to-day duties but not suited to the rigours of the partnership track.[55]

The lawyer in question said that the proposed policy changes would have a profound negative effect on women with family responsibilities. In spite of her reluctance to speak out and her concern for anonymity, she wanted to get her message across: life is getting very difficult for lawyers in large firms, especially if they are women with small children. When I asked who was imposing these demands, she said: "I don't like labels but I think it is sort of a useful label. I call them 'young, aggressive males.' They're late thirties, early forties, maybe late forties, not older than that, and they're driving the bus." She saw these moves as part of a larger trend, one which reflected concern about a high partner/associate ratio that would water down the incomes of controlling partners. If new policies were implemented, only the most productive lawyers would become full partners while the remainder would spend their working lives as employees.

Despite Kristeva's idealism about the experience of motherhood, many women face a daily competition between the time of production and the time of reproduction. They are expected to follow feminine ideals, subordinating their own interests in the service of others, both at home and at work. Many employers see motherhood itself as the rationale for reduced commitment among women and the justification for their subordinate position in the workplace.[56] One woman was shocked by the attitudes of her male colleagues after the birth of her child. In their minds, motherhood was equated with reduced performance at work. One lawyer began addressing her as "Mom" and the others complained that she was never there any more because she had stopped coming into the office at seven in the morning. A second woman had worked for a number of years in an all-male firm where she said she had enjoyed the full support of her colleagues until she announced her first pregnancy. The firm had no formal parental leave policy, but the other lawyers assumed that she would return to work three or four weeks after the birth of her baby. By the time I spoke to her, she had three children and was practising law in her own isolated corner of the firm with very little backing from her colleagues:

> I was told that I'd inconvenienced the office ... Each time I was pregnant, I was afraid to tell them – the lawyers. I knew that, after I told them the first time ... the second time I knew it would be bad, in the sense that they wouldn't be happy. And the second time I was told: "Well don't expect us to cover your files." And then by the time I had my daughter, when I told them I was pregnant with my daughter, I remember the look, and it was like – I might as well have told them I had cancer or AIDS. Nobody said: "Congratulations." There were all these looks of horror. (Family lawyer, small firm, called to the bar 1984)

These kinds of negative reactions are common. Several women with experience in large firms said that senior partners were appalled when they announced their pregnancies. In most cases, these women or their friends were fired from their jobs when they became pregnant. In one of the earliest interviews for this project, I talked to a woman who had been forced out of a large firm during her pregnancy. She told me that she had met a number of women in similar positions while she was on maternity leave and suggested that I interview some of these women.[57] One of them related the following story:

> I told them at around two-thirty on a Wednesday and he [one of the partners] turned sort of blue and red and purple and managed to spit out "congratulations" and then left. And at six-thirty that night – I knew it was going to be bad but I had no idea it would take less than twenty-four hours – he came and said: "I couldn't fire you for being pregnant because that's illegal but if, on the other hand, I were to, say, notice a marked decrease in the quality of your work between now and the time you're due, and you were to be let go for those reasons, now that of course wouldn't be against the law, would it?" (Corporate commercial lawyer, sole practice, called to the bar 1987)

She went on to tell me that she had had a first rate performance review just before this encounter and that the firm had been anxious to promote her. After some pressure on her part, she was granted a four-month paid maternity leave, but, two weeks before she was scheduled to return to work, she was called in and told that her position had been terminated. The next woman who got pregnant was fired before she had her baby and a third woman left quietly as soon as she found out that she was pregnant. For many large firms with high overhead, women's cyclical time is deemed to be incompatible with expected levels of productivity.

Time devoted to family matters is also seen as a threat to women's productivity and those who are single parents face tremendous pressure when they try to tailor their family needs around their workplace schedules. One of these women talked about her commitment to her two small children, demonstrating her sense of divided responsibility in the face of crisis:

> And I remember one day my daughter was sick. I got called for that, at the same time as a big meeting was happening to decide numbers, millions of dollars. I think it was in the order of hundreds of millions of dollars ... I remember just breaking into tears ... I ended up having to be home because my daughter was quite sick. Then I found out my phone was cut off because I had been so preoccupied with work and the family things that I hadn't even noticed that I hadn't paid the bill. I went over to the neighbours' [house] and phoned the people here ... [they] weren't very supportive ... I just phoned the people I had been working with in another department ... I remember the woman. I think I burst into tears talking to this woman and I love her ... She said: "Wait, stop. You sound frantic." ... She said: "Nobody else can be A's mommy right now. I can go to the meeting and I can tell you what happened at the meeting but you're the only one who can be home and be A's mommy." (Government lawyer, called to the bar 1992)

If motherhood is a major impediment in the lives of busy women, then young lawyers without added responsibilities should be able to balance their commitments at work and home. However, many of the new lawyers in this study were caught in a cycle of overwork that was a continuation of the patterns they had established during their law school and articling years. One woman, recently married, said: "On the weekend I'm cleaning, I'm cleaning, I'm doing laundry, I'm doing the grocery shopping. I have not yet found and – I mean – I have to find time for myself." She went on to describe her experience with marriage counselling, poor health, and a mental breakdown that she attributed in large part to her demanding schedule. A second new lawyer who had also weathered marital problems and extreme tension at work expressed similar sentiments:

> Things are a lot better now. I went to my doctor about a year ago and was flipping out basically, and asked to be referred to a psychologist,

asked to be put on something to get me to sleep at night. I never did take them, but he did give me a prescription. I mean – it was to the point – I mean – I was in bad shape. I knew, because I went to the doctor. But he offered to write a note for a leave. I mean – he could see it. I didn't take him up on it. I figured I could work through it. (Insurance lawyer, small firm, called to the bar 1997)

When I interviewed this woman, she had been working in a firm controlled by very conservative men, but she had finally garnered enough experience and self-confidence to apply for another job. She was about to move into a new area of law, but the tension from her previous experiences was still evident.[58]

A third young lawyer had inadvertently set up practice in a hostile legal community where she was ostracized by other lawyers in the area. After a few years of practice, she had left the community and taken a new position. When I interviewed her, she had just started her new job but was haunted by the demands of her previous life. She told me about a recurring dream that signified the depth of her anxiety: "I kept having these dreams – you know. This one dream would always come around. I don't know if you've ever experienced that, but it was this one dream that I would run, run, run, and I would go backwards. And I would run, run, run, and I kept going backwards."

Many women in the study had concentrated on their legal practices without the distractions of young families. Some of them had found their commitment to the law and related community work to be highly satisfying, but others had experienced intense work-related stress that left them exhausted and embittered. One of these women told us in her first interview that she was very happy in her current location – a small firm where she worked a minimum of sixty hours a week and took responsibility for many of the firm's administrative duties as well. She said that she had no life beyond her legal work but that she found it rewarding and would be happy to remain with the firm for many years. When we returned four years later, she had moved to a new location where she shared a small practice with another lawyer. Her billings had fallen off in the previous practice because of provincial cutbacks to Legal Aid so she had been fired. Her income was more modest in the new position, but she no longer worked weekends or twelve-hour days. She told us that her family and friends were delighted to "have her back." She recalled her feelings of profound disappointment when she received news of her dismissal:

They [the partners] just came in and said – you know – "That's it." So it came definitely as a shock. I felt extremely betrayed, given my years at the firm ... I had felt that I was, professionally, quite a respected member of the firm ... Then when I found out a couple of days later that they hadn't let everyone go ... I felt extremely betrayed by that, like extremely, extremely betrayed. I'd never go back! Never! I always say, if anyone told me I had to go back and do that again, I'd just start to cry ... I hadn't realized how much the whole kind of lifestyle work thing had affected me ... I found it stressful. I was under stress all the time. I was always stressed out and I didn't really see that as a bad thing. (Criminal lawyer, small firm, called to the bar 1987)

In her previous position, this woman had led a life where she was willing to conform to the dictates of linear time. Her working days had been long and stressful, leaving her with the feeling that she could never accomplish everything, but, in spite of the pressures, she said she had enjoyed her work. She had deferred to the decision-making powers of the partners in her firm, and she had voluntarily assumed extra duties that should have been covered by an administrative assistant. Paradoxically, her actions reflected commitment to the "feminine ideal" because she had been willing to sacrifice her own interests to attend to the needs of others. She was willing to focus on these immediate obligations without consideration for her own long-term career prospects, adopting a cooperative, unquestioning approach that typified relational time. In her new location, she shared office space on a completely autonomous basis, and the relief that she felt was evident in her relaxed manner.

A second woman was forced out of her senior level government job after refusing to implement radical cutbacks. She had twenty years of experience when we interviewed her for a second time, but she was in the process of developing new skills with a view to moving in a different direction, either within law or in a related area. Four years earlier, she had been happy to accept the challenge of a difficult assignment, but she had also hinted that she might leave the public service. At the second interview, she described her work as "a much more contained part of her life" and told us that the voice on her earlier tape was that of a different person. This woman had been free to establish her own priorities during her twenty years in legal practice. Unimpeded by family and domestic obligations, she had organized her time in a linear way as she advanced through the hierarchy to a senior position where most of her colleagues were men. Although she supervised a large group of women and was eager to accommodate their family needs, her personal management style did not incorporate aspects of self-sacrificing relational time. During the critical period between interviews, she dealt with a series of disappointments that she experienced along with her male colleagues. Her overall experience does not fit neatly into any of the theoretical frameworks focusing on women's time.

Like the previous woman, this lawyer had graduated from law school with a sense of idealism and respect for the profession, but both women had become disillusioned during their years in practice. A similar sense of disappointment was clear from our interview with a lawyer who had chosen to move in a different direction following the death of a close family member. She had begun her law career with high ideals, recalling in her first interview that Perry Mason had been her role model because he was decisive, ethical, and theatrical. She had achieved her goal of becoming a first-class litigator and looked forward to the day when she could become a judge. In the follow-up interview, she was much more reflective and her healthy scepticism had turned to bitter disappointment. She no longer felt an obligation to work long hours, she had made a conscious effort to enjoy her leisure time, and she had lost respect for the entire justice system. The impact of the death was clear from her comments:

> I was very idealistic and this was the career that I wanted from the time I was a child and I fought to retain that ideal for a very long time ... I was interested in hearing this tape [of my previous interview] because my life for me now divides into two parts: there was how I was and how I felt before I lost "X" and how I was after ... And so the interesting thing for me out of that tape was that I wasn't – I'm not a different person ... And that was tremendously comforting actually for me to know I didn't really lose a piece of myself. (Civil litigation lawyer, large firm, called to the bar 1987)

This woman had worked for a number of years in an environment dominated by linear time, but she had never become fully integrated into the system. At one point, she said: "We put on the clothes, we play the game," presenting herself and other women as temporary actors – Portia's descendants in an unfamiliar culture. She had resisted pressures to become a partner and her underlying reservations about professional ambition had been sharpened by the grieving process. She had given herself licence to focus more fully on the interests in her life shaped by cyclical time. Like the previous lawyer, she had fashioned a new identity for herself by reducing her commitment to the goals and ideals of the profession.

Personal illness has also played a role in decisions to cut back on working hours. Another senior government lawyer had weathered several rounds of cutbacks but, in the process, had become ill. In her first interview, she had reported that she worked about sixty hours a week and that employees in her department who wanted to advance to senior levels were expected to work a minimum of fifty-five hours a week. She had chosen not to have children and saw her career as a sequence of linear advancements. Although she was still working a twelve-hour day four years later, she no longer took work home on weekends, and, like the woman who had dealt with the grieving process, she had purposefully scheduled time for fun. Responding to our queries about her change in attitude, she said: "I couldn't remember if I defined myself as a workaholic or not [in the earlier interview] because it was fuzzy to me. [She did.] I would say that, if I was looking at my work schedule now ... compared to then, it's a little – it's lighter. It's not quite as intense. And quite frankly I learned a hard lesson in that regard." She went on to discuss her illness that had been triggered by work-related stress.

This woman has been prepared to work long hours measured in linear terms as she pursued her career goals. Before her illness, she was willing to let linear time spill over into the cyclical time of weekends. Yet illness, like death, is not controlled by linear time. Often unanticipated, it can rupture the most carefully laid plans. Like the previous government lawyer, this woman had chosen a path that mirrored those of her male colleagues. Even though she was forced to take time off during her illness, she has resumed the duties that will enhance her career, cutting only the weekend work from an otherwise busy schedule. She still appears committed to linear time.

Conclusion

When Portia appeared in men's dress, she became, for a brief moment, an esteemed member of the legal fraternity, unimpeded by her femininity. The women in this study have also adopted formal legal dress. The robing ceremony has granted them professional legitimacy, and some of them continue to robe regularly for their court appearances. However, legal robes also have strong metaphorical value because they signify membership in an elite corps. Portia provides the model for young women attempting to fit in to the profession, but many of their more experienced colleagues have found that the robes are ill-fitting and inadequate in a culture bound by men's rules. They no longer work their magic because they have failed to provide protection in a system that is, in many ways, flawed.

The right to robe is granted to graduates who possess the requisite human capital, but less visible credentials are to be found in the social capital that guarantees professional success. Access to time is a critical component of social capital because it allows lawyers to delegate all nonpractice obligations to spouses and support staff. Since time is so important and because it is not equally available to women and men, this chapter is devoted to a qualitative analysis of temporal pressures in the lives of the women in my study. Their parenting responsibilities often clash with the time required for their legal practices so their comments are embedded in a discussion of changing theoretical views of time.

Conceptualizations of time as linear or cyclical are essential as a starting point for this discussion, but recent feminist efforts to expand this dualistic approach are also critical to an understanding of women's lives. In spite of our best efforts to overcome the dualisms inherent in many early theories, time seems to remain, at least at the normative level, divided along gender lines. As a result, the women in this study, like women everywhere, are not only pressured to meet the demands of linear, "masculine" time within their legal practices, but they are also expected to forfeit some of their control over time, particularly if they also have family responsibilities. These responsibilities are not seen to be as pressing for their male colleagues.

Some feminists view women's scheduling talents in a positive light, suggesting that they weave time into a lifetime tapestry or that they are uniquely innovative in their approach to family time and organizational demands. In reality, they are often caught somewhere between these competing domains. Many of the women who told their stories in this chapter described incredibly complex daily schedules involving infants, older children, husbands, and nannies. The women themselves held the keys to organization within these networks before, during, and after their own long working days. A few of them managed to fit brief periods of exercise or relaxation into their weekly schedules, but most of them said that they had no time for themselves. Two of the women in this study had negotiated a successful job-sharing schedule in a medium-size law firm, and several government lawyers had arranged extended periods of leave. These kinds of creative approaches to scheduling are rare in the profession at present, but, given the growing levels of time pressure, men as well as women are beginning to long for more balanced family lives. Large firms continue to impose high expectations and their time norms have spilled into other legal settings, but leaders in the profession are beginning to realize that the part-time option merits attention.[59]

Carmen Leccardi's vision of women's time as lived time, incorporating family time, cyclical time, body time, and personal time, provides one of the most inclusive visions of their very complex lives.[60] While this is an impressive package, it fails to take account of the most prized time of all – the minutes that can be tallied by the computer, measuring out the precious time of the billable hour. Until the profession changes its expectations about the double burden of career and family responsibilities, accepting pregnancy and parenthood as valued aspects of life, women will continue to attempt the precarious balance of doing it all. This pattern is evident among working women everywhere, but it is most pronounced in professions such as law.

6
Careers and Curricula Vitae

Career: one's advancement through life, esp. in a profession (noun); move or swerve about wildly/go swiftly (verb).[1]

Curriculum vitae: a brief account of one's education, qualifications, and previous occupations.[2]

The linear trajectory known as a traditional career has dominated the career theory literature until recently, providing the model for a successful working life. Strongly rooted in a measured temporal framework suggesting Newtonian time, it was conceptualized in the early 1960s as "a succession of related jobs arranged in a hierarchy of prestige through which persons move in an ordered (more or less predictable) sequence."[3] The passage of time and the strategic timing of successive career stages are critical markers of success according to the linear model of career.[4] Time-space metaphors are evident in the images of ladders, lines, escalators, and plateaus that characterize many of these theories.[5] The geography of careers is mapped out by imaginary intersections of latitude and longitude, framing the paths of individuals intent on meeting established norms for performance.[6] This idealization reflects the careers of men, particularly if they are engaged in managerial or professional pursuits, and it is most commonly found in bureaucratic organizations.

This vision also summons up the middle-class work-life norms that prevailed in industrialized countries during the mid-twentieth century – a "career mystique" fractured by a "gender divide" that idealized women's roles in the home and an "age divide" that prescribed men's career progression from their educational training through their years of employment to their carefully timed retirement dates.[7] Accordingly, women were expected to live their adult lives in the shadow of the male career, and, in spite of profound changes in the gender composition of the labour force, as Phyllis Moen and Patricia Roehling maintain, this "career regime" – "the cultural bundle of roles, rules, and regulations that built up around the mystification of this lockstep organization of paid work" – is still the pattern that comes to mind when we speak of careers.[8]

These early theories evolved over time, adding family roles and life course transitions to the model as women began to move into the labour market in the 1970s. However, Michael Arthur, Kerr Inkson, and Judith

Pringle argue convincingly that, even with modifications, traditional career theories are deficient in two important ways: they focus on status and salary while ignoring the subjective meaning of career advancement and they fail to acknowledge the interplay between careers and the larger economic context in which they unfold.[9] In short, careers are much more complicated than the monochromatic record of achievement that appears in bulleted form on the standard résumé or curriculum vitae.[10]

Arthur, Inkson, and Pringle invoke the metaphor of the theatre to capture the complexity of career development in contemporary industrial societies:

> Our thesis is that as we build our careers, we are all actors. But we are ceasing to be (as we have been encouraged to think) agents for the powerful institutions which try to write our scripts and direct our actions. The scripts of monotonous work, or careful ascent through a series of company job descriptions, or steady specialization in a typecast occupation, or (for women) relegation to the margins of employment because of discontinuities of service, are disappearing. Actors don't like those scripts, because although their parts may be all right for a while, over a life-time they are essentially one-dimensional and boring.[11]

This view emphasizes the importance of individual initiative in shaping careers, suggesting that upward mobility is not the only path available. People can choose lateral moves as well, sometimes crossing the boundaries between industries, occupations, or geographic locations. The model of linear perfection, in fact, often gives way to a spiralling career pattern, at times moving downward, remaining static, or connecting with interests beyond the workplace and breaking away from formal employment for defined periods of time.[12] By invoking the temporal aspects of career, we can imagine the linear path as a perfectly straight, Newtonian arrow aimed clearly in one direction.[13] Deviations from this model result in an uneven, twisted, perhaps broken arrow that is too flexible and misguided to focus on a target.

This warped, aimless, or truncated career line is particularly appropriate as a conceptual framework for women's careers.[14] By conventional standards, it is a distortion of the idealized path, but feminist theorists see it as a valuable alternative to the straight-arrow career. Joan Gallos urges us to explore the balance between love, work, and career in women's lives,[15] and Judi Marshall stresses the importance of adjusting the theoretical lens to make room for the variations that often constitute women's career paths:

> From a feminist perspective we need then to re-vision career theory because it is rooted in male values and based on disguised male psychology;

it neglects or devalues the feminine. New theories of career must give equal value to male and female aspects of being. This is necessary to accord women equality in all areas of life and to develop the potential of the female principle in society, including its significance as an aspect of men's identity. We therefore need to take models of women's psychology to the heart of career theory. Recent developments have modified its basic arrow design; we now need to recreate the core.[16]

Marshall's view of a re-visioned career is both welcome and long overdue, but, just as the 1950's "organization man" helped to shape the career norms of the time, women's lived experiences are essential building blocks for a radically different vision of career. Moen and Roehling see the lingering career mystique as an impediment in this regard, stalling the critical policy changes needed to take account of growing work and family pressures. These pressures are not the sole province of women but the old views are persistent. As they note, the new metaphor stresses balance, but it is grounded in the assumption that women will do the balancing.[17] This pattern is most pronounced in dual-career families where women turn their attention to home and family, often at the expense of career mobility, while men continue along the richly rewarding path to success. However, recent work suggests that a shift in these patterns may be occurring. Sonya Williams and Shin-Kap Han's analysis of middle-class American families reveals that, among couples, men are still more likely to have "stable" careers, but some of them have chosen to follow paths once travelled exclusively by women while increasing numbers of women now pursue full-time careers.[18] The gender divide may be breaking down, but the age divide is still firmly locked in place.

Women in male-dominated professions are an important part of this moving picture. As lawyers, they constitute the first generation to experience life in the culture of the learned gentleman so their stories provide valuable material for evolving theories of career. In spite of the optimism expressed by Arthur and his colleagues, if so-called career actors are aspiring partners in large law firms they have very little control over the script, and, if they are women, they are often found on the margins of professional life.[19] As Cynthia Fuchs Epstein and her colleagues have noted, women in these firms continue to face "multiple glass ceilings" in their quest for partnership.[20] They have moved into the profession in growing numbers over the past few decades, but the barriers are still evident. For example, men and women graduate in equal numbers from the University of Michigan Law School, but women are less likely to enter private practice. Within private practice, the gender balance begins to shift after four years and at critical stages thereafter as women gradually drop out. Men are twice as likely to attain partnership, and, when they do, their salaries are 32 percent higher than those of comparable women. In some cases, women abandon careers to deal with family needs, but the gender differences in partnership status and salary levels are apparent even when men and women have the same work histories.[21] These patterns have been widely documented in Canada as well. Women face discrimination at every level and their careers suffer as a result.[22] As Michael Ornstein has demonstrated, the mean incomes of men in the Ontario legal profession outstrip those of women at every turn, becoming more pronounced as they proceed through their careers. Data from the 2001 census indicate that the $4,000 gender gap for lawyers aged twenty to twenty-nine grows to $24,000 for those in the forty-to-forty-four age bracket and expands still further to $67,000 for the fifty-five-to-fifty-nine age group.[23]

Undoubtedly, women's family responsibilities affect their career patterns, but discriminatory practices are also rooted in institutional norms. Women are seen as less effective practitioners than men so they do not receive the same levels of encouragement or support. Fuchs Epstein and her colleagues have documented the most extreme exclusionary practices in large law firms where powerful time norms determine daily schedules, intrude on family time, and, in the process, sculpt the most-valued career profiles. Like Moen and Roehling, they use the word "mystique" to describe the institutional memory of many law firms, which is kept alive by senior partners' stories about their willingness to work long hours in the golden days before lawyers were called home to be with their children.[24]

Strong mentoring is one of the most valuable keys to career success because it provides access to knowledge, networks, and social capital in the complex culture of the large law firm. In spite of evidence suggesting that women derive unique benefits from mentoring, men are more likely to be favoured in this regard. Jean Wallace's work confirms the value of mentoring for women in various legal settings, particularly with respect to their feelings of social integration.[25] Her findings also show that a woman's career can be affected by the gender of her mentor. Women who are mentored by women derive emotional benefits, presumably because their mentors understand the effects of family pressures on their practices, but women mentored by men have significantly higher incomes than those mentored by women.[26]

These findings suggest that women's values differ from those of men, even at the highest levels of legal practice, but, for many women, success has hinged on a denial of their own basic values and outward commitment to prevailing organizational norms. As lawyers, these women adopt masculine styles of practice in order to fit into the culture. Heather Höpfl and Pat Hornby Atkinson draw an interesting parallel between these behaviours and the medieval regulation of inheritances according to European Salic law. Since these laws excluded women, they could only inherit by standing in for male heirs.[27] In effect, women who chose this route became surrogate men, just as Portia disguised her gender to gain acceptance as a judge.

The large law firm has been singled out as the most demanding legal environment, but the women in this study represent a cross-section of lawyers so they are located in private firms of varying sizes, sole practices, government departments and agencies, clinics, court houses, and large corporations. Some of them may not see themselves as career bound, but most of them encounter pressures to perform. The large firm sets the standards for performance, and its time norms spill over into other settings, building a vision of career success achieved only through long hours and single-minded devotion to the job.[28] This vision provides the framework for the discussion that follows – an account of the career patterns fashioned by women in this study in response to conflicting norms at home and in the office.

A Continuum of Careers

Some of the women in my study talked about their problems with career advancement in large firms, but, given the wide variation in professional specializations and practice types reported by other women, patterns of professional involvement cannot be reduced to a simple typology of careers. In fact, because women's careers defy categorization, they offer a rich variety of potential paths, adding a realistic dimension to the simple linear model. In order to accommodate the broad range of career paths, I have envisioned each of the 110 women along a continuum stretching from the classic linear career to the most extreme variation on this theme. Women whose careers best emulate the linear trajectory devote much of their energy to their legal practices, but, as we move along the continuum, we find that family obligations, friendship networks, volunteer commitments, personal interests, and changing health statuses tend to draw women away from an exclusive focus on their work. Each woman on this imaginary line has her own complete curriculum vitae, embracing both work and non-work interests.

In the section that follows, I describe the careers of women at both extremes of the continuum and in the intervening spaces. Interviews with twelve women provide the material for this discussion because they represent a range of careers reflecting diverse backgrounds and long-term goals.[29] Table 6.1, which is shown at the end of this section, gives an overview of the career paths of these women, along with information about the length of their careers, the number of children reported by each woman, their career interruptions, and their views of future directions. By adopting the linear model as a standard, the discussion begins with the women who most closely match this model and gradually moves along the continuum to careers that are often unplanned, unstructured, or bound for new directions. A careful review of their case histories identifies factors that have helped to shape their career paths, providing a picture of life beyond the workplace and positioning their careers in the context of life course events.[30] At the end of this section, I deal briefly with the women who have left the profession during the ten-year period covered by this research project. Many of them responded to my requests for updated information, but they have scattered in many directions and several of them are impossible to trace.[31]

This review also allows us to glimpse extraneous influences – pregnancy, parenting, family obligations, marital breakdown, personal illness, and, in some cases, death – as critical events that often provide opportunities for reflection and reassessment of career objectives. Traditional career theories discount the effects of these factors or see them as impediments to advancement, but Judi Marshall casts them in a positive light, using language that evokes images unique to the lives of women: "Female values offer career theory a more *cyclic* interpretation of phases, based on notions of ebb and flow, of shedding and renewal. These are important counterpoints to the cumulative, building metaphor ... They involve giving something up, letting achievements go, in order to create anew and differently. This requires considerable faith that future creativity will be possible and an ability to embrace and engage with uncertainty."[32]

Marshall's approach provides a useful framework for my analysis of the careers of women in various legal practices, whether they choose the linear path or simply follow the twists and turns that are more common markers of career passage. Using this expanded vision of career also necessitates a more complex conceptualization of time, which embraces both timing and temporality. Commitment to a linear path requires meticulous attention to timing: lawyers in large firms are expected to devote the initial six to ten years of their working lives to this path as they negotiate the steep ascent to partnership status. However, a more comprehensive definition of career incorporates a vision of temporality. Marshall touches on this aspect when she refers to cycles and phases, but, at a broader level, it captures the unrelenting forces of life course events – birth, aging, and death.[33] These aspects of time beyond the workplace combine with the more obvious temporal demands, and they are evident in the lives of the women in this study.

The Classic Linear Career

I remember people in interviews would say: "Where do you see yourself five years from now?" and I thought: "Good God!"

Table 6.1

Career paths for twelve lawyers on the continuum from linear to non-linear career type

Name	Career path	Career length (years)	No. of children	Career interruptions	Future directions
Sheila	Government → Judge	24	2 step	None (delayed entry)	Established now
Barbara	Associate → Partner large firm	26	2 step	None	Unclear but restless
Marilyn	Vice-president private industry	19	1	None (delayed entry)	Open to suggestions
Kristen	Associate → Partner large firm	16	1	Two years in non-legal position	Unknown
Jessica	Associate → Partner large firm → "Special partner" same firm	16	2	"Retired," September 2001 to February 2003	Unknown
Ellen	Associate → Partner large firm → Judge	24	3	Three years in other types of practices	Established now
Jenny	Associate large firm → In-house legal consulting → Pursuing a political career	15	3	None	Unknown
Claire	Associate → Partner mid-size firm → Mediator-lawyer	17	2	Left legal practice after 15 years	Mediation
Megan	Associate mid-size firm	18	2	None	Open to suggestions
Natalie	Small firm → Sole practice	10	1	None	Established now
Stephanie	Associate mid-size firm → Sole practice	17	2	None	Established now
Heather	Associate mid-size firm → Sole practice	13	1	None (delayed entry)	Unknown

Something that has always bothered me is that I think I judge women harshly if they do have a career plan and their ambition is sort of logged for them. I think women are very hard on other women.

Both of the women quoted above have reached senior levels in the administration of justice. One of them appeared to move effortlessly through a series of legal positions with the Ontario government, while the other one worked in law firms of varying sizes before advancing to the bench. They seemed to have had vague career plans, but both said they had been very naïve about mapping out the steps and following a direct linear path. One of them said that she had wanted to be a judge from her first day in law school, but she had no idea of the process involved in achieving her goal.

The first woman is known as Sheila in the discussion of careers that follows. The stories of two other women also suggest linear patterns of advancement. Barbara had carved out a successful practice in a large law firm, and Marilyn had chosen a route through successive levels of a major corporation. Sheila spent seven years doing secretarial work before returning to school to complete, first, an undergraduate degree and, ultimately, a law degree. She did not recall setting out with a career plan in mind, but she had considered joining a large firm on graduation. However, she opted instead for a position as an assistant Crown attorney for the Ontario government, and her bureaucratic career was set. She became a senior policy advisor a few years later, and, over the next thirteen years, she advanced rapidly through various legal departments within the civil service, devoting much of her extracurricular time to professional associations. At the culmination of her government career, she was appointed to the judiciary. She married along the way and her partner had adult children, but she had not interrupted her career to have children.

Her views of career advancement are interesting because she has followed a classic linear route, but she told me that she had never looked at her career in a strategic way. When I asked if she had guided her career, she said: "I've just sort of fallen into what comes along." When I said: "You haven't contrived things?" she said: "No, no, not at all." She was quite modest about her accomplishments, suggesting that, as one of the first women in a government legal department, she was very visible so her successes were noticed. As a result, she received encouragement along the way and, with every move, was contacted and asked to apply for the next position. She was proud of the fact that she had never applied for any of these jobs but that she had known how to take advantage of opportunities when they presented themselves. Her interview was one of the funniest and most interesting encounters that I had during the course of this research. She was definitely not a dull bureaucrat, and I was not surprised when I read the news of her appointment to the bench. Since her appointment, she has gained publicity for presiding over several high-profile hearings.

Barbara was located in a prestigious office tower with an imposing view of the waterfront. She was extremely cordial, providing lunch and engaging in easy conversation before the taped interview. Her career, like Sheila's, had also followed a traditional linear path. However, when I interviewed her four years after our initial meeting, she had begun to consider her career in the context of other events in her life:

> I guess the interesting thing for me is that this year is my twentieth anniversary in practice and it sort of gives one time to pause and reflect. Over the past four years, I have developed another specialty in my practice and I'm certainly enjoying it ... On a sort of more negative aspect, I feel that, within the law firm there has become tremendous pressure to meet unrealistic billing targets in terms of billable hours and a lot of people are feeling extremely stressed over it.

She had graduated from law school in her mid-twenties and moved immediately into a large, established, urban firm where she developed a successful corporate commercial practice. In her first interview, she had been very positive about her work, explaining that she had been fortunate to learn from a senior lawyer in the firm and had advanced very quickly through the ranks, achieving partnership status six years after entry. During these years, she had also married and, like the previous woman, acquired two stepchildren. At this point, she talked briefly about the increasing demands for long hours within the firm but seemed optimistic that the partners would not impose unreasonable billing requirements on their cadre of lawyers.[34] Her concerns were sharpened a few years later when one of her family members became ill, necessitating travel and time away from her job. During this period, even though she worked from a distance, the firm was less than understanding about her family commitments.[35]

At the conclusion of the interview in 1998, I asked her if she thought I would find her at the firm in five years' time. She replied that there would be a fifty-fifty chance that she would still be there. She had lowered her self-expectations, passed up the performance-based bonuses, and come to terms with her decision, saying: "When I went through the loss of face that I felt when I came down in the allocation system, I learned that I had to sit back and figure out who I was and what was good about me."[36] Like so many other women in the study, her identity was closely tied to her professional achievements and her status in the eyes of her legal colleagues. At another point in the interview, she expressed concern about temporal issues, saying: "I think I've hit middle age for sure because I'm getting restless. I haven't figured out what I want to do but I think there's something in me to do something else, because I just don't find what I'm doing right now as fulfilling as it once was." Her comments suggest that her linear career was on the verge of changing direction, but she is still a partner and has passed the twenty-five-year mark.

Neither Sheila nor Barbara had spent time caring for small children, so they had had relative freedom to advance within the profession. However, many of the women in this study have managed to balance parenthood with their legal careers, either in large firms or in the public sector. Marilyn's experience as in-house counsel exemplifies this pattern. She had followed a well-defined career path for a number of years, but the birth of her child brought a new focus to her life.[37] Like Sheila, she had delayed her entry to law school after experiencing an early period of indecision and dropping out of high school because, as she said, "I just thought it would be – I don't know – a fun thing to do." Five years later, she returned to night school, completed high school, and went on to university. Torn between a master's degree in business administration (MBA) and a law degree, she decided in favour of law school. She articled with a large firm and appeared headed for a career in corporate commercial litigation, but, during her first year with the firm, a chance encounter led to a position in the legal department of a large, international technology firm where she adjusted to the business environment quickly, using her grasp of legal concepts to deal with corporate matters. Her comments indicated that she was on an upward path and enjoying the trip:

> So I started there doing sort of corporate commercial, so I was doing Eurobonds and real estate, joint ventures ... bankruptcy – so sort of the finance stuff, corporate finance, and then – I was on a fast track as they called it there, so then I said: "Well, I'd like to try some marketing because marketing is where it's at – so, not moving out of law but just moving into supporting the marketing area ... And that I didn't like as much because that was much – I perceived it was much more of a rubber stamp.

Like Sheila, she was a bright, enthusiastic person, enjoying the prospect of something new around the next corner without obviously initiating the change. Three years later, she was invited to join a competing firm and that was where I found her, ten years into a very promising career. She had drifted away from her legal focus and was navigating her way through the corporate network. She is still with the firm and she has a very demanding job involving a great deal of community work, but she is extremely well organized and she does not work the extended hours that are common in large law firms. In a profession committed to long hours, her nine-hour workday and weekend freedom seem to present an enviable alternative.

Her progress up the career ladder represents a strong linear path, and, even though she did not begin with a definite agenda, she had reached the level of vice-president and was poised to climb even higher. However, the birth of her son after many years of career advancement brought about a remarkable change in her attitudes towards success, and her shift in priorities was evident in our discussion. She referred to him several times, talking about the utter joy she felt when she was with him. At one point, she said: "He's the bee's knees ... He's my little puppy ... There's no way – I mean it breaks my heart to go on a business trip. There's just no greater experience in the whole world [than motherhood] ... I walk in the door every night. As soon as the key's going in I can hear him: 'Momma?' I get right down on the floor. He runs across there and throws himself in my arms. And we just have a smooch!"

She was still focused on her career and she hinted that upcoming changes in the firm might increase her travel time, but she stressed that she would keep the travel to a minimum in order to be with her child as he grew up. When I asked if she would leave the firm, she said that she might if the right opportunity came up but added: "I can't say that I'm really sitting here thinking or plotting." At the end of the interview, she returned again to the topic of her son, saying: "He's just such a joy! And there's just such little – you know – the questions ... you know – I mean he's only four years old. Can you imagine? We're going to have so much fun!" I said: "If it came to a tossup between the job and the child's needs, would the job go?" She replied without hesitation: "There's no question! No question!"

These kinds of spontaneous comments suggest that motherhood is a powerful event for many women, even those who initially appeared committed to a career above all else. To some extent, they validate Julia Kristeva's visions of motherhood as an integral part of a woman's experience. Of course, there were women in this study who had not had children, many of them by choice, but I was intrigued by the numbers of women who became very emotional at the mention of their families. This pattern was particularly obvious when they tried to calculate the number of hours that their children spent with other caregivers in an average week or when they talked about the sanctity of their evening time with their children as they prepared them for bed.

Their divided loyalties reflect strong societal norms promoting conflicting visions of motherhood and career success.[38] These divisions provide the basis for media suggestions that high-achieving women are leaving behind their careers to stay home full-time with their children. Interpreted as a "new traditionalism," this pattern appears to be the product of media fabrication based on a few high-profile cases.[39] It does not rest on a strong bed of empirical research. One recent study concludes that some women in senior managerial roles have left after experiencing extreme performance stresses on the job during the years when their families need them most. The decision is not a "choice" or a vote for a return to traditional roles as media reports suggest, but it is, perhaps, an admission that work-family policies are still inadequate to the task of accommodating women and their families.[40] Marilyn is one of these women. Her work record has been outstanding, and, given her level of energy, she would experience extreme conflict before deciding to stay home full-time. Her career is still moving in a positive direction, but the presence of her child places her one notch along the continuum from the true linear career.

Variations on the Classic Career
Other in-house lawyers in this study have told us that their counterparts in private practice often envy them their security and control over their time. In-house legal positions continue to attract lawyers who want to leave behind the demanding hours of large firms. These positions were once considered second-rate, but they have gained new status, and the salaries for in-house lawyers have increased to levels that are competitive with those offered by large law firms.[41] Government legal departments have also tried to accommodate family needs in the past, but, even in these settings, the workload has become more demanding over the past decade. However, most lawyers would agree that the most unforgiving environment is to be found in the very large Bay Street firms in Toronto. Nine of the lawyers interviewed had had successful practices in these kinds of firms, and eight of these women had taken time to have at least one child.[42] A look at the careers of two of these women, Kristen and Jessica, gives us an indication of the impact of childbearing on a woman's professional involvement, shifting them slightly farther along the continuum than the other career lawyers. These two women have some common characteristics: they both came from legal families and they were called to the bar in the same year. When we interviewed them the last time, they had each completed ten years of practice and had recently started their families. They were also considering alternative careers.

Kristen's story demonstrates the impact of motherhood on a career marked by a strong upward thrust in its initial stages. Her career plans had taken shape during law school when a respected professor sparked her interest in a particular area of law and she decided to apply to one of the large firms where she could practice her specialty. She joined the firm with the expectation that she would follow the traditional path through the ranks to full partner. Describing herself as one of several "Type Triple A perfectionist personalities" in the firm, she told me that she had worked incredibly long hours during her early years, arriving at her desk at six-thirty every morning and staying until the work was done.[43] She had achieved partnership status on cue, but when I asked her if she still felt a strong sense of career commitment, she said: "I feel differently about things. If I were to be totally honest with you, I would say that I don't want to be here for the rest of my life or even for the rest of my career." In response to a question about negative aspects of her job, she cited long days, heightened client expectations, pressures to docket billable hours, and partners' excessive concern about profits as major stressors in her life. Her life away from the firm was more rewarding at that point. She had strong extended family support and a very solid marriage, and she told me that she had recently decided to have children. On the subject of career, she said: "I went right through undergrad, law school, articling, work. I've never taken a break from it. And I sort of think, in retrospect – not that I would have taken a year off or anything like that – that's not me. I wouldn't have felt right about doing it but I might have been channelled into something else ... I feel, in a sense, trapped in a career that is really not making me altogether happy."

When we looked for her four years later, we found that she had left the practice of law and moved into a setting where she could make use of her legal background. She had also had a child and her life had changed markedly. Although she expressed regret at the loss of daily contact with her legal colleagues, she said that she had left on very good terms, and she was visibly relieved that she had taken steps to ease her burden. Her decision to leave was based partly on her growing dissatisfaction with her work, but the birth of her child had also had a profound impact on her priorities. She said: "It leads you to think a lot more about choices and about lifestyle and that sort of thing and I just found myself in the last couple of years becoming increasingly disillusioned with the practice ... and that, coupled with the fact that I really do want to spend time with my son and have these years that I'll never have again."

However, she continued to express mixed feelings about her legal career. She said that she had recently had lunch with a group of colleagues from the old firm and they had all talked about the "golden handcuffs" that kept them tied to their jobs. She concluded with the observation that "they don't have the option to get out and it is hard because you're making a great income, it's a steady source, it's an environment that, despite the headaches, has some comfort and some security attached with it." In spite of her reservations about the climate in the big firm, she must have found its appeal too strong to resist because she returned to her old firm three years later and worked out a schedule designed to accommodate her family obligations.

Jessica said that she had not begun her job search with definite career plans. She had considered working as a crown prosecutor but eventually settled on a career in the litigation department of a large firm. When I interviewed her the first time, she had just been made partner and her response to a question about work and family plans was interesting. She said:

> I think if I had really thought about having children – and I've always wanted to have children – I've wanted to have children more than I've ever wanted to have a career. And it just seemed like this – when I went into law school I turned into a career-oriented person and professional-oriented person rather than a family-oriented person. I guess what happened was I just – well I wasn't in a relationship with anyone, family wasn't imminent, so I just said: "Well, I'll just keep going with this career." And that side of me just took off and I didn't think about the other part. And now, you know, however many years later, ten years later from when I started law school, the family part is coming up and you've got this professional part too and it's the balancing act. But I wouldn't have gone into – I wouldn't have – if I had my time back – I probably still would have done a law degree. I probably wouldn't have stayed in Toronto working in a Bay Street firm.

Her comment about turning into a "career-oriented person" suggests that she can somehow reshape her identity at will. At the time of the interview, she was planning to start a family, apparently ready to move from her career orientation to her untested role as a parent. She was clear about her priorities, saying: "I'm absolutely prepared to earn 50 percent of what I'm earning but I'm not going to be working the amount that I work [now]. In fact I'll probably be working half of what I work." She went on to say that, if the firm did not agree to her terms, she would quit completely and consider a different career. In fact, her view of her legal accomplishments was anything but traditional. She said: "I've done it. I've been here. You know, they've made me a partner where I can go up and can eventually sit on the committee that runs the place but I don't feel that I have anything else to conquer."

Four years and two children later, she told my assistant that she was much happier with her life, saying: "I guess I've done sort of a flip in my life in terms of what's important and they're the number one thing in my life and my profession is more to me like a – I still really love what I do but it's more of a job." She had also become very disillusioned about the treatment of women in large firms, and she was considering a career move. She was still working ten-hour days in the office most of the time, leaving at six to have dinner at home and put her children to bed before opening her briefcase and working for another hour and a half.[44] Like a number of other women in the study, she told us that her daily involvement in the social life of the firm disappeared with the birth of her children. Since her time was so precious, she worked steadily in her office with occasional breaks for fitness classes. Her final words revealed a great deal of ambivalence about her life in the firm when she said, in response to a question about attitudes towards women, "I'm not bitter about it at all. I'm here. I worked my way through. I'm fine. But I know what the reality is and I've decided to sort of put up with it ... I earn a good living ... *It's all very stressful constantly but it's all perfect. It's just perfect."*

The Large Firm as One Stage in a Career

Several of the women in this study have had successful mini-careers with large firms but, for various reasons, have decided to move into other types of practice. Ellen and Jennie told very different, but equally fascinating, stories of careers marked by this kind of pattern. When I went to interview Ellen for the first time, I found her in a very modest office in a large city. She told me that she had been there for four years, and, as her story unfolded, it was clear that this had been no ordinary career path. She had been practising law for fourteen years and had changed firms four times before landing in her current location. She struck me as a very bright woman who performed at her best as long as she was challenged. She was also prepared to work hard and mentioned several times that she tended to be a workaholic. Her career had assumed a linear shape during her tenure in a large firm, but it had meandered in other directions along the way. When I commented on this pattern, she agreed, saying: "It's been all over!" When I asked where it would go next, she said: "I have no idea. I'm happy here for now."

After being called to the bar, she had been employed in two very different settings – first in a small firm ("a good experience ... I needed more of a challenge intellectually") and then, briefly, in a very large Bay Street firm. Two years out of the bar, she had accepted a position with another large firm and seemed ready to advance up the ladder to partner. She loved the environment, got along well with everyone, found the work interesting, and, in her words, "became a workaholic again." By the time she joined this firm, she had married and was pregnant with her second child so she was delegated by the other women in the firm to negotiate a reasonable maternity leave policy. From a career point of view, her family plans were surprising because she had told me earlier that she had never intended to marry or have children. When I asked her about this change it was clear that, like Marilyn and Kristen, she had found motherhood to be unexpectedly fulfilling:

I loved children but – you know – I decided that I was going to do a career instead and so I went off on that track and I worked like hell, steadfastly saying: "No children and never would have one," until I hit thirty and went: "Ah!" And I still thought: "I just won't be able to stay away from work that long." But you know, I had [baby's name] and I was absolutely blown, unbelievable, over the moon! It just changed my life! It was the most amazing miracle! I just could not – couldn't believe it!

She took her entire maternity leave when her second child was born and then returned to her gruelling schedule. Shortly after she was made partner, her third child was born and life became much more complicated. When I asked if these increasing family demands had hurt her career, she assured me that they had not because she simply hunkered down and worked harder than ever. Life in the large firm had definite appeal, but the workload had begun to have its effect on her well-being:

I had been there for six years and I was a partner in the litigation department and I had a beautiful office – not much like this one. It was full of marble. I had a southern view over the lake. It was lovely. I felt fine while I was there ... [At this point she said she had been invited to apply for a job in a different setting.] When I came home and told my husband about the offer, he said: "What did you tell them?" And I said: "I'm not interested." And he said: "Why not?" And I said:, "Because I'm happy doing what I'm doing." And he said: "You've done nothing but complain for a solid year about what you're doing" ... I started to think about it and – you know – the firm had become much more sort of business oriented and bottom line and docketing and all this kind of stuff was creeping in. And the people I really liked who had been in management were being replaced by the business manager side – you know.

After careful reflection, she decided to accept the offer, but the new venture was not what she had expected so she spent the next two years in a kind of legal limbo. She decided against a return to the large firm because she had lost interest in the kinds of files that she had been given there. Once again, her thirst for challenge and change had led her in a new direction. Although she did not say so during our interview, the position she was occupying was a temporary one. In fact, she was very positive about the progress of her career and her involvement in family life. At the end of the interview, she said: "I have everything. Isn't it like – it's like a magic life. It's true." When I suggested that she had endured a great deal along the way and that she was very talented, she countered with: "But you know, everything drops in my lap. I am lucky ... I cannot say I can take any credit for the way my life has gone because it just – at the same time I'm presented with certain choices and I choose that one for sometimes ridiculous reasons and it always works out somehow."

Like Sheila, she discounted her own contribution to her career, preferring to see it as the product of forces beyond her control. When I asked where she thought things would go next, she said: "I have no idea. I'm happy here for now."

Shortly after our interview, Ellen had decided that she could no longer remain with the agency employing her. At that point, she was a single mother with three children, and, even though she loved her work, she was struggling financially. She learned via the legal grapevine that, if she decided to apply for a judicial appointment, her application would be given serious consideration. Once again, she saw her career being guided not by her own initiative but by simple good fortune, saying: "It's being in the right place at the right time ... some people might think ... having the kind of career that I did was a real disadvantage." She applied for the position and was appointed within a few months. When I visited her in her chambers a few years later, she was enthusiastic about her new role, in spite of the added time constraints. She said: "I feel that I have more problems managing this because I have more family, you know. I often say to other women judges: 'Do you think the boy judges have to go through what I do? Before I got here this morning I did this, this, this, this, this, and this – and do you think any of the boy judges had to delouse their kids' hair before they came in to work this morning?'" She went on to say that her male colleagues in the judiciary were extremely supportive and that there were policies in place to accommodate family schedules. It was just different for women. Once again, at the end of the interview, I said: "Tell me, is this it? You've been everywhere, you've had lots of different bits to your career. Is it going to be a judge [for the rest of your career]?" Her response was typical:

> I have no idea. I love it. And do you know, it's such a treat to be able to come to work every day and think: "I wonder what's going to happen today?" There's always some twist – there's some – you know, it's real people and their lives and you get inside them and it's tragic, some of it, and it's funny at other times ... Some of this stuff is hilarious ... and other stuff is just tragic and gut wrenching but it's also fascinating – you know. It's so interesting. And the law is interesting. It's just that there isn't enough time to do it well.

She had left behind the cramped little office and was happily ensconced in chambers, at least for the moment.

One of the interesting aspects of interviewing for this study lay in the surprises that we encountered when we approached the lawyers' offices for the first time. There are no such surprises in the corridors of Bay Street. Offices are arranged in elegant suites covering several floors of a tower, well-groomed receptionists page lawyers as they deal with a stream of incoming calls, and lawyers are brisk and business-like, often choosing boardrooms rather than their offices for their interviews. The magazines in the waiting rooms are standard business publications, and, occasionally, nervous students in business suits sit waiting for their articling interviews. However, the real surprises are to be found far beyond the Toronto financial district. One of my favourites was located in a town outside the urban fringe. It was a small stucco house on a side street, and, as I approached it, I thought that there must have been a mistake because there was no sign indicating that a lawyer might be in residence. However, I entered and climbed the stairs to a second level, walking into an office where two people sat working. I asked for the lawyer on my list, and they told me that she was on the telephone. One of them found a chair and set it in an awkward position between their desks. She arrived a few minutes later, dressed in jeans and a sweatshirt, and ushered me to her office at the back of the building. It became immediately clear that this woman was different from her urban counterparts. My notes for this interview said: "She has always been willing to effect change when she does not like her working environment. I think her story would make a very effective introduction to a chapter on *career creativity*. She has done much more than adapt!"

This lawyer, dubbed Jenny, had her first child while she and her husband were undergraduates, and they had two more children by the time she finished law school. She articled and began her practice in a large Toronto firm, balancing family responsibilities with her legal work while her husband completed his education. She said that they had been incredibly busy and stressed but that they had learned to share their parenting duties equally, and she remembers those years with great fondness. She remained with the firm for five years, but she was never interested in becoming a partner because, as she said, "I just couldn't picture myself sitting around a table trying to come to decisions with twenty-some odd other people, or forty. At one partner meeting, they took over an hour to decide where to put a toaster!" She said she had enjoyed her time with the firm, assuring me that she had always been treated fairly and given every opportunity to advance. However, she was interested in the business side of law, and, when she was offered a position as in-house lawyer with a telecommunications company, she decided to move on. She told me that she experienced sexual harassment for the first time in her life during her two-year stint with the company. It became clear that women would not be allowed to advance in that environment so she left the firm and accepted a second in-house position as a senior manager in the telecommunications industry. Her comments about the new environment were scathing:

I spent the next two years in the most chauvinistic, male chauvinistic, sexist, unbelievable environment I thought could possibly – I didn't think it could exist! And the most upsetting thing I found was that most of the women, most of the *senior* women, were just as male chauvinistic as the rest. They were – uh – a number of them had ended up in the positions that they had because of having engaged in various relations ... But they also assumed – the women in this environment – that women weren't as good [as men]. And these were people in positions of senior management!

She said that she felt very badly because she had always assumed that women who complained about sexual harassment were, in some way, responsible for their treatment, but, having come face to face with discriminatory practices, she realized that she had just been lucky in avoiding this kind of abuse for many years. She said: "I was led to believe that there was no reason to believe that I couldn't do anything because I was a woman, but I don't agree with that any more. I think there are lots of things – problems for us. I know lots of women lawyers who struggle – a woman at a big law firm just a couple of weeks ago – she's a fairly senior partner in a big firm – and it's just a horrible experience she's going through!" She went on to talk about the unique pressures experienced by women in large law firms and the failure of professional bodies to address these issues effectively:

Every time we refer to it as a women's issue, we just reinforce the attitude ... And unfortunately, the law firms don't get it. I mean – even my old firm – which I said was wonderful for me – is proving to be extremely difficult for a number of women ... The woman I was speaking with just the other day, a couple of weeks ago – she's almost in tears and she's been with this firm for a long time ... she said that it has become so much worse in the last five years.

Having come to terms with the difficulties faced by women in many large firms, Jenny decided to make use of the experience she had gained in the telecommunications sector and head in a completely different direction. She and her husband moved to the small community where she embarked on an entirely new form of legal practice, describing it this way:

I knew at that point that I didn't want to go into another environment – I didn't want to be somebody's employee and I didn't want to be somebody's partner ... and so I had decided that I wanted to do something differently. The whole way we've set up our practice is very much an alternative to traditional law firms and in-house practice. So from a business perspective, we spend a lot of time at clients' premises. We almost never charge by the hour. It's almost all on a retainer basis. It's like part-time in-house counsel basically. That's what we do for a number of clients.

Her low profile on the town's street was deliberate. She did not want local, walk-in legal business and she did not get it. Instead, she worked quietly in her office, putting on her dress clothes when necessary and flying off to various locations to ply her trade as visiting in-house counsel. When she described her move from jeans to business clothes, I thought again of Portia and the need for costuming to promote the right image.

When I asked about a possible career strategy, suggesting that she might have been engaged in a chess or checkers game without any particular focus on a career pinnacle, she said: "I didn't start off law thinking of doing this. No question. But it was less chess or 'checkerboardish' than an evolving path. Because I came upon the idea of doing something like this, when I was in my law firm, I wasn't really able to pin down what it was that made sense until after having been in-house for a few years in a couple of different environments." On the subject of women's views of career, she echoed Jessica's sentiments, saying: "A lot of men I know are just happy to do their jobs and most of the women I know are not happy unless they're happy. They're a little bit more particular about what they want and so I know lots of women now who are partners who are saying: 'Okay, I've done this' ... I don't hear that from many of the men I know."

We closed the interview with the usual question about long-term plans, and she assured me that, in spite of her recent successes, she would not continue to practise law in the same way for many more years. She suggested teaching as an option and perhaps a blend of her business and law interests as an appropriate course in an MBA program, saying: "I'm a big believer in, if I'm not really happy doing what I'm doing, and I'd rather be doing something else, I'll be pretty quickly doing something else. I'm having a great time." When my research assistant conducted the follow-up interview, she was still running her business but had moved away from the hands-on practice of law. She had engaged other lawyers to do the legal work and was concentrating on the management side of the business. She has recently turned to politics. Her activities are publicized on a website and she is about to move in a new direction. She is still young, her children are in the process of leaving home, and I expect to see her career evolve in many more creative ways as she works her way through life. Her experience epitomizes the positive aspects of career change that Judi Marshall emphasizes.[45] She is keenly aware of the male values that shape life in many large firms, and she is intent on avoiding the gender inequities that often hide behind the most eloquent mission statements as she steps confidently along her own career path.[46]

Life in Medium-Size Firms

Many of the women in the study had chosen to work in smaller firms for various reasons. They may have practised a type of law that was better suited to this environment or they may have wished to avoid the long hours culture that characterizes large firms. Their careers were less likely to follow a steep linear trajectory than those of women in large firms, and they were more likely to have moved around from one firm to another in search of the perfect situation. None of them left these firms to pursue careers in large firms. Claire and Megan described paths that are typical of careers in medium-size firms. Claire was based in an urban setting, having changed positions several times before moving away from a traditional law practice completely, and Megan was firmly established in a small town firm, content with the balance between her legal work and her family life.

When I first met Claire, she was at home on maternity leave following the birth of her second child. She told me that she had entered law school with a vague idea about the type of law she would like to practise, but, like many of the women in the study, she had no firm picture of her legal career even upon graduation. Almost by chance, she began a career in litigation with a medium-size general law firm where, as she recalled, she had enjoyed the company of other young hard-working colleagues. The firm dissolved after a few years, and she joined a second firm of similar size, but, in this case, the atmosphere was much less hospitable. She became pregnant while she was there and her male partners reacted with outright hostility, claiming that a maternity leave would be far too costly for the firm and that she would have to compensate them for time away from their families while they covered her files. This experience left her feeling angry and disillusioned about the practice of law as she headed off to her maternity leave. At the time of the interview, she was undecided about her future and when I asked how she saw her career in light of the standard linear model, her response was interesting:

> I guess I have always modelled my career on that male linear pattern – but it's not critically important. I guess you reach the point, and maybe becoming personally happy is a big part of it, where – you know, my most important source of self-esteem is no longer in the office. Although it is a critically important one for me still and I really do want to continue to progress, I don't view progressing in any particular direction as being the goal. In other words, I'm not seeking to become senior partner, corner office, the way I suspect many male lawyers may. It's more important to me to just continue to develop my career so that I'm always challenged, I'm always doing a good job, I always care about what I'm doing and obtain gratification from it – and I always have time to spend with my family.

Her comment about the source of her self-esteem shifting away from her work suggested that she might already be looking elsewhere for challenging interests. Four years later, she told us that she had moved to a third firm after her maternity leave, stayed two years, and moved again. This time she appeared to be content with her practice and her partnership status, in spite of the fact that she was working long hours and carrying more than her share of family duties. She told us that there was no pressure to put in long hours at the office, as long as the overhead was covered. When I asked how she saw her career unfolding in the future, she was vague and her use of a divorce analogy was unsettling:

> I don't know. I actually don't. I guess my past has predisposed me to not think about the long term. I'm here right now. I'm very happy. It's going well ... [My husband] could be out of a job. This partnership could split up. I have no way of knowing but I guess I've learned to not worry. I don't worry any more about any of that because I've always – every time – landed on my feet just fine ... I'm very independent. I'm sort of like somebody who's been divorced twice. I came into this relationship with this firm very wary, very reluctant to join the partnership even though it was perfect.[47]

In spite of her state of relative contentment, she seemed to suggest that life could still take a negative turn without warning. In fact, there were ominous signs on the horizon that were not obvious at the time of the interview. Three years later, her world came crashing down. Her practice had expanded dramatically and she had become heavily involved in community affairs, but she was stretched to the breaking point. She rarely had time with her children, and, although her partner had assumed a larger share of the domestic work, he was tired of carrying the load alone and her marriage was severely threatened. As she told me later, "I melted down one night after a partners' meeting. I went home that night and never came back." She was about to embark on a year of therapy, soul-searching, and a protracted healing process.

Her experience has raised questions in my mind about the profound importance of professional identity for practising lawyers.[48] It seems that women in particular are expected to meet impossible ideals, both as professionals and as responsible mothers.[49] Claire's observations, two years after her crisis, are very revealing in this respect:

> What I first thought was going to be a short mental health break turned into a year-long sabbatical. At first I didn't know what to make of any of it. I should go back and read the diary that I kept during this time but it was a time of great uncertainty. *For weeks I wouldn't go outside because*

I didn't know who I was. I was afraid of seeing people who might ask me what I was doing or how was work. I wasn't "Claire-downtown lawyer" anymore, nor was I "Claire-superb-stay-at-home mom" like the other moms. I was just Claire. At first I hated going to pick the kids up at school because I didn't know what to say to people. I was so embarrassed and ashamed![50]

By the end of the year, she and her family had worked their way through a maze of issues and emotions while she struggled to regain her confidence. The process was a slow one, but now, several years later, she seems to have lost the fear that life might break apart again at any moment:

Along the way, I realized that I could not go back to doing what I had done all along. I had no stomach for being an adversary any more. I wanted to do something more creative, more positive, more in keeping with the way I felt about relationships and life. I went to see a career counsellor ... I called every mediator I knew (not many) and many that I did not know. I decided to enrol in an ADR [alternative dispute resolution] course. As the program progressed, I came to have confidence that this was the right path for me. I opened up shop and started taking cases, and the practice just grew from there.

She has left the practice of law and devotés all her time to her mediation interests. Her income has dropped, but her marriage has been revived and she has achieved a new level of contentment with her work, her family, and herself. She recently sent me a letter in which her final words were: "It has been such a glorious time. We have all fallen in love. (It isn't perfect of course!!!) And we have this bond ... I think we all grew and were so strengthened." The letter was followed by a brochure publicizing her new enterprise in which she appeared as a smiling, confident practitioner, headed in a different direction.[51]

Her journey demonstrates the value of an inductive approach as a way of envisioning expanded theories of career. It is devoid of conventional time-space metaphors and its strength lies in the endless possibilities for exploration. Both Marshall and Gallos emphasize the importance of viewing unique career paths in positive terms rather than as corruptions of the accepted model. Claire's experience confirms the value of this approach. Her hiatus could be seen by some people as a period of unproductive inactivity, but Judi Marshall would view it as a time for "incubation or regeneration," paving the way for a new life.[52] In fact, Claire herself uses images of death to describe her despair and says that, in many ways, she had experienced rebirth.

Megan's path was quite different from Claire's. On graduation from law school, she decided to do her articles with a large firm, as she said, "to see what it was like." She told me that she had enjoyed the experience, but the firm dissolved at the end of her articling year so she decided to relocate, choosing a solicitor's position in a small town firm. When I met her, her practice was a blend of real estate, wills, and estate planning. Unlike Claire, she had been with the same firm for thirteen years and appeared quite content. She had chosen the firm because she felt that it was very "professional," like the large firm where she had trained, and the partners were "forward thinking" and "aggressive." She said that they supported a work-family balance for their staff, and they had accommodated her during her maternity leaves, although she felt that the women in the firm would benefit from a formal maternity leave policy. She said: "There are no paid benefits. It's all covered through unemployment insurance because I'm an employee. Had I been a partner, I would have funded it entirely myself."

She was quick to tell us that she did not want to be a partner because she was not interested in managing staff or attending partners' meetings, she did not want to make the financial commitment, and she did not want to sacrifice time with her family. In fact, at both interviews she expressed a strong desire to move to a part-time practice, but she had concluded that it would be problematic:

> I'd love to work part-time but it's just really difficult ... Clients expect you to be there. And if there are issues, if you have deals closing, you have to be there to answer their questions. I may – what I'm going to try to do is probably work on a part-time basis but on a flexible basis. If I don't have a deal closing, if I've cleared my day, if I've put in all my hours for the week in four days, then I take the day off. It's not that you have to be there for the issues. The other part of it is – for your remuneration. If you're not there, you're not getting that work too. That's a trade-off I guess and that's a personal decision ... I'm going to be missing issues or new clients possibly and I'm willing to go for that at this point in my career.[53]

She had been very fortunate in working out a schedule that accommodated her family's needs. They had an excellent nanny, her husband typically arrived home ahead of her after work, and he generally had more time to devote to the children. As she said, "I have simple goals. I want to be home every night with my family for supper. I want to have a sit-down meal. The TV is downstairs. We never have dinner in front of the TV. And then we talk. I need to know what they did during the day and get back in touch with them." Her position on the continuum was like the balance point on a fulcrum. She said that she would not be happy as a stay-at-home mother, but she did not want her law practice to take precedence over her family. This desire for balance was evident in her response to questions about her career. She said: "I enjoy my career. I love working here but sometimes it's a job too. It's a means to an end. It's a means to allow me to do things with my family, or the travel. So it's not the focus. The children are more – make me more fulfilled certainly than the job does."

At this point, I asked her if she would encourage her daughters to be lawyers and she hesitated, then said that law would be fine if it made them happy. This comment led her to reflect on her own personality and she concluded: "I don't know that I have the spark for the law as such. What I enjoy out of the career is helping people – which makes me think maybe something more in the social work field might have been better, or psychology, that kind of thing ... I don't know that I have the same passion that you see with some lawyers." At both interviews, she talked about moving into a different kind of work, ruminating about the possibility of returning to school or taking a sabbatical in another country or going into business with her husband. In spite of the relative stability of her practice over time, she had avoided the linear route and was prepared to consider options that Judi Marshall would view as positive and creative.

Sole Practice

One-fifth of the women in this study had spent all or a significant proportion of their working lives as sole practitioners. Some of them had chosen this route and others had been forced into it when they were released from larger firms. In several cases, they were asked to leave when they became pregnant or they were the victims of cutbacks during periodic downturns in the economy. The women in sole practice were concentrated in three specific areas – family, real estate, and criminal law. A few of them had corporate commercial practices, but none of them specialized in civil litigation. Approximately half of them were located in outlying communities where they practised family law or did basic solicitors' work, and the remainder, especially the criminal lawyers, practised in large urban centres. Three of these women practised in very different settings. Natalie is one of the few women practising criminal law in an outlying area of the province, Stephanie practises corporate commercial law in a large city, and Heather's small town practice consists mainly of family law.

When Natalie was called to the bar she decided to return to the small community where she had grown up, marry, and establish her legal practice. During her articling year, she found that she loved criminal law so, when she applied for a job, she specified criminal law as her primary interest:

I went for an interview and got a job with that firm and my personality blended with the two gentlemen who worked in their criminal department. It was just an instant hit so I went to work for them in criminal – doing criminal work predominantly – but they had never had a female practising in their firm, let alone in criminal law. They thought that I would just tire of it quickly and so it was their suggestion that I do family law as well – the pink ghetto they called it – so I would always have a fallback. And I despised it! I hated it from the first file to the last file that I covered! ... I'd rather have a root canal! ... I found more of my clients were respectable, cash-paying clients coming in with family issues and they were worse to deal with than my heroin addict even though I would say to him: "I don't believe a God-damned thing you're saying!"

She had found her niche early in her career and would have been happy to stay with the firm but things took a decidedly nasty turn when she announced two years later that she was pregnant:

The firm didn't like a pregnant woman who wanted to take full maternity leave. I had a battle royal with them. I was entitled by law – I was a salaried employee – to take the full maternity leave and I fought them on it from the day I left [on maternity leave] until the week before I returned ... Some male personalities were very old fashioned in the firm. They were the high billers and sort of held the ship together and they were pressuring the others to say – you know – get her back here. What is she doing at home with a child?

The senior partners tried to persuade her to resign before her maternity leave was over so she took her year at home, mulled over her options, and ultimately agreed to accept their terms for dismissal. She will always be convinced that the birth of her child had made her a liability to the firm:

They were starting to pass a rumour around the office that it didn't appear that my heart was in my work, that I turned out to be more maternal than anyone thought I would be and maybe I should just come back working part-time or ... It's crap! I got this kind of weird vibe about the fact that they're just trying to get me out so I beat them to the punch and said: "Well, why don't you just buy me out?" ... I took some cash from them and said: "I'll just leave." As a condition of that, he [a senior partner] wanted me to sign a letter that it was my choice to leave the firm, that I truly didn't intend to return to the practice of law with them full-time. I didn't sign it. They knew they were in the wrong. They had treated me like dirt ... they said: "We'll keep quiet. Don't tell anybody that it's because of maternity reasons."

She said that the next woman hired by the firm was pressured early in her pregnancy to either drop back to part-time work or leave the firm altogether. Like Natalie, she had negotiated a settlement and left shortly after the birth of her baby. Experiences like these are not unusual. A number of the women in this study talked about their own experiences with pregnancy or those of other women, while most of the women in large firms made conscious decisions to postpone parenthood until after they had become partners. Their stories emphasize the fact that legal practice is a business, and, given the pressure to generate profits, many senior partners regard motherhood as an impediment.

Natalie moved into sole practice after the birth of her son and has remained there. Her practice is heavily dependent on Legal Aid funding so it does not generate high billings, but she loves criminal law. She also plays an active role in her local law association and takes part in various community organizations. Her major focus, however, is on her family life – her husband and her growing son.[54] She summed up her feelings in her second interview, saying: "I really believe that I like my work. I feel happy most of the time ... when I don't want to go to work it's because something's telling me that I don't want to go to work, whether it's nice weather or whatever, so I listen to my other self and then I don't sell out and go sell real estate ... I don't care about the money. I want to live to support what I like – which is to travel. And I love food, I love to cook, and I love to go out to restaurants."

Stephanie's urban office differed from Natalie's small town setting, but their stories were, in many ways, similar. She had decided during her articling year in a large firm to aim for a smaller practice, but she liked corporate law and the firm provided a good training ground. Since she eventually wanted to have children, she decided to accept a position with a second large firm where she hoped to develop some contacts before moving to a smaller firm. The experience was valuable, but it came to an abrupt end when, after four years with the firm, she announced her pregnancy. Like Natalie, she provoked an icy reaction:

I think I was very fortunate in getting good quality work and good quality training. I was the only woman in the department for the longest time and there tended to be one other at some point but it was a revolving door. Six months later she'd be gone and there would be another one. Six months later she would be gone and it would be another one ... I mean – the firm doesn't have the greatest reputation in terms of the way it treats associates but I think for my initial stretch there – I don't think I was treated any better or worse than any of the male associates ... I think they just worked people hard and got rid of them, which is not an uncommon setup in those firms. I was fine there until I announced that I was pregnant.

She went on to describe a series of events involving verbal abuse and rumour mongering within the firm. In the end, she took her maternity leave, but her position was terminated two weeks before she was due to return to work.[55] These kinds of experiences illuminate the dark side of women's career paths, reminding us that their decisions to move are not always creative alternatives to the male model. Stephanie told me that her treatment was not unusual, given the firm's record of dealing unfairly with pregnant lawyers. When someone suggested that she consider a submission to the Ontario Human Rights Commission, she declined: "I said: 'Look, I'm just going to go away quietly.' That's what everyone does. I can tell you so many stories ... It was just a question of – they were very quick in branding you as a troublemaker which means you get black-listed. And if you – I didn't know at that time that I would end up in solo practice. I couldn't risk my being – you know."

When I interviewed her the first time, she was located in a modest office some distance from the centre of the city. She had two small children and her career was, for the time being, secondary to her husband's business plans. I asked her to tell me about her own career, if indeed she regarded it as a "career in the professional sense." She told me that she wanted to be available for her children as they were growing up and her plan was to hire other lawyers who would be willing to do part-time contract work:

> What I would like to do is eventually hire other lawyers so that the overflow of work – contract lawyers, not employees ... and who I'd like to get are women with young children because I think the profession does not accommodate women with young families and I guess the purpose – I mean it's not entirely altruistic – I'd like to get someone who wants to work ten or fifteen hours a week that I can farm out specific pieces of work to ... This wouldn't be under one roof. You do all your work at home and I'll buy your services. And the idea from my point of view is beneficial because, in a contract position, you don't take on the obligations of source deductions and remitting tax and a regular salary whether there's work or not.

When I described the linear career model and asked her for her opinion, she was quite explicit about her divided roles and her need to maintain her professional identity:

> I think it's a great concept but it's fundamentally irreconcilable with having a family. Ten women from my year – we all had babies the year I had my first. Between March and August, there were ten of us, ten babies and so we have discussed this at length ... I kid around that I don't know

whether I have the best of both worlds or the worst of both worlds ... I have a brain. I am smart. We do draw our identity from it [the practice of law], especially those of us who have been practising. I think I would find it terribly hard to be at home and say: "Well, you know, I'm at home right now." I find this need to say: "Well I did practise for so many years and I had my own practice" and it's a terrible thing to say but I think it's true.

When we returned four years later, her children were both in school and she had cut back her working day in order to be available for them after school. Her husband was still more involved with his profession than she was. She had taken a leave of absence from several professional committees and regretted the loss of her key networks. Since she had reduced her hours on the job, she had less business to handle and had had to postpone her earlier plan to hire contract lawyers. She was also toying with the idea of making a major career change that would lead her out of the practice of law. She said:

I still basically like what I do, although there was a moment, probably in the last six months that I could pinpoint at that specific moment the novelty of working definitely wore off ... but I still basically like what I do and I hadn't realized how much until I suddenly thought – again, this is within the last month or so that this opportunity has come up – of maybe not doing this any more and I thought: "Oh, wait a second, I don't know. I'm so used to getting up in the morning and putting on a suit and coming in and doing this."[56]

Heather also had a sole practice, but her background was very different from Stephanie's. She had grown up in a small Ontario town, and, when she entered law school as a mature student, she was a single mother in search of economic security for herself and her child. She had worked previously as a law clerk in a small general firm so she planned to practise real estate law when she graduated. Her motivation for choosing a law career was interesting. She said: "The reason I went to law school was because my father had always wanted to be a lawyer but he was from a very poor family and was not able to go. So I definitely went to please him, but I stayed to please myself. I really liked law school, although I had no idea what it was going to be like to be a lawyer." She was called to the bar at a time when the real estate market had slumped so she accepted a position with a small firm in need of a family lawyer.

When I met her, she was located in the town where she had grown up. She had been a sole practitioner for eight years, devoting 80 percent of her time to family law. She said that her practice was very stressful, partly because she absorbed tension from her clients and partly because other family lawyers in her community tended to favour an adversarial approach that she despised. She had enjoyed a settled, balanced life close to her large extended family, but she was beginning to experience some stress-related health problems. When I asked her if she thought she would continue to practise family law for many years, she said:

> I can't imagine that. [Why not?] Because of the stress. Actually, I've often heard lawyers, senior lawyers, saying – you know – the litigation bug eases. It becomes less and less a part of your practice or what you want to do, the older you are, the longer you've been practising. And I can likely see that. They say family lawyers burn out in eight to ten years. [And you've had eight years] Yup. [So what would the alternatives be?] Well, that's a good question. Either becoming an educator, I guess, in the area. [A judge?] A judge, yes, or some public service area.

When my assistant returned to her office three years later, her practice had not changed much. She was still practising family law, without any obvious prospect of a judicial appointment. A recent check indicated that she is still in the same location. Her career does not resemble the upward linear path of some of her urban counterparts, and it does not appear that she ever intended to follow that route. She had been offered a position in a Toronto firm early in her career but had declined, saying that she wanted to raise her child in a small town. Her child has grown up and left home now, but she still finds great comfort in her family networks close by.

Women in Search of New Lives

Finally, eleven of the original women in this study have now left the profession.[57] Some of them had very promising legal careers when I first met them, but others were already considering new paths. Two of them were government lawyers, three of them had worked in small- to medium-size firms, four women had sole practices, one woman had been an in-house lawyer, and one had been employed with a community agency. Why did they leave? Several women disliked the pressure to perform, both in private firms and in government departments, all but one of them had children, and some of them simply did not like the practice of law.[58]

One of these women, whose pseudonym is Amanda, told an interesting story about her brief legal career. She was at home with her nine-month-old baby when we interviewed her, obviously happy to be away from the office environment. Law had never been a vocation for her. She said that she had decided on law school ahead of medical school because she did not like blood.[59] After her call to the bar, she practised civil litigation in a large firm but did not enjoy the experience so she moved to a high-tech firm as in-house lawyer. Six months later, she found that she was pregnant. She said that her immediate supervisor was very understanding when she broke the news, but the senior managers were not pleased. They suggested that she drop back to a part-time position after the baby's birth, but she decided against it because she thought it would be a full-time position disguised as part-time. She added: "The same men who weren't happy that I got pregnant were still there so I knew – I heard through a friend of mine who was still there – that they were all saying: 'Well, you know, why doesn't she just hire a nanny? Why does she have to work part-time?' And I knew that attitude was there. I didn't want to get involved."

She chose instead to stay at home with her child but found that she was not getting enough stimulation so she picked up some part-time legal work that allowed her to get out of the house one day a week. She said that she had no definite plans for the next few years, except that she wanted to have more children. When I asked what her dream career would be, she surprised me, saying: "I would do something in another country, helping people with World Vision or something like that. I'm a big softy. I love kids. I would do something that is not business at all ... some sort of missions work with World Vision or – I mean that's what I've always dreamed of doing since I was a kid." When I suggested that that route might be a sidetrack down the road, she said: "I got very sidetracked with life." She also said that she was considering a teaching degree or a master's degree in law. I have been unable to locate her but am not surprised that she is no longer on the Law Society's rolls.

Conclusion

The career theory literature is still anchored in a masculine vision of career as an unbroken, upwardly mobile path to status, money, and power. This outdated career model does not accommodate women's lives, and it describes the employment history of only a small proportion of men. It is oversimplified and one-dimensional – a single corner of the curriculum vitae that is designed to incorporate all aspects of life. Families would be better served by career expectations that allowed them time to deal with the other dimensions of their lives, particularly during the childrearing and eldercare years. This kind of flexible arrangement would provide a truly equitable approach to career-building and family life.[60]

In spite of its limitations, the linear career model is still prized in large law firms and other legal settings, but the entry of women to this once exclusively male club has raised a number of issues about the profession's willingness to accommodate the needs of busy families. The women in studies such as this one have valuable information to contribute in their descriptions of the interactions between their legal lives and their other interests. As the body of literature grows and policy-makers respond, the uninterrupted career path may be replaced, in many cases, by more humane approaches to the curriculum vitae.

Judi Marshall has suggested that new theories are needed to encompass the kinds of careers that women develop, either by design or by circumstance, but it is difficult to conceptualize a one-size-fits-all alternative to the linear career. However, women in male-dominated professions have an important role to play in this regard. If they enter legal practice, particularly in large prestigious law firms, they may clash head-on with the masculine values inherent in the long hours culture where careers are built on complete dedication to the firm and freedom from domestic responsibilities. Since they are not always seen as serious contenders for partnership, they encounter barriers to advancement, both subtle and obvious. Their predecessors were, in many cases, energetic women who proudly "did it all." For example, a recent media report profiles a senior partner in a large Toronto firm who says she is intent on changing the corporate culture to accommodate family needs but who goes on to say that she established herself in the profession when she was a single mother of twins and that she took only seventeen weeks of maternity leave.[61]

These kinds of accounts need to be supplemented by more realistic descriptions of women's lives in the legal profession. An inductive approach will provide alternative career visions based on a composite of career paths viewed in the context of lifetime events and valued rites of passage. This has been my focus in this work and I see it as an ongoing exercise. Careers are dynamic and the best way to track them is to keep listening to the stories that emerge when people describe their working histories. The experiences of women in the legal profession will help to generate new career theories, serving as guides in other occupations and professions. Heather Höpfl and Pat Hornby Atkinson see this approach as an effective way of deconstructing career mythology, noting that careers rarely follow the linear ideal. While women may face unique barriers to career advancement, men also experience disappointments and suffer the consequences of poor decision-making.[62] These men stand to benefit as well, and a choice of alternative career paths will act as a corrective, adding balance to the lopsided career and family patterns currently evident in many dual-career families.

The concept of time is also critical to an understanding of women's careers. Much has been written about gender differences in perceptions of time, but the pertinent aspects are the disjunctions between timing and temporality in the mapping out of women's career lines. Three strong themes prevail in this chapter: the role of temporality in the shaping of careers, the pressures to pay attention to timing in accordance with the principles of the linear career model, and, most importantly, women's responses to these competing pressures. Temporality is the dimension of time that encompasses life course events, and a wide-angle lens is needed to comprehend its scope. Women confront issues of temporality when they postpone parenthood in favour of career advancement or face their colleagues with news of a pregnancy. Several of the women in this study struggled to deal with these issues. Jenny and her husband worked hard to nurture and support their three small children as they completed their education and pursued their separate careers. Other women negotiated maternity leaves with their firms, worried that they would be bored at home and then discovered the overwhelming joy of motherhood. Too often, women described the open hostility and intolerance of senior partners and managers when they announced their pregnancies. Some of the women expressed regret that they had postponed pregnancies, and several of them described their experiences with repeated miscarriages. The women in this study also dealt with issues of temporality when they experienced marital breakdown and the prospect of single parenthood.[63] Several of the women had reached the stage marked by mid-life pressures – their own futures, personal illness and burnout, parents' illnesses, or the deaths of spouses or parents. One of them captured the essence of temporality when she described a very dark period in her life, saying: "I finally understood that if something really matters to you, you must be willing to treat it as though it were a matter of life and death. At the time, my dad was dying, my marriage was dying, and my career was all but dead, and so the metaphor was very meaningful. I think I was dying too and I look back at this time as something of a rebirth for me."

Timing is critical in the development of a career and unanticipated pregnancies are often seen as evidence of bad timing. One woman told us that a male colleague suggested that she should have been "more careful sexually" and another one was informed by a senior partner that her sterling record of performance might somehow become tarnished by the time her baby was due, justifying her dismissal. These kinds of comments are always made in private, leaving the women without recourse, but they are undoubtedly examples of sexual harassment. We did not ask leading questions about harassment in the interviews, but several other women reported incidents that confirmed our suspicions that it was widespread. Jenny's report of the expectations of sexual favours in corporate settings suggests that the timing of her career advancement could have been speeded up if she had chosen to play the game, and Jessica's observations provided further evidence of prejudice against women:

It starts when you tell them you're pregnant. It's just a change in attitude towards you and it's truly believed and it's not just in law. It's believed in business everywhere. If there are two equally capable people and there's a choice between a man and a woman, they would want to hire the man because the woman is seen as someone who, in a year's time, is going to be off having babies ... It's not going to change. I don't think it's going to change. I think you just sort of have to get out and do what you want to do or put up with it.

Later in the interview, she said that people also assign blame to women who are not pregnant, saying: "They'll say, 'Oh PMS – bad day.' Oh yeah. But when guys are having a bad day, it's stress. Oh they have such diffi-cult lives. [Interviewer: That would be considered harassment in any other workplace.] Oh and it still would be here. It's still harassment."

Unreasonable billing expectations and limited access to key files also provide evidence of differential treatment, particularly in the biggest firms. These forms of discrimination are difficult to prove, but their influence leaves many women stalled at junior levels of practice.[64] Barbara had attained partnership and was able to reduce her hours, but she was very concerned about the impact of a proposed policy change on the women with young children who would not be able to meet the demands with-out jeopardizing their families. Once again, women would stand accused of faulty timing and would either remain as hard-working career associ-ates or would search for other opportunities.

Finally, women's responses to these pressures are interesting. Many of them ignore the compulsion to time their careers and remain committed to a broader temporal view of the curriculum vitae. Their decisions to explore new areas of interest or devote more time to their families are not made lightly, but, without the support of their firms or their col-leagues, they are often forced to abandon their legal careers. One woman in a senior position told me that she always advises the women lawyers in her firm to spend the childrearing years at home because, as she put it, "the career will wait." Unfortunately, the career does not always wait. Women who take these kinds of breaks are seen as a liability to the firm, and they risk losing their place in the tightly scheduled track to part-nership status.[65] Interestingly, the women who achieve the highest career levels do not always acknowledge the expectations associated with advancement, tending instead to dismiss their successes as simply the result of good luck. Both Sheila and Marilyn laughed off suggestions that they had been ambitious or highly skilled, saying rather that they had just been fortunate. In the words of one senior lawyer, "I really didn't know what I wanted to do ... I just ended up here and I've been very lucky."[66] Perhaps a lifetime career is a capricious thing, guided not so much by careful planning as by a lucky role of life's dice.

7
Cracking the Codes

Women with children are treated in a more discriminatory
way than women in the law profession generally and certainly
men in the profession. The billing rate is less, the access to
partnership is less for women and this is exacerbated with
respect to women and family responsibilities.[1]

> – Professor Gerald Gall, citing Law
> Society of Alberta survey, 2004

I think it is perfectly possible for women to have children,
maintain an active role with those children and still develop a
practice to a degree which allows you to apply for silk and
get it.[2]

> – Cherie Booth, QC, addressing
> Minority Lawyers Conference, 1997

Over a century ago, Clara Brett Martin made history as the first woman
to be admitted to the Ontario Bar but other women were slow to follow.
It was not until late in the twentieth century that their numbers in the
profession expanded to equal those of men. During the post-Second World
War years, women's roles in general underwent a dramatic transformation, giving rise to an unprecedented period of feminist ferment. The elitist masculine culture that had prevailed in the legal profession provided
fertile ground for discussions about gender equality, and the sharp rise
in women's numbers sparked lively debate in venues ranging from law
school classrooms to the boardrooms of large firms. Many women in this
study were part of the first wave of law school applicants, but variations
on their stories emerge with each new crop of graduates. The most experienced women were called to the bar in the late 1960s so they arrived
on the scene when the feminist movement was just beginning to gather
steam. The professional gentlemen had yet to feel the full effect of its
blast.

My intent in this book has been to provide a glimpse of the legal system – the schools, the law firms, the government offices, the corporations, and the courts – through the eyes of these women – 110 in all – as
they make their way through their daily lives and their professional
careers. From the outset, I wanted to know if their experiences signalled
broad changes in the culture of these institutions. Have the expectations
for performance been modified over the past thirty years as women have

advanced in the system or charted new approaches to the management of time, professional work, and family life? The answer is a very guarded "yes," only because, by their very presence, they have raised alarm bells and provoked responses from law societies and bar associations. They have also laid bare a vein of prejudice in firms that have remained committed to a masculine approach to practice. The profession has a long way to go before it can boast of true equality reflecting the ideals of the Canadian Charter of Rights and Freedoms. Law schools espouse equality and firms proudly display their equity policies, but women are still handicapped and, if they come from working-class or racialized backgrounds, they may be doubly disadvantaged, facing the same barriers as those who are disabled or lesbian or, in some way, different from their mainstream colleagues. Many law firms declare their intentions to accommodate family needs, but women who have postponed their childbearing years or faced angry partners with news of their pregnancies understand the power of the profession to control their lives. However, I marvel at their tenacity in the face of these challenges. Whether they know it or not, they are engaged in a profound process of social change.

These women are a pioneering group in many ways. Accounts of their experiences can contribute to a growing literature devoted to the study of the male-dominated professions in general. Other women have broken new ground in areas such as medicine, dentistry, veterinary practice, pharmacy, engineering, or academia.[3] Judging by numbers alone, many of these professions have moved well along the road to feminization, but traditional values and attitudes are deeply entrenched in the masculine cultures that have shaped expectations for performance and promotion. The process of feminization is a complex one, and is part of a gradual accommodation of women's unique needs and a recognition that their contribution to professional life has merit. I am not suggesting that masculine attitudes and practices should be overtaken by countervailing norms that reflect only women's interests but, rather, that somewhere between these two poles an equitable point of balance exists. Experiences reported by the women in this study provide viewpoints and visions that will enhance the scope of this literature. Their stories will also be familiar to researchers focusing on careers in other competitive settings – the management ranks of large corporations and the hierarchies of publicly funded institutions.

Since women in law and other male-dominated professions have begun to challenge accepted practices, their actions will have far-reaching implications at the policy level. Their entry to the professions has followed on the heels of an unprecedented rise in women's labour force involvement in Canada, in the United States, and across all industrialized countries. Public concern about the impact of these trends on family life has inspired a broad body of literature designed to address alarming levels of work-family conflict.[4] Much of this work reflects a commitment to policy change, but the next giant step involves the implementation of progressive legislation and contractual terms of employment guaranteeing equal opportunity for all employees, especially if they have family commitments. Beyond this step lies the greatest challenge: a gradual acceptance of new norms that honour the lives of individuals as parents and partners with loyalties that transcend their daily working lives.

Portia and the Learned Gentleman

As I reach the end of this enterprise, I am increasingly aware of the powerful interconnection between social class and gender in the legal profession. At the most superficial level, women are faced with competing images of professional success – the privileged nineteenth-century gentleman replicated in the senior ranks of some established law firms and the fictional Portia who moves from unlessoned girl to wise counsel in Shakespeare's *The Merchant of Venice*. Most of them will follow a path that falls well short of the learned gentleman's charmed life, inspired instead by Portia and the brief but powerful encounter with the law that makes her story so appealing. She has assumed mythical proportions in discussions of women's legal careers, and her actions offer a vision of success to women who might otherwise limit their expectations for professional achievement.[5] Her presence in this book is haunting – a metaphor with a mixed message that highlights the transparency of women's performances and the ways in which they court professional failure when they turn their attention to family matters or deviate in any way from the prescribed patterns of practice.

The legal fraternity, like other professional groups, claims superior occupational ranking because it harbours a unique body of knowledge that blossoms into practical legal reasoning in the hands of skilled lawyers. In a characteristic attempt to build status and protect its territory, the law has, in the past, made use of its knowledge to exclude designated groups of people from its ranks.[6] The architects of these professions justified gendered patterns of exclusion by labelling women's practical domestic skills as the product of their *status* knowledge, and thus considered of limited value in a world where professional expertise rested on access to rational, scientific knowledge.

Women who enter the profession today possess a bank of legal knowledge that equals or surpasses that of their male counterparts, but they must also demonstrate to clients, courts, and the general public that they can use it effectively in their daily practices. The posting of credentials is an important signal in this process, but outward demeanour and dress are also necessary markers of professional expertise. Where Portia relied

on deceit and enjoyed a brief moment of judicial glory, women who practise law must continue to convince others that they are competent practitioners of their craft. Legal robes are one of the props available to them
as they attempt to overcome disadvantages associated with their size, their
age, and their gender. Men also declare their legal competence when they
robe for court, but they never have to explain to judges that they need
breaks to nurse babies or that the late stages of pregnancy have made
their vests impossibly tight. Legal robes were designed for men, and they
remain a symbol of professional legitimacy in courts that are steeped in
patriarchal tradition.

The women in this study reported a range of feelings about their legal
robes. Some said that they enjoyed the chance to speak out in a masculine
setting and others stressed the importance of robing for a solemn task.
Most of them said that the robes conveyed a sense of legitimacy, even if
they saw the judicial setting as unnecessarily elitist. Many of them said
that they felt odd or out of place when they wore their robes for the first
time, but they acknowledged that the costume made them feel "like real
lawyers." Their acceptance into the profession has been slow and, at times,
grudging because, like Portia, they have entered an arena marked by cultural ambivalence towards learned women. One seasoned lawyer confirmed these contradictions when she recalled the actions of a tactless judge
who dismissed her from his courtroom because she was wearing a dress.
When he said, repeatedly, "I can't hear you Ms. _____ ," she finally realized that he was refusing to include her because of her clothing – a plain,
dark coloured dress with a high collar and a hemline well below her knees.
She left the courtroom, puzzled by a situation in which her male colleague
was acceptable in a business suit but her feminine attire was deemed inappropriate. This kind of judicial blundering is becoming less common, but
it confirms the lingering presence of outdated symbolism when women
are silenced until they appear in masculine or, at best, neutral dress.

Legal Culture and the Law School
Our interviews revealed that these women chose law, not because they
knew about the inner workings of the profession or planned careers that
would transport them to powerful positions, but because, on the whole,
they had excelled at school and they were looking for a challenging profession that would provide a secure, well-paying job with a measure of
status attached to it. Economic security was uppermost in the minds of
many of them. Most of them had no prior knowledge of law so their
indoctrination was a protracted process leading to a gradual awareness of
underlying cultural patterns. Most of their professors were men who held
traditional views of the law, but a strong feminist consciousness was developing in some of the most prominent law schools during the 1980s. Many

women, such as the ones in this study, avoided feminist issues, but the debate exposed layers of culture bound by conservative attitudes and expectations for performance – specifically a focus on corporate law emphasizing the importance of networks, both in law school and in legal practice. They would learn that social capital was a powerful resource, available to lawyers with the time and the inclination to develop strong collegial bonds and earn the trust of their superiors.

Their experience in law school was not as daunting as we might expect, given the reports from the first generation of women in large American law schools. Many of the women in this study were confused at first because the pedagogy and the volume of material provided a sharp contrast to their undergraduate courses. However, in general, they managed to gain confidence during second year as they began to appreciate the merits of learning to "think like a lawyer." Their most common complaint was that law school was boring. The results of this study confirm some of the findings from recent American studies, specifically the work of Lani Guinier at the University of Pennsylvania and Robert Granfield at Harvard.[7] These studies move beyond simple gendered divisions and consider the effects of other background variables in shaping law school experience. Social class is a particularly potent determinant of success, and, in this respect, the image of the professional gentleman still lingers in Canadian law schools. The mature students in this study were often painfully aware of financial constraints and family obligations that set them apart from their younger, more affluent classmates. A few women also reported incidents of racial stereotyping in law school, and one of the lesbians in the study was very frank about the hostile climate she encountered.

This study also highlights features that are missing from most other current works. Since it focuses only on women in the profession, it provides a view of critical events in their lives that their male counterparts would not have experienced. For example, several women recalled the overwhelming fatigue accompanying pregnancy, lactation, and family demands during their law school years, and these factors were often compounded by long-distance commuting. Several women developed serious health problems as well. For some of them, law school provided a preview of the stressors that lay ahead as they approached professional practice.

The chapter on legal education provides a historical backdrop for the discussion of theory and findings in this study. The theme of social class is never far from the surface as we move from the image of the nineteenth-century professional gentleman through the lives of these women to the present and the potential for further segmentation within professional ranks. It is no accident that many of the mature students in this study attended the University of Windsor and went on to develop modest practices, while women who concentrated on corporate law at the

University of Toronto or the University of Western Ontario invariably moved into large firms. Recent reports indicate that the most prestigious schools, led by the University of Toronto, intend to raise their fees beyond the level of affordability for most aspiring law students.[8] Only the very affluent and the scholarship winners will be able to attend these schools. The move is partly motivated by the need to attract the best legal minds to permanent faculty posts, but it also serves to channel the students with higher class backgrounds into the most prominent law firms, both in Toronto and New York.

Time in the Lives of Women Lawyers

International concern about the clash between work and family time has increased dramatically over the past thirty years, and the dual-earner family has assumed normative prominence in many industrialized countries.[9] While many parents struggle to balance busy schedules, dual-career families face the most serious levels of time stress, and, within the professions, law has earned a reputation as being one of the most demanding. Pressures to increase billable hours to impossibly high levels have been widely documented in academic journals, legal publications, and media reports. The onus is particularly heavy for women because they typically add the organization of household affairs to the work of their legal practices. The women in this study are not exceptional in this regard, so time in all its manifestations forms a central core of the discussion throughout the book.

Women in general express concern about their overloaded schedules, and their frustrations shine through in their responses to statements about levels of time crunch. The lawyers in this study experience higher levels of time-induced stress than other groups of employed women, and their scores on specific items from the index of time crunch are even more telling. These items tap feelings of inadequacy in the face of daunting schedules, particularly when there is insufficient time left for family and friends. In general, the lawyers do not see themselves as workaholics. They are, rather, women faced with a situation where they are powerless to effect change. When we probed further for the reasons behind these frustrations, we found that lack of time for family was a major factor. Many of them said that extended family members took second place to their children, and their social networks were severely constricted. As one woman said, "there's just too much to do and not enough time!" A few women registered consistently low scores on the time crunch index and some others had attempted to cut back on their professional demands across the course of this study, but the majority were caught up in busy lives characterized by a lack of time for themselves and/or their partners. Their organizational skills were superb, but, once the priorities were drawn, there was barely enough time for adequate sleep, daily family routines, and the mounting files at work.

While these patterns rest on immediate pressures across the course of a working day or week, I have also tried to unravel the complicated strands of time in the lawyers' lives. Barbara Adam's work is pertinent to this discussion, especially her vision of time as a kaleidoscope of patterns, marked by sequence and duration, thought and memory, cycles and rhythms. At the most immediate level, it is about daily schedules and, by extension, the timing of career moves, but it also embraces the temporality that stretches across the life span, periodically evident in rites of passage such as graduation, marriage, or parenthood.[10] Time is also a key aspect of social capital because it provides opportunities for career enhancement that lie beyond the demands of a normal working day.[11]

Adam and others have challenged the dualistic theories that draw simple dichotomies between such ideal types as *linear* and *cyclical* or *monochronic* and *polychronic* time. Many theorists have also been tempted to connect gender to specific kinds of time, arguing, for example, that the linear time of the workplace represents men's time while women's time follows a more cyclical pattern. To some extent this pattern is true. Feminist writers have tried to distance themselves from these dualisms, but many of them acknowledge the power of norms to pattern behaviour. Most of them would agree that the linear time used to establish the tempo of the workplace and frame long-term goals is born of men's experience. These kinds of traditions often harden into expectations that can have powerful effects on attitudes and practices. If linear time is defined as masculine then it is a short step to cast women's time in traditional terms, reflecting outdated ideals for feminine behaviour. Women are then expected to focus on day-to-day concerns, leaving larger goals in the hands of their male colleagues. If professional women try to claim their share of linear time, they fly in the face of accepted practices.

Women who combine careers with motherhood manage the most complex schedules imaginable and, because they are so competent, it is generally accepted that they should continue to bear these burdens. Carmen Leccardi is right when she bundles several concepts together, seeing women's time as *biographical* or *lived*.[12] Family time, body time, cyclical time, and personal time are all juxtaposed against the linear time that prevails in the workplace and, increasingly, in the organization of family activities. Her vision of women's time is not constrained by dualistic definitions. Each woman's biography is unique, and it changes shape as she progresses through the life course. This theme is evident in the organization of daily life, and it persists when we consider women's curricula vitae as unique life records. For this reason, inductive research provides the best tool for chronicling these patterns as they develop over time.

Time Lines and Career Patterns

Daily time commitments provide the building blocks for careers, and women's long-term paths reflect their busy schedules, often departing radically from the unwavering line of the ideal career. This pattern, characterized by a Newtonian vision of linear progress, became the accepted path for middle-class men during the years before women moved into the labour force in large numbers. Phyllis Moen and Patricia Roehling identify the inadequacies of this "career regime" as a way of framing careers in general, arguing strongly for innovations in public and corporate policies to provide career flexibility for both women and men. Recognizing the outdated status of the so-called "career mystique," they conclude that "the reality is that children are not simply a distraction. Many parents would like to spend more time with their children ... There can never be equality of opportunity in the workforce for men and women and for mothers and fathers given the career mystique and the gendered distribution."[13]

Moen and Roehling's work elaborates on models of career proposed during the mid-1990s by feminist scholars searching for new career visions that would honour women's values and position them on equal footing with their male colleagues.[14] These kinds of career revisions are long overdue in the legal profession because women continue to face barriers to career advancement that are both obvious and subtle.[15] Since these barriers are so deeply embedded in the cultures of many law firms, they are often taken for granted, both by senior partners and many aspiring lawyers. Women part company with the professional gentleman or his heirs when they disrupt their careers with maternity leaves or reroute their working lives in pursuit of tangential interests.

Theories of time come into play here as well. Instead of attending to the *timing* of their careers, many women experience aspects of life that reflect the tempo of *cyclical* time and expand their career paths to provide a vision of *temporality* that spans the life course.[16] The birthing and rearing of children, the time spent with an aging parent, or simply the time for career breaks and contemplation all contribute to this larger composition of the curriculum vitae. Perhaps the pared down linear career would be more aptly termed the *curriculum operis* because it concentrates almost exclusively on work and related interests.

Feminist theorists who reshape the linear career to accommodate broader interests have signalled a new and valued vision, offering traditionalists an alternative to the strategic pursuit of financial rewards, elevated status, and access to power as career essentials. Like the tendency to view time as a gendered phenomenon, the normative view of career grew out of men's experience, leaving women with two alternatives – either to abandon peripheral interests and behave like men or to follow a broader path by including family concerns in their lives. Either way, they never quite measure up to the ideal. Heather Höpfl and Pat Hornby Atkinson suggest that we can best appreciate this "mythology of career" by listening to people as they review their own career experiences:

> Career stories are rarely stories of sustained success and achievement, of gains without costs, or of continuity and progress. For most people, men and women alike, careers are constructed in prospect and accounted for in retrospect. People make the wrong decisions, get caught in the political cross-fire, make unacceptable sacrifices, suffer remorse, lose face, lose faith even, and experience all the range of emotions that a system of life planning might produce when translated into everyday experience. Unlike the tidy plans that seem to guide a "career," life experiences are much more messy.[17]

As the women in this study told their stories, it became clear that many had endured these kinds of obstacles. One lawyer in her early forties used the metaphor of a long distance swim to describe her career. Sometimes she moved forward with the kind of ease that a calm sea provides, but, from time to time, she encountered currents and waves that threatened to engulf her. She saw the accepted vision of the ideal career as an upwardly bound line, but her description suggests that she was prepared to dive off the line into the deep waters below. This kind of action requires much more courage and imagination than the safe, secure, unwavering track.

Some of the women in late middle age looked back on satisfying careers, but they all insisted that they had not been calculating in their approach. Like the woman mentioned earlier, they were prepared to weather the tides as they faced new challenges. The younger women in this study were still testing the waters, unsure about the direction their lives would take. Women who had chosen to have families seemed too busy with everyday concerns to spend much time contemplating the next career move. Perhaps they were, for the time being,[18] drawn into a pattern exemplifying the stereotypical vision of women's time as focused on immediate concerns ahead of long-term strategies. One of the most cogent comments came from a lawyer who was midway through the process, balancing parenthood with a busy practice. She was the only person to suggest the need for major systemic changes to the gendered patterns of responsibility among working couples. In the law and other professions, these practices have endured, forming a protective coating around men's careers:

> I end up very frustrated and this applies to the women in law issue. I know there have been a number of studies. Bertha Wilson was involved in one and it was entirely focused on women in law firms and I found

myself saying: "No, no, no! I don't think that's the issue. I think that the issue has to be *people* in law firms and *parents* in law firms." And every time I see an article in a magazine talking about daycare being a *women's* issue and the glass ceiling for *women* – it's actually those people who end up taking responsibility for home and family and are not in a position to work twenty hours a day. That's not just a women's issue!

Her words are profound and deserve to be placed front and centre in our lives, flashing like an Internet pop-up, reminding us that equality in the home is just as important as equality in the workplace and, in fact, that the two are interdependent. An insidious but disturbing trend has developed over the past few years. A great deal of media space has been devoted to the theme that women, especially those in senior corporate and professional positions, can find fulfilment at home with their children. There has been no comparable message aimed at men in high places.[19] For women like the stressed lawyers in this study, this route may be tempting, but it is not the answer to parental scheduling problems. It violates all the principles of gender equity.[20]

Looking Ahead

All signs seem to point to increasing levels of segmentation within the legal profession. Until the late 1970s, lawyers' sons (and, occasionally, their daughters) could enter law school in Ontario even if their marks were less than stellar, but, when LSAT scores became part of the admission requirements, students with high rankings began to flood into the schools. Mechanisms for admitting mature students were also implemented, ensuring places for promising candidates who would otherwise be excluded from the law school rolls. Women were often the beneficiaries of these policies, and many of them went on to pursue rewarding careers. However, this brief period of relative democratization may be drawing to a close. With dramatic fee increases on the horizon for the most prestigious schools, only the most affluent families will be able to launch their children on careers in the top law firms.[21]

Once again, women stand to lose because even those who gain entry to the best jobs may be consigned to second-tier positions, researching and writing briefs for senior partners whose family commitments are limited. Of course, many lawyers have aspired to less lofty heights, happy to work in small offices doing criminal law or drafting wills and administering real estate transactions. Others have chosen to follow civil service careers or move to in-house legal positions.[22] These patterns will undoubtedly continue, but, in order to provide equal access to a range of career options, entry to the best schools should reflect students' academic qualifications and their potential contribution as lawyers, not their parents' income levels.

Recent reports indicate that the gap between lawyers in small firms and those in charge of the largest firms continues to widen. In a 2004 survey of lawyers across Canada, 10 percent of partners in small firms reported annual incomes of less than $50,000 while increasing numbers of partners in large firms earned more than $300,000 a year. The survey also found that the most affluent senior partners were located in Ontario where 8 percent of them reported incomes in excess of $400,000.[23] These patterns became even more pronounced in a 2005 survey indicating increasing frustration among lawyers in small firms or sole practice but a steady increase in income levels for lawyers at the top of the largest firms.[24] Apparently, a new generation of professional gentlemen remains firmly in control at the elite end of the legal community.

Social class runs like a powerful undercurrent through much of the discussion in this book. It is evident in the buildings, the boardrooms, and the carefully tended networks of legal contacts. It is veiled in the cultural expectations that reflect parental wealth, private schooling, and connections made early in life.[25] Since my work focuses on women's experiences, it deals with the effects of social class in the lives of women in the profession. I regret that I have been unable to offer more than a cursory nod to issues of diversity – the effects of race, ethnicity, sexual orientation, or disabilities on legal practice. These attributes can be disabling on their own, and, when combined with gender effects, they can lead to gross inequities in access to professional positions. Constance Backhouse expresses similar regrets about her study of women and law in nineteenth-century Canada as she picks up the threads in the introduction to her historical analysis of racism.[26] Much work remains to be done on issues of diversity in the Ontario legal profession. Like women, Blacks, Jews, and other designated out-groups have been historically barred from legal training, so it is reasonable to assume that members of these groups have, from time to time, faced disappointment in their search for professional status.

Although race is a key attribute that sets some aspiring lawyers apart from their peers, it remains elusive, both conceptually and in real life. Joanne St. Lewis provides an excellent account of the dilemma posed by race in the preamble to her discussion of the racialization of women of colour in legal doctrine.[27] Official publications speak gingerly of "diversity" and rely on euphemisms to identify members of "multicultural" communities as "visible minorities" or "people of colour" or, in the early Canadian census categories cited by Backhouse, simply as "black," "red," or "yellow."[28] Several of the women in my study would have qualified for racialized status, but only three of them were identifiable members of so-called visible minorities.[29] Four others reported mixed race backgrounds, but, based on appearance alone, they would not have found a place on the nineteenth-century census-taker's limited palette.[30]

Future work in this area will require careful attention to sampling design. Just as the legal profession should mirror the demographic profile of the larger society, a solid random sample of the profession should include accurate proportions of lawyers from diverse backgrounds. Robert Granfield aimed for this kind of statistical accuracy by drawing a large sample of students from Harvard Law School, but it is worth noting that Harvard students do not typify the population of law students across the United States.[31] Without access to a representative sample, it would be equally difficult to establish a profile of law students in Ontario. In fact, this task would be complicated by the lack of complete records. The Law Society of Upper Canada did not collect data on the racial characteristics of bar admission students until 2002, and, even now, this information is based on applicants' voluntary self-identification as members of "visible minorities." Given these problems, the accurate identification of racialized students would appear to be an insurmountable task. According to the Law Society of Upper Canada records, visible minorities represented 19 percent of the Ontario population in the 2001 census and a creditable 16.5 percent of the bar admission course in 2002. By May 2005, their numbers had declined to 15 percent of the class. Yet who are the members of these so-called visible minorities? Would the women in my study with Irish or Scottish grandfathers and First Nations or Chinese grandmothers find their way into the records or would they choose to ignore the question? As Constance Backhouse has observed, "the concept of 'race' through time illustrates beyond controversy that the very notion is built upon shifting sands."[32] Fiona Kay and her research associates have taken steps to overcome some of these limitations in their 2003 survey of the Ontario legal profession.[33] Their findings indicate that lawyers in racialized communities are over-represented in the lowest income brackets, are absent from senior positions, and are found in the least prestigious types of practice.[34]

In terms of numbers, members of racialized communities have reached a position paralleling that of women in the late 1970s, on the eve of feminist conflict within Ontario law schools. Awareness of race issues has grown more slowly than concerns about women's equality, but various agencies, both federal and provincial, have taken steps to advance the interests of racialized groups. In Ontario, the Women's Legal Education and Action Fund (LEAF), an organization of feminist lawyers founded in 1982, has played a major role in the promotion of equality, particularly in the area of constitutional reform.[35] The Law Society of Upper Canada, like other law societies across the country, offers support and encouragement to students from Aboriginal communities. According to the Law Society's records, these students comprised 1.5 percent of the 2005 bar admission course – a representative proportion, given the fact that Aboriginal persons constitute 1.6 percent of the Ontario population. At a national level, one of the most novel projects is to be found in the Akitsiraq Law School, a one-time program established in Nunavut in 2001 with support and encouragement from the University of Victoria. "Akitsiraq" translates as "to strike out harmony/wrong-doing, to render justice." It serves as an inspiration for Aboriginal people and other racialized groups across the country.[36]

This kind of symbolism helps to combat petty prejudices that are all too common in everyday life. In a similar way, a framed poster entitled "Canadian Women and the Law: Search for Justice" that hangs on the wall of my office, offers hope for the next generation of women in the legal profession. It was designed to commemorate Women's History Month in 1999, and it presents a glowing record of women's achievements, from Clara Brett Martin's entry to the profession in 1897 to the 1989 appointment of Juanita Westmoreland-Traoré, honoured as the first Black woman to become dean of a law school (University of Windsor). The twenty-six faces on this poster represent a range of ages, racial backgrounds, and connections to the profession. The poster marks important milestones – the appointment of Justice Bertha Wilson to the Supreme Court of Canada in 1982, followed by Justices Claire L'Heureux-Dubé, Beverley McLachlin, and Louise Arbour. Since then, the Honourable Madam Justice McLachlin has served as chief justice of the Supreme Court of Canada and Justice Louise Arbour has moved on to become United Nations High Commissioner for Human Rights. Justices Rosalie Silberman Abella and Louise Charron have recently joined the ranks of Canada's highest court, bringing a combined history of experience with equality law and human rights issues.[37] These appointments are heavy with symbolism, sending a strong signal that women merit equal status with men, both in the legal profession and across the spectrum of Canadian society and the international stage. Portia's legal reputation fades into obscurity when we consider the impact made by these women and their counterparts at all levels of the justice system. Their robes are not borrowed and their reputations are their own. They are lessoned, schooled, and very practised.

Appendix:
Where Are They Now?

This study spans a twelve-year period in the lives of the earliest women interviewed. Women in the second group were interviewed for the first time in 1996, and those in the third group were contacted in 1999. Over the years, many of them have encountered the rites of passage and unpredictable events that mark the passage of time – birth, death, illness, the departure of children, marriage, divorce, relocation, and a range of career changes. Many of the women have kept in touch, responding quickly to my periodic requests for information with e-mails, letters, and telephone calls. I have tracked many others through the Law Society of Upper Canada's membership list and the Canadian Law List, but some of them have vanished from the official lists. Between 2004 and 2006, I made several attempts to contact all of the women but was unable to reach everyone. The following tables are designed to provide the best possible picture of their lives as they unfolded over the course of the study. Eleven women or 10 percent of the sample have either left the profession or disappeared from the records. One woman has retired from active practice and one woman died recently. In the original questionnaire, responses for "size of firm" included six categories. In these tables, the categories have been collapsed to include sole practitioners, small firms (2-9 lawyers), medium firms (10-49 lawyers), large firms (50-74 lawyers), and very large firms (75 lawyers or more).

Table A.1

Toronto area lawyers: Work and family changes, 1994-2006

	1994 Practice/Family	1998 Practice/Family	At last report
1	Sole practitioner No children	Same Ready to go on maternity leave	On Law Society of Upper Canada list **Not practising law** Three children
2	Partner-elect Very large firm No children	Partner Same firm Two children	Special partner Two-day work week Three children
3	Partner Small firm No children	Sole practitioner No children	Same Reduced work hours Married, one stepchild
4	Partner Small firm Two children	Judge	Same Loves her job Three children
5	Sole practitioner One child	Same	Same
6	Associate Small firm No children	Sole practitioner Married Three stepchildren	Working part-time in public corporation
7	Senior government lawyer No children	Government Different location	Government Different location Anticipating retirement
8	Associate Medium firm Two children	Partner Different location Medium firm	Mediator-lawyer On Law Society of Upper Canada list **Not practising law**
9	Senior government lawyer No children	Same Advanced since previous interview	Same Looking forward to retirement
10	Senior government lawyer Two adult stepchildren	Judge	Judge Loves her work
11	Senior government lawyer Three adult children	Sole practitioner Very large firm	Same Planning active retirement

▶

	1994 Practice/Family	1998 Practice/Family	At last report
12	Partner Very large firm Two children	Same	Same
13	Associate Small firm No children	Same	Same
14	Partner Very large firm Two children	Same	Judge
15	Partner Very large firm One child	Same	Legal consulting business
16	Government lawyer Two children	Same	Same Has returned to art and writing interests
17	Sole practitioner No children	Same	Has hired an associate Considering new career One stepchild
18	Government lawyer On leave One child	Same	On Law Society of Upper Canada list **Not practising law**
19	Sole practitioner Three children	Judge	Judge
20	Partner Small firm One child	Same Second child	Same Collaborative family law Good work-life balance
21	Employee Small firm Two children	Associate Same firm	Same Collaborative family law Good work-life balance
22	Sole practitioner Two children	Same	Same Good work-life balance
23	Sole practitioner One child	Same	Same Devoting more time to life outside law
24	Partner Medium firm One child	Vice-president Private industry	Same Has shifted from legal practice to management

▶

	1994 Practice/Family	1998 Practice/Family	At last report
25	Government lawyer Two children	Same	Same
26	Sole Practitioner No children	Same Part-time	On Law Society of Upper Canada list **Not practising law**
27	Partner Small firm Three children	Associate Medium firm	Considering a different career
28	Associate Small firm No children	Partner New small firm	Same Good work-life balance
29	Partner Very large firm Two stepchildren	Same	Same Advocate for women lawyers
30	Partner Very large firm No children	Corporate position Not practising law One child	Special partner in previous firm Good work-life balance

Table A.2

London lawyers: Work and family changes, 1996-2006

	1996 Practice/Family	2000 Practice/Family	At last report
31	Associate Small firm No children	With government Has left Ontario One child	Organized crime prosecutor
32	Sole practitioner No children	Same Hoping for judicial appointment	Same Practice has improved
33	Associate Small firm Two children	Sole practitioner Has moved to different community	Same Has hired an associate Active in law association
34	Employee Social Service Agency No children	Same One child	Busy, challenging work Two children Strives for balance

▶

	1996 Practice/Family	2000 Practice/Family	At last report
35	Associate Small firm One child	Same	Sole practitioner
36	Judge Two stepchildren	Same	Work is very demanding Doing master's degree

37	Associate
	Small firm
	One child
		Sole practitioner
		Has moved to
		  different community
			Home-based practice
			Doing some teaching
			  and volunteer work

38	Sole practice No children	Part-time employee at law clinic	**Retired**
39	Part-time associate in small firm Two children	Part-time Sole practitioner	Same
40	Associate Medium firm No children	Associate Small firm In new community	Same Thriving practice One child
41	Partner Very large firm One child	Head of department in same firm	On leave Doing master's degree

42	Sole practitioner
	Active in Law Society
	  of Upper Canada
	Three adult children
		Same
		No private clients
		Government work
			Has reduced practice to
			  spend time with family
			Active in Law Society
			  of Upper Canada

43	Partner Medium firm Three children	Same Four children	Same
44	Sole practitioner No children	Associate Small firm In new community	Partner Different firm Two children
45	Sole practitioner Two adult children	Same	Moved to new location Collaborative family law
46	Sole practitioner No children	Same	Partnership with one other lawyer Plans to retire in 2010
47	Partner Small firm Two children	Same Three children	Same

▶

	1996 Practice/Family	2000 Practice/Family	At last report
48	Partner Small firm Two children	Same	Sole practitioner Government prosecutor
49	Partner Large firm No children	Same	Same Doing less law, more administration
50	Government lawyer Two children	Same	Works three-day week Trying to balance work and family
51	Sole practitioner in mediation Two children	Same	Same Teaches alternative dispute resolution
52	Partner Medium firm Four children	Same	Same
53	Judge No children	Same	Reports satisfaction with her judicial duties
54	Partner Large firm No children	Same One child	Has moved to a different law firm
55	Sole practitioner One child	Same	Not on Law Society of Upper Canada list **Appears to have left legal practice**
56	Employee Law clinic Two children	Same Moved to a different community	Same
57	Partner Medium firm One child	Same On child, two stepchildren	Judge
58	Associate Large firm Two children	Partner in same firm	Same
59	Associate Medium firm One stepchild	Same Likes associate level Two children	Sole practitioner Values time with her family
60	Associate Medium firm Three children	Same Four children	In-house counsel

Table A.3

Lawyers across Ontario: Work and family changes, 1999-2006

	1996 Practice/Family	2000 Practice/Family	At last report
61	Associate Small firm No children	Same	Changed firms Two children
62	Partner Very large firm Two children	Same	Same
63	Trust company officer Not practising law No children	Left labour force in 1999 Two children	Has recently begun practising law with a small firm
64	Government lawyer On leave Two children	On Law Society of Upper Canada list Employment status unclear	On Law Society of Upper Canada list **Appears to have left legal practice**
65	Partner Medium firm Two children	Same	Same
66	Government lawyer No children	Promoted in 1999	Same Guards work-life balance
67	Part-time employee Medium firm Four children	Left practice in 1999	At home with family **Not practising law**
68	Government lawyer Two children	Same	Promoted to senior government position
69	Began practice in 1997 Left in 1998 One child	No longer on Law Society of Upper Canada list	Has moved No forwarding address **Not practising law**
70	Partner Medium firm No children	Same	Same
71	Sole practice Two children	Same	Same Stress-related illness Work-family struggle
72	Associate Medium firm Two children	Same	Same

▶

	1996 Practice/Family	2000 Practice/Family	At last report
73	Part-time employee Small firm One child	Same	Not on Law Society of Upper Canada list No forwarding address **Not practising law**
74	Partner Small firm No children	Same	Same
75	Employer Small firm One child	Same	Teaching at local college Hired associates in her office
76	Partner Medium firm One child	Same	Same
77	In-house counsel Two children	Same	In-house counsel in different firm Also does legal writing
78	Associate Small firm One child	At home with family	Part-time In-house counsel Three children
79	Part-time employee Small firm Four children	Same	In-house counsel Public corporation
80	Partner Small firm Two children	Same	Same
81	Contractual In-house counsel Three children	Same	In a different community Still practising law Involved in politics
82	Sole practitioner Three children	Same	Same
83	Partner Small firm Four children	Same	Very positive report Very busy but balanced Strong family ties
84	Partner Small firm (four-day work week) Three children	Same	Happy with work and family commitments Elected to political office

▶

	1996 Practice/Family	2000 Practice/Family	At last report
85	Part-time Sole practitioner Three children	Same	On Law Society of Upper Canada list **Appears to have left legal practice**
86	In-house counsel No children	Same Different company	Has gained confidence Has two children
87	Partner Small firm Three children	Same	Same
88	Sole practitioner One child	Same	Same Content with her legal practice
89	Sole practitioner No children	Same	Same
90	Associate Small firm Three children	Same	Same Not happy about her legal practice
91	Sole practitioner Wanted to leave law No children	Same	Same
92	Partner Small firm One child	Same	Not on Law Society of Upper Canada list **Appears to have left legal practise**
93	In-house counsel No children	Same	Same
94	Sole practitioner Two children	Same	Same
95	Associate Small firm One child	In-house counsel	Same Likes autonomy of work Law is "just not fun"
96	Sole practitioner Two children	Judge	Likes her work Misses her clients Work-family struggle
97	Staff lawyer Legal clinic One adult child	Same	Same

▶

	1996 Practice/Family	2000 Practice/Family	At last report

98	Associate
	Small firm
	Two children,
	  one stepchild
		Same	Renewed energy after
			  career break in 2004
			Work-family balanced

99	Partner Small firm One child	Same	Health problems **Died in 2006**
100	Sole practitioner No children	Same	Same

101	Partner
	Small firm
	One child
		Same	Heavily involved in
			  Law Society of
			  Upper Canada work
			Would like to be a judge

102	Sole practitioner No children	Same	Same
103	Vice-president Private industry One child	Same	Same Likes the fast pace of corporate life
104	Sole practitioner Bar association duties Three children	Same	Same
105	In-house counsel No children	Same	Same but has changed companies
106	Partner Small firm One child	Same	Has changed law firms
107	Sole practitioner One child	Same	Same
108	Sole practitioner No children	Same	Same Helps Legal Aid clinic Plans to retire soon
109	Sole practitioner One child	Same	Same

110	Partner
	Small firm
	Two children
		Employed in Legal
		  Aid clinic
			Temporarily working
			  with Aboriginal
			  organization

Notes

Chapter 1: Introduction

1 This woman is a partner in a large firm. She reappears in Chapter 6 under the pseudonym of Kristen.

2 These professional distinctions were derived from British traditions where barristers stressed their superiority over attorneys, described variously as "an inferior class of men," "ill-bred," and "disreputable." See W. Wesley Pue, "Guild Training versus Professional Education: The Committee on Legal Education and the Law Department of Queen's College, Birmingham in the 1850s" (1989) 33 American Journal of Legal History 241 at 243-44. For more detail on the education of early lawyers, see R.D. Gidney and W.P.J. Millar, *Professional Gentlemen: The Professions in Nineteenth-Century Ontario* (Toronto: University of Toronto Press, 1994) at 5-7.

3 See Constance Backhouse, *Petticoats and Prejudice: Women and Law in Nineteenth-Century Canada* (Toronto: Women's Press for the Osgoode Society, 1991) at 293, for an excellent discussion of Clara Brett Martin's career.

4 I report this comment, not to discredit farmers' wives but to emphasize the tendency to perpetuate stereotypes on the basis of appearance.

5 See, for example, Julie Lesser, "The Balancing Act" (August 2004) Career Verdict: The Magazine for Law Students 23.

6 Scott Coltrane, "Elite Careers and Family Commitment: It's (Still) about Gender" in Jerry A. Jacobs and Janice Fanning Madden, eds., *Mommies and Daddies on the Fast Track: Success of Parents in Demanding Professions*, special edition (November 2004) 596 Annals of the American Academy of Political and Social Science 214.

7 Susan W. Hinze, "Women, Men, Career and Family in the US Young Physician Labor Force" in Nancy Ditomaso and Corinne Post, eds., *Diversity in the Workforce, Research in the Sociology of Work*, vol. 14 (Oxford: Elsevier JAI, 2004), 185; Jerry A. Jacobs and Sarah E. Winslow, "Overworked Faculty: Job Stresses and Family Demands" in Jacobs and Fanning Madden, *supra* note 6 at 104; Mary Blair-Loy and Amy S. Wharton, "Mothers in Finance: Surviving and Thriving" in Jacobs and Fanning Madden, *supra* note 6 at 151; Mary C. Noonan and Mary E. Corcoran, "The Mommy Track and Partnership: Temporary Delay or Dead End?" in Jacobs and Fanning Madden, *supra* note 6 at 130.

8 Cynthia Fuchs Epstein, Carroll Seron, Bonnie Oglensky, and Robert Sauté, *The Part-Time Paradox: Time Norms, Professional Lives, Family, and Gender* (New York and London: Routledge, 1999).

9 Jean E. Wallace, "Motherhood and Career Commitment to the Legal Profession" in Ditomaso and Post, eds., *supra* note 7 at 219.

10 This movement is described in more detail in Chapter 4 herein.

11 Thoughtful lawyers are aware that legal terminology can be incomprehensible and intimidating for members of the general public. In a rare departure from convention, Madam Justice Denise Bellamy wrote her recent report of the Toronto computer scandal in interesting, easily understood language. See James Rusk, "The Report That Reads Like a Novel" *Globe and Mail* (27 December 2005) at A11.

12 These ideas appear in draft form in an earlier paper. For more detail, see Jean McKenzie Leiper, "An 'Unlessoned Girl, Unschooled, Unpracticed': Women Lawyers, Legal Robes and the Transformation of Identity," paper presented at the Renaissance Law and Literature Conference, Oxford University, Oxford, United Kingdom, July 1998.

13 I am grateful to one of my reviewers for recognizing the importance of Portia's story and suggesting that her experience with the robes be used as an overarching metaphor for the book.

14 See Erika Rackley, "Reassessing Portia: The Iconic Potential of Shakespeare's Woman Lawyer" (2003) 11 Feminist Legal Studies 25.

15 Margaret Thornton, *Dissonance and Distrust: Women in the Legal Profession* (Melbourne: Oxford University Press Australia, 1996) at 22.

16 For more detail, see Heather Höpfl and Pat Hornby Atkinson, "The Future of Women's Career" in Audrey Collin and Richard A. Young, eds., *The Future of Career* (Cambridge: Cambridge University Press, 2000) 130 at 138.

17 For an expanded discussion of Bourdieu's work, see Fiona M. Kay and John Hagan, "Cultivating Clients in the Competition for Partnership: Gender and the Organizational Restructuring of Law Firms in the 1990s" (1999) 33(3) Law and Society Review 517 at 525.

18 See Carol Gilligan, *In a Different Voice: Psychological Theory and Women's Development* (Cambridge, MA: Harvard University Press, 1982).

19 For more detail, see Gidney and Millar, *supra* note 2 at 171 and 200.

20 Clara Brett Martin's anti-Semitic views have been discussed at length in recent work. For more detail, see Backhouse, *supra* note 3 at 323.

21 For an excellent historical treatment of racism in the Canadian legal system, see Constance Backhouse, *Colour-Coded: A Legal History of Racism in Canada, 1900-1950* (Toronto: University of Toronto Press for the Osgoode Society for Canadian Legal History, 1999). See Radha Jhappan, ed., *Women's Legal Strategies in Canada* (Toronto: University of Toronto Press, 2002), for a comprehensive collection of works dealing with women's struggles for legal equality in Canada. The Law Society of Upper Canada has also commissioned some excellent work on diversity in the legal profession. See Fiona M. Kay, Cristi Masuch, and Paula Curry, *Diversity and Change: The Contemporary Legal Profession in Ontario* (Toronto: Law Society of Upper Canada, September 2004); and Michael Ornstein, *The Changing Face of the Ontario Legal Profession, 1971-2001* (Toronto: Law Society of Upper Canada, October 2004).

22 Citations included in Chapter 4 herein reveal the extent of the growing literature on work-family conflict.

23 Jerry A. Jacobs and Kathleen Gerson, *The Time Divide: Work, Family, and Gender Inequality* (Cambridge, MA: Harvard University Press, 2004).

24 Arlie Russell Hochschild, *The Second Shift: Working Parents and the Second Shift at Home* (New York: Avon Books, 1989).

25 See Carroll Seron, *The Business of Practicing Law: The Work Lives of Solo and Small-Firm Attorneys* (Philadelphia: Temple University Press, 1996) at 32-33.

26 Karin Jurczyk, "Time in Women's Everyday Lives: Between Self-Determination and Conflicting Demands" (1998) 7(2) Time and Society 286 at 288-89.

27 For a discussion of traditional career approaches, see Michael B. Arthur, Kerr Inkson, and Judith K. Pringle, *The New Careers: Individual Action and Economic Change* (London: Sage, 1999) at 3.

28 Phyllis Moen and Patricia Roehling, *The Career Mystique: Cracks in the American Dream* (Lanham, MD: Rowman and Littlefield Publishers, 2005) at 12.

29 *Ibid.* at 8.

30 *Ibid.* at 188-90. See also Jeffery A. Thompson and J. Stuart Bunderson, "Work-Nonwork Conflict and The Phenomenology of Time: Beyond the Balance Metaphor" (2001) 28(1) Work and Occupations 17, for a critique of balance imagery.

31 See, for example, Jacobs and Fanning Madden, *supra* note 6.

32 Noonan and Corcoran, *supra* note 7.

33 See Alfred A. Hunter, *Class Tells: On Social Inequality in Canada*, 2d ed. (Toronto: Butterworths, 1986) at 125.

34 An early reader of this manuscript noted that I move between "I" and "we" when describing aspects of the research project. This pattern is intentional because, although I was responsible for the initial design and implementation of the study, I have had excellent research assistants so I include them wherever they have played a significant part in the research process.

35 Most of the women were happy to take part in the study, and some of them spoke out in public about their involvement. Other women have had unpleasant experiences or expressed concern about practices in their firms so they need reassurance about the confidential nature of the work. Each woman was provided with a copy of the tape from her initial interview, and women who are quoted at length in this book have had an opportunity to read the transcribed quotation in the context of the discussion.

36 Neither of these lawyers are part of the sample.

37 For sampling details, see Jean McKenzie Leiper, "It Was Like 'Wow'!: The Experience of Women Lawyers in a Profession Marked by Linear Careers" (1997) 9 Canadian Journal of Women and the Law 115.

38 Two points are worth noting here. First, we contacted several women in northwestern Ontario but received no response. Second, although the sampling was random, I wanted to include at least one Aboriginal lawyer in the study. Strictly by chance, two women had Aboriginal connections, and I was delighted when a third woman, the last one to be interviewed, reported that she was Ojibway.

39 See J. Seidel, R. Kjolseth, and E. Seymour, *The Ethnograph: A User's Guide* (Corvalis, OR: Qualis Research Associates, 1988).

40 For more information, see Qualitative Solutions and Research Pty Ltd., *QSR NUD*IST 4 User Guide* (Thousand Oaks: Sage, 1997).

41 Other researchers have done very comprehensive studies based on surveys and interviews with men and women in the legal profession. See, for example, John Hagan and Fiona Kay, *Gender in Practice: A Study of Lawyers' Lives* (Oxford: Oxford University Press, 1995); and Joan Brockman, *Gender in the Legal Profession: Fitting or Breaking the Mould* (Vancouver: UBC Press, 2001).

42 For an excellent discussion of the politics of questionnaire design, see Joan Brockman, "'A Wild Feminist at Her Raving Best': Reflections on Studying Gender Bias in the Legal Profession" (2000) 28(1/2) Resources for Feminist Research 61.

Chapter 2: "The Portia of Our Chambers"

1 William Shakespeare, "The Merchant of Venice" in Alfred Harbage, ed., *William Shakespeare: The Complete Works* (New York: Viking Press, 1986) at 230.

2 Shakespeare's first production of *The Merchant of Venice* was mounted in 1597 and was based partly on the 1558 text by Fiorentino called *Il Pecorone*. For a detailed description of the genesis of the play, see Alice Arnott Oppen, *Shakespeare: Listening to the Women* (Henley Beach, Australia: Seaview Press, 1999) at 184.

3 Harbage, *supra* note 1 at 237.

4 Arnott Oppen, *supra* note 2 at 184.

5 For more detail, see Clara Clayborne Park, "As We Like It: How a Girl Can Be Smart and Still Popular" in Carolyn Ruth Swift Lenz, Gayle Green, and Carol Thomas Neely, eds., *The Woman's Part: Feminist Criticism of Shakespeare* (Urbana: University of Illinois Press, 1980), 100 at 110; and Carol Leventen, "Patrimony and Patriarchy in *The Merchant of Venice*" in Valerie Wayne, ed., *The Matter of Difference: Material Feminist Criticism of Shakespeare* (Ithaca: Cornell University Press, 1991) 59 at 68. See Daniel Kornstein, *Kill All the Lawyers? Shakespeare's Legal Appeal* (Princeton: Princeton University Press, 1994) at 77 for a dissenting view of Portia's strengths.

6 See, for example, Lisa Jardine, *Reading Shakespeare Historically* (London: Routledge, 1996) at 63.

7 See Leventen, *supra* note 5 at 71; and Michael Shapiro, *Gender in Play on the Shakespearean Stage* (Ann Arbor: University of Michigan Press, 1994) at 102.

8 For more detail, see Thomas Kuehn, *Law, Family and Women: Toward a Legal Anthropology of Renaissance Italy* (Chicago: University of Chicago Press, 1991).

9 See Leventen, *supra* note 5 at 62-64.
10 Kornstein, *supra* note 5 at 81.
11 Carol Gilligan, *In a Different Voice: Psychological Theory and Women's Development* (Cambridge, MA: Harvard University Press, 1982); Carrie Menkel-Meadow, "Portia in a Different Voice: Speculations on a Women's Lawyering Process" (1985) 1 Berkeley Women's Law Journal 39; and Bertha Wilson, "Will Women Judges Really Make a Difference?" (1990) 28 Osgoode Hall Law Journal 507.
12 Ian Ward, "When Mercy Seasons Justice: Shakespeare's Woman Lawyer" in Clare McGlynn, ed., *Legal Feminisms: Theory and Practice* (Aldershot: Ashgate/Dartmouth, 1998) 63 at 66, 69-70.
13 Erika Rackley, "Reassessing Portia: The Iconic Potential of Shakespeare's Woman Lawyer" (2003) 11 Feminist Legal Studies 25 at 40.
14 Keith M. Macdonald, *The Sociology of the Professions* (London: Sage, 1995).
15 See, for example, Magali Sarfatti Larson, *The Rise of Professionalism: A Sociological Analysis* (Berkeley: University of California Press, 1977); Anne Witz, *Professions and Patriarchy* (London: Routledge, 1992); and Macdonald, *supra* note 14.
16 For a comprehensive history of British legal robes, see J.H. Baker, "History of the Gowns Worn at the English Bar" (1975) 9 Costume 15; and J.H. Baker, "A History of English Judges' Robes" (1978) 12 Costume 27.
17 Historians provide evidence that professions such as law were well organized and politically active as early as the thirteenth century in most European countries. See, for example, W.N. Hargreaves-Mawdsley, *A History of Legal Dress in Europe* (Oxford: Clarendon Press, 1963) at 1; and Brian P. Levack, *The Civil Lawyers in England, 1603-1641* (Oxford: Clarendon Press, 1973) at 1.
18 For more detail, see Macdonald, *supra* note 14 at 157-86; and Elliot Freidson, *Professionalism: The Third Logic* (Chicago: University of Chicago Press, 2001) at 152-76.
19 For more detail, see E. Greenwood, "The Attributes of a Profession" (1957) 2 Social Work 44; and George Ritzer and David Walczak, *Working: Conflict and Change*, 3rd edition (Englewood Cliffs, NJ: Prentice-Hall, 1986).
20 For more detail, see Sarfatti Larson, *supra* note 15 at 49-54; and Eliot Freidson, *The Profession of Medicine* (New York: Dodd, Mead and Company, 1970).
21 Sarfatti Larson, *supra* note 15 at xvii.
22 Macdonald, *supra* note 14 at 30-31 [italics added].
23 *Ibid.* at 160.
24 Freidson, *supra* note 18 at 23.
25 *Ibid.* at 25.
26 *Ibid.* at 80-81.
27 Max Weber, *Economy and Society* (London: University of California Press, 1978) at 342.
28 See, for example, Sarfatti Larson, *supra* note 15; Frank Parkin, *Marxism and Class Theory: A Bourgeois Critique* (London: Tavistock Publications, 1979); and Witz, *supra* note 15.
29 R. Murphy, *Social Closure* (Oxford: Clarendon Press, 1988).
30 Macdonald, *supra* note 14 at 128.
31 Witz, *supra* note 15 at 46.
32 See Constance Backhouse, *Petticoats and Prejudice: Women and Law in Nineteenth-Century Canada* (Toronto: Women's Press for the Osgoode Society, 1991) at Chapter 10, for a discussion of Clara Brett Martin's struggle to become Canada's first woman lawyer in 1897.
33 Harbage, *supra* note 1 at 232.
34 Shakespearean audiences were aware of a further level of gender confusion when young male actors played Portia and Nerissa who were in turn masquerading as men. For more detail, see Shapiro, *supra* note 7. See Marjorie Garber, *Vested Interests: Cross-Dressing and Cultural Anxiety* (New York: Routledge, 1997) at 72, for a description of the "triple" entendres in this passage.
35 Harbage, *supra* note 1 at 235.
36 Jardine, *supra* note 6 at 62-64.
37 Paula Berggren, "The Woman's Part: Female Sexuality as Power in Shakespeare's Plays" in Swift Lenz, Green, and Thomas Neeley, *supra* note 5 at 20.

38   Harbage, *supra* note 1 at 233.
39   Jardine, *supra* note 6 at 63.
40   Harbage, *supra* note 1 at 242.
41   See Berggren, *supra* note 37 at 19; Claiborne Park, *supra* note 5 at 109.
42   Angela Pitt, *Shakespeare's Women* (Newton Abbot: David and Charles, 1981) at 92.
43   Harbage, *supra* note 1 at 233.
44   The question was not addressed if the women did not wear their robes regularly or if I felt that it would interrupt the flow of the discussion. Since it was an unusual question, I typically began with a brief explanation and then asked: "How do you feel when you put on your robes?" or "How did you feel the first time you put on your robes?"
45   Women's size is frequently mentioned in contradictory terms when they assume powerful roles. The Chicago judge assigned to Conrad Black's case was described by her father as "only five feet tall," but he went on to say: "You'd never guess that out of this little squirt comes a fistful of dynamite." See Paul Waldie, "Black's Judge 'A Fistful of Dynamite'" *Globe and Mail* (29 November 2005) at B20.
46   Joanne Entwistle, "The Dressed Body" in Joanne Entwistle and Elizabeth Wilson, eds., *Body Dressing* (Oxford: Berg, 2001) cited in Fiona Cownie, *Legal Academics: Culture and Identities* (Oxford and Portland: Hart Publishing, 2004) at 187.
47   See Chapter 3 herein for a definition of culture.
48   Not all of the lawyers shared her enthusiasm. One young criminal lawyer said she felt "scared a bit" when she first appeared in court but added that "it made me feel ... different in a way that I shouldn't feel different." Aware of the elitism that could creep into the system, she went on the compare her job with the trades, suggesting that legal practice was more like a craft than a profession.
49   Another lawyer told me that the first time she appeared in court, she met one of the senior partners from her firm on her return, and he blurted out: "You look so cute in your robes!"
50   Margaret Thornton, *Dissonance and Distrust: Women in the Legal Profession* (Melbourne: Oxford University Press Australia, 1996) at 137. Thornton's observations parallel Lisa Jardine's view that learned women have been expected to tread a thin line between chastity and "sexual knowingness." See Jardine, *supra* note 6 at 63.
51   Thornton, *supra* note 50 at 16.
52   See Carole Pateman, *The Disorder of Women: Democracy, Feminism and Political Theory* (Stanford: Stanford University Press, 1989) at 18 and 75.
53   Thornton, *supra* note 50 at 226. See also Richard Collier, "(Un)Sexy Bodies: The Making of Professional Legal Masculinities" in McGlynn, *supra* note 12 at 26-31, for an extension of Margaret Thornton's views on the representation of women in the legal profession. Collier argues that the male/female divide ignores important differences among men in the profession.
54   See Sandra Lee Bartky, "Foucault, Femininity, and Patriarchal Power" in Katie Conboy, Nadia Medina, and Sarah Stanbury, eds, *Writing on the Body: Female Embodiment and Feminist Theory* (New York: Columbia University Press, 1997) 129 at 136.
55   Bartky, *supra* note 54 at 142; Michel Foucault, *Discipline and Punish: The Birth of the Prison* (New York: Vintage Books, 1979) at 138; and Thornton, *supra* note 50 at 79.
56   "Claire" is a pseudonym, which is used in reference to this woman again in Chapter 6 when she talks about the trauma she experienced as she moved from legal practice to a new life.
57   See Collier, *supra* note 53 at 26, for a discussion of the business suit as a symbol of masculine power in the legal profession.
58   John Harvey provides an excellent historical discussion of the empowering effects of men's black clothing in contrast to women's colourful or white clothes. See John Harvey, *Men in Black* (Chicago: University of Chicago Press, 1995) at 195.
59   For a comprehensive discussion of women as "reluctant adversaries" in the legal profession, see Joan Brockman, *Gender in the Legal Profession: Fitting or Breaking the Mould* (Vancouver: UBC Press, 2001) at 128.
60   Cownie, *supra* note 46 at 187.

61 See, for example, Thornton, *supra* note 50 at 155.
62 Hargreaves-Mawdsley, *supra* note 17, documents regional and seasonal variations in legal dress from the thirteenth century to the end of the eighteenth century in western European countries.
63 Baker, "History of the Gowns," *supra* note 16 at 18.
64 Thornton, *supra* note 50 at 222.
65 Sarfatti Larson, *supra* note 15; and Weber, *supra* note 27.
66 Witz, *supra* note 15; and Macdonald, *supra* note 14.

Chapter 3: Educating Women in the Law

1 Florence A. Scheftel, "The Study of Law As a Means of Culture for Women" (1911) 1(2) Women Lawyers' Journal 10 at 11.
2 Constance Backhouse, *Petticoats and Prejudice: Women and Law in Nineteenth-Century Canada* (Toronto: Women's Press for the Osgoode Society, 1991) at 321.
3 *Ibid.* at 318-19.
4 See Mary Jane Mossman, "Women Lawyers in Twentieth Century Canada: Rethinking the Image of 'Portia'" in Regina Graycar, ed., *Dissenting Opinion: Feminist Explorations in Law and Society* (Sydney: Allen and Unwin, 1990) 88.
5 For a discussion of exclusionary patterns in the English legal profession, see Richard L. Abel, *English Lawyers between Market and State: The Politics of Professionalism* (Oxford: Oxford University Press, 2003) at 120-22.
6 See Karen Berger Morello, *The Invisible Bar: The Woman Lawyer in America 1638 to the Present* (New York: Random House, 1986) at 3; and Cynthia Fuchs Epstein, *Women in Law*, 2d ed. (Urbana and Chicago: University of Illinois Press, 1993) at 49, for more detail.
7 See Carrie Menkel-Meadow, "The Comparative Sociology of Women Lawyers: The 'Feminization' of the Legal Profession" (1986) 24(4) Osgoode Hall Law Journal 897 at 902.
8 Margaret Thornton, *Dissonance and Distrust: Women in the Legal Profession* (Melbourne: Oxford University Press Australia, 1996) at 48.
9 Mary Jane Mossman, "Portia's Progress: Women as Lawyers Reflections on Past and Future" (1988) 8 Windsor Yearbook of Access to Justice 252 at 254.
10 See Mossman, "Women Lawyers in Twentieth Century Canada," *supra* note 4 at 82, for a discussion of the "persons" debate and the admission of women to law schools in other Canadian provinces. The issue of women as "non-persons" was contested in several jurisdictions, affecting their right to vote, their property rights, and their acceptance into the learned professions. Margaret Thornton describes the process in Australia in *Dissonance and Distrust, supra* note 8 at 56.
11 For an excellent presentation of Clara Brett Martin's career, see Backhouse, *supra* note 2 at 293.
12 For more detail, see Mary Jane Mossman, "Gender Bias and the Legal Profession: Challenges and Choices" in Joan Brockman and Dorothy Chunn, eds., *Investigating Gender Bias: Law, Courts and the Legal Profession* (Toronto: Thompson Educational Publishing, 1993) 147; Mary Jane Mossman, "Lawyers and Family Life: New Directions for the 1990's (Part One)" (1994) 2(1) Feminist Legal Studies 61; and John Hagan and Fiona Kay, *Gender in Practice: A Study of Lawyers' Lives* (Oxford: Oxford University Press, 1995) at 9.
13 See "The Changing Face of the Legal Profession," which can be accessed online at http://www.lsuc.on.ca/news/a/fact.
14 Clara Brett Martin came from a middle-class family. She and her eleven siblings were tutored at home, and they all attended university. For more detail, see Backhouse, *supra* note 2 at 295.
15 See R.D. Gidney and W.P.J. Millar, *Professional Gentlemen: The Professions in Nineteenth-Century Ontario* (Toronto: University of Toronto Press, 1994) at 6-10; and Robert L. Fraser, ed., *Provincial Justice: Upper Canadian Legal Portraits from the Dictionary of Canadian Biography* (Toronto and Buffalo: University of Toronto Press for the Osgoode Society, 1992). See also W. Wesley Pue, "Planting British Legal Culture in Colonial Soil: Legal Professionalism in the Lands of the Beaver and Kangaroo" in Linda Cardinal and David Headon,

eds., *Shaping Nations: Constitutionalism and Society in Australia and Canada* (Ottawa: University of Ottawa Press, 2002), 91, for a discussion of attempts to establish "Britishness" in new colonies.

16 Moore, Christopher. *The Law Society of Upper Canada and Ontario's Lawyers, 1797-1997* (Toronto: University of Toronto Press, 1997) at 171 and 200.

17 *Ibid.* at 176.

18 See Mossman, "Gender Bias and the Legal Profession," *supra* note 12 at 150-51; and Fuchs Epstein, *supra* note 6 at 385.

19 For more detail, see Joan Brockman, *Gender in the Legal Profession: Fitting or Breaking the Mould* (Vancouver: UBC Press, 2001) at 4-7; Fiona M. Kay and Joan Brockman, "Barriers to Gender Equality in the Canadian Legal Establishment" (2000) 8 Feminist Legal Studies 169 at 171-73; Fiona M. Kay, "Crossroads to Innovation and Diversity: The Careers of Women Lawyers in Quebec" (2002) 47 McGill Law Journal 699 at 706-9; Mary Kinnear, "That There Woman Lawyer: Women Lawyers in Manitoba 1915-1970" (1992) 5(2) Canadian Journal of Women and the Law 411; W. Wesley Pue, *Law School: The Story of Legal Education in British Columbia* (Vancouver: University of British Columbia Faculty of Law, 1995) at 223-33; and Lois K. Yorke, "Mabel Penery French (1881-1955): A Life Re-Created" (1993) 42 University of New Brunswick Law Journal 3.

20 See Thornton, *supra* note 8 at 47 and 4.

21 Helena Kennedy, *Eve Was Framed* (Oxford: Oxford University Press, 1992) at 43. Baroness Kennedy was called to the bar in 1972 and, in spite of her initial reservations, has accumulated an array of honours, including Queen's Counsel, a life peerage, bencher's status, and a number of honorary doctorates.

22 For more detail, see Abel, *supra* note 5 at 149-50.

23 See, for example, Paul Carrington and James Conley, "The Alienation of Law Students" (1989) 75 Michigan Law Review 887; Marina Angel, "Women in Legal Education: What It's Like to Be Part of a First Wave or the Case of the Disappearing Women" (1988) 6 Temple Law Review 799; Rand Jack and Dana Crowley Jack, *Moral Vision and Professional Decisions: The Changing Values of Men and Women Lawyers* (Cambridge: Cambridge University Press, 1989); and Catherine Weiss and Louise Melling, "The Legal Education of Twenty Women" (1988) 40 Stanford Law Review 1299.

24 Mona Harrington, *Women Lawyers: Rewriting the Rules* (New York: Alfred A. Knopf, 1994) at 47.

25 Sonja A. Sackmann et al., "Single and Multiple Cultures in International Cross-Cultural Management Research," in Sonja A. Sackmann, ed., *Cultural Complexity in Organizations: Inherent Contrasts and Contradictions* (Thousand Oaks, CA: Sage, 1997) 14 at 25 [italics added].

26 See Radha Jhappan, ed., *Women's Legal Strategies in Canada* (Toronto: University of Toronto Press, 2002) at 14-16, for a discussion of the critical legal studies school.

27 Paul W. Kahn, *The Cultural Study of Law* (Chicago: University of Chicago Press, 1999) at 40.

28 *Ibid.* at 24.

29 Catharine A. MacKinnon, *Toward a Feminist Theory of the State* (Cambridge, MA: Harvard University Press, 1989) at 161-63.

30 Ann C. Scales, "The Emergence of Feminist Jurisprudence: An Essay" (1986) 95 Yale Law Journal 1378.

31 MacKinnon, *supra* note 29 at 25.

32 Richard A. Posner, *The Problematics of Moral and Legal Theory* (Cambridge, MA: Belknap Press of Harvard University Press, 1999) at 43.

33 MacKinnon, *supra* note 29 at 242.

34 See Joanne St. Lewis, "Beyond the Confinement of Gender: Locating the Space of Legalized Existence of Racialized Women" in Jhappan, *supra* note 26 at 312-14.

35 Menkel-Meadow, *supra* note 7 at 898-99.

36 See also Thornton, *supra* note 8 at 268, for an excellent discussion of feminization in the legal profession.

37 See Catharine MacKinnon, *Feminism Unmodified: Discourse on Life and Law* (Cambridge, MA: Harvard University Press, 1987) at 74.

38 Menkel-Meadow, *supra* note 7 at 912.
39 Mossman, "Lawyers and Family Life," *supra* note 12. Mossman was responding to Judith Kaye's suggestion that the profession had moved through three stages – the "pioneer" stage, the "superwoman" stage, and the stage marked by challenge. See Judith S. Kaye, "Women Lawyers in Big Firms: A Study in Progress toward Gender Equality" (1988) 57 Fordham Law Review 111 at 126.
40 For a brief summary of this literature, see Susan Erlich Martin and Nancy C. Jurik, *Doing Justice, Doing Gender: Women in Law and Criminal Justice Occupations* (Thousand Oaks, CA: Sage, 1996) at 137-40.
41 Janet Rosenberg, Harry Perlstadt, and William R.F. Phillips, "Now That We Are Here: Discrimination, Disparagement, and Harassment at Work and the Experience of Women Lawyers" (1993) 7(3) Gender and Society 415.
42 Canadian Bar Association, *Touchstones for Change: Equality, Diversity and Accountability*, Report of the Canadian Bar Association Task Force on Gender Equality in the Legal Profession, chaired by the Honourable Bertha Wilson (Ottawa: Canadian Bar Association, 1993) at 32 and 55-74.
43 Ellen Anderson, *Judging Bertha Wilson: Law As Large As Life* (Toronto: University of Toronto Press, 2001) at 348-49; and Canadian Bar Association, *supra* note 42 at 185-200.
44 Menkel-Meadow, *supra* note 7 at 916.
45 John Hagan and Fiona Kay, "Hierarchy in Practice: The Significance of Gender in Ontario Law Firms" in Carol Wilton, ed., *Inside the Law: Canadian Law Firms in Historical Perspective* (Toronto: Osgoode Society for Canadian Legal History by University of Toronto Press, 1996) 530; and Robert L. Nelson, "The Future of American Lawyers: A Demographic Profile of a Changing Profession in a Changing Society" in Richard L. Abel, ed., *Lawyers: A Critical Reader* (New York: New Press, 1997) 20.
46 See Fiona M. Kay and John Hagan, "The Persistent Glass Ceiling: Gendered Inequalities in the Earnings of Lawyers" (1995) 46(2) British Journal of Sociology 279 at 293-303; and Fiona M. Kay, Cristi Masuch, and Paula Curry, *Women's Careers in the Legal Profession: A Longitudinal Survey of Ontario Lawyers, 1990-2002* (Toronto: Law Society of Upper Canada, September 2004) at 107.
47 For more detail, see Kay and Brockman, *supra* note 19 at 180-86.
48 See Fiona M. Kay and John Hagan, "Cultivating Clients in the Competition for Partnership: Gender and the Organizational Restructuring of Law Firms in the 1990s" (1999) 33(3) Law and Society Review 517 at 525. See also Kay and Brockman, *supra* note 19 at 182.
49 For more detail, see Pierre Bourdieu, *Distinction: A Social Critique of the Judgment of Taste* (London: Routledge and Kegan Paul, 1979) at 114.
50 Carroll Seron, *The Business of Practicing Law: The Work Lives of Solo and Small-Firm Attorneys* (Philadelphia: Temple University Press, 1996) at 32-33.
51 Fiona M. Kay and John Hagan, "Building Trust: Social Capital, Distributive Justice, and Loyalty to the Firm" (2003) 28(2) Law and Social Inquiry 483 at 485 and 510.
52 For an excellent discussion of cultural capital, see Fiona M. Kay and John Hagan, "Raising the Bar: The Gender Stratification of Law-Firm Capital" (1998) 63(5) American Sociological Review 728 at 730-31. See also Hilary Sommerlad and Peter Sanderson, *Gender, Choice and Commitment: Women Solicitors in England and Wales and the Struggle for Equal Status* (Aldershot: Ashgate Publishing Company, 1998) at 121-51, for a discussion of cultural capital in "The Men's Room."
53 Seron, *supra* note 50 at 32.
54 Kay and Hagan, *supra* note 52 at 741.
55 See Mossman, "Lawyers and Family Life," *supra* note 12 at 70.
56 For more detail, see Kay and Brockman, *supra* note 19 at 186-93.
57 Sheilah Martin and Gaylene Schellenberg, *Equality of Women in the Legal Profession: A Facilitators' Manual* (Ottawa: Canadian Bar Association Standing Committee on Equality, 1996).
58 Anderson, *supra* note 43 at 343-44.
59 See, for example, Law Society of Upper Canada, *Preventing and Responding to Workplace*

Harassment and Discrimination: A Guide to Developing A Policy for Law Firms (Toronto: Law Society of Upper Canada, March 2002); and Law Society of Upper Canada, *Guide to Developing a Policy Regarding Flexible Work Arrangements* (Toronto: Law Society of Upper Canada, March 2003).

60 For example, Catalyst Research, *Women in Law: Making the Case* (New York and Toronto: Catalyst, 2001).

61 Alfred Harbage, ed., *William Shakespeare: The Complete Works* (New York: Viking Press, 1986) at 236.

62 Sharyn Roach Anleu, "Women in the Legal Profession: Theory and Research" in Patricia Weiser Esteal and Sandra McKillop, eds., *Women and the Law: Proceedings of a Conference, September 24-26, 1991* (Canberra: Australian Institute of Criminology, 1993) 193 at 196.

63 Carol Gilligan, *In a Different Voice: Psychological Theory and Women's Development* (Cambridge, MA: Harvard University Press, 1982). See Carrie Menkel-Meadow, "Exploring a Research Agenda of the Feminization of the Legal Profession: Theories of Gender and Social Change" (1989) Law and Social Inquiry 289 at 316; and Naomi R. Cahn, "Styles of Lawyering" (1992) 43 Hastings Law Journal 1039, for discussions of Gilligan's thesis.

64 See Carrie Menkel-Meadow, "Portia in a Different Voice: Speculations on a Woman's Lawyering Process" (1985) 1 Berkeley Women's Law Journal 39 at 50-55; and Menkel-Meadow, "Comparative Sociology of Women Lawyers," *supra* note 7 at 897 and 915.

65 See Jennifer L. Pierce, *Gender Trials: Emotional Lives in Contemporary Law Firms* (Berkeley: University of California Press, 1995) at 140-41.

66 See Brockman, *supra* note 19, Chapter 5, for an excellent discussion of the adversarial system.

67 Ann Scales makes a strong case for a radical feminist critique of Gilligan's thesis. See Scales, *supra* note 30 at 1380-84.

68 Cynthia Fuchs Epstein, *Deceptive Distinctions: Sex, Gender, and the Social Order* (New Haven, CT: Yale University Press, 1988); and Robert Granfield, "Contextualizing the Different Voice: Women, Occupational Goals, and Legal Education" (1994) 16(1) Law and Policy 1.

69 Deborah L. Rhode, "Gender and Professional Roles" (1994-95) 63 Fordham Law Review 39 at 44.

70 MacKinnon, *supra* note 37 at 39.

71 For a critique of MacKinnon's work, see Roach Anleu, *supra* note 62 at 196.

72 *Ibid.* at 198.

73 See Cahn, *supra* note 63 at 1068.

74 See Ann Shalleck, "The Feminist Transformation of Lawyering: A Response to Naomi Cahn" (1992) 43 Hastings Law Journal 1039 at 1072 and 1074.

75 See Rhode, *supra* note 69 at 50.

76 Black-letter or academic law springs from the doctrinal tradition, reflecting a vision of the law as separate and distinct from moral or political issues. For a clear description of black-letter law, see Fiona Cownie, *Legal Academics: Culture and Identities* (Oxford and Portland: Hart Publishing, 2004) at 49-50.

77 For more detail, see Ruta Stropus, "Mend It, Bend It, and Extend It: The Fate of Traditional Law School Methodology in the 21st Century" (1996) 27 Loyola University Chicago Law Journal 449 at 453-54; and Pue, *supra* note 19 at 163-67.

78 See Max Weber, *Economy and Society* (London: University of California Press, 1978) at 342.

79 Keith M. Macdonald, *The Sociology of the Professions* (London: Sage, 1995) at 160. See also Bob Gidney, "'Madame How and Lady Why': Learning to Practise in Historical Perspective" in Ruby Heap, Wyn Millar, and Elizabeth Smyth, eds., *Learning to Practise: Professional Education in Historical and Contemporary Perspective* (Ottawa: University of Ottawa Press, 2005) 13. Gidney differentiates between scientific knowledge or "knowledge about" and the "knowledge-in-use" that informs professional practice.

80 The bar admission course was discontinued in 2005 and replaced by a Licensing Process for Admission to the Bar of Ontario, in conjunction with ten months of articling.

81 Gidney and Millar, *supra* note 15 at 73, describe the lineage and connections of the early

benchers of the Law Society of Upper Canada. Without exception, they represented the most powerful and prestigious families in Upper Canada.

82 *Ibid.* at 173. Gidney and Millar provide an excellent discussion of the rise of the legal profession in Ontario and the debates surrounding the establishment of Osgoode Hall Law School.

83 Proponents of academic law in Ontario were influenced by the Harvard model. For more detail on the Harvard experience, see Robert Stevens, *Law School: Legal Education in America from the 1850s to the 1980s* (Chapel Hill and London: University of North Carolina Press, 1983) at 51.

84 Wright had adopted Christopher Langdell's methods during his postgraduate year at Harvard.

85 See C. Ian Kyer and Jerome E. Bickenbach, *The Fiercest Debate: Cecil A. Wright, the Benchers, and Legal Education in Ontario, 1923-1957* (Toronto: Osgoode Society for Canadian Legal History, 1987), for an excellent discussion of Wright's career.

86 See Jamie Cassels and Maureen Maloney, "Critical Legal Education: Paralysis with a Purpose" (1989) 4 Canadian Journal of Law and Society 99, for a history of legal education in Ontario.

87 The University of Western Ontario's Law School has recently introduced a mandatory first-year course called "Legal Ethics and Professionalism." See "Western First to Make Legal Ethics Required First-Year Course" (Spring 2005) Western Alumni Gazette 29.

88 See Cassels and Maloney, *supra* note 86 at 108. Their work focuses on law schools in common law jurisdictions in Canada.

89 The law school admission test (LSAT) is a standardized test developed in the United States. See Dawna Tong and W. Wesley Pue, "The Best and the Brightest? Canadian Law School Admissions" (1999) 37(4) Osgoode Hall Law Journal 843, for a good discussion of LSAT scores and grade point averages as appropriate entrance requirements for Canadian law schools.

90 See Abel, *supra* note 5 at 153-58, for a discussion of meritocratic processes and continuing class privilege in England.

91 For more detail, see Larry Chartrand, Dolores Blonde, Michael Cormier, Kai Hildebrandt, Christopher Wydrzynski, and Edward Czilli, "Law Students, Law Schools, and Their Graduates" (2001) 20 Windsor Year Book of Access to Justice 211 at 232; and Statistics Canada, "Study: Access to Professional Programs amid the Deregulation of Tuition Fees, 1995 to 2002," *The Daily* (27 September 2005), which is available online at http://www.statcan.ca/Daily/English/050927/d050927a.htm.

92 For more information, see Cassels and Maloney, *supra* note 86.

93 See William C. Kidder, "Portia Denied: Unmasking Gender Bias on the LSAT and Its Relationship to Racial Diversity in Legal Education" (2001) 12(1) Yale Journal of Law and Feminism 1 at 11-17.

94 Harry A. Arthurs (chair), *Law and Learning: Report to the Social Sciences and Humanities Research Council of Canada by the Consultative Group on Research and Education in Law* (Ottawa: Social Sciences and Humanities Research Council of Canada, 1983) at 154 [Arthurs Report].

95 See Constance Backhouse, "Revisiting the *Arthurs Report* Twenty Years Later" (2003) 18(1) Canadian Journal of Law and Society 37; and Roderick A. Macdonald, "Still 'Law' and Still 'Learning'" (2003) 18(1) Canadian Journal of Law and Society 22.

96 See John C. Kleefeld, "Rethinking 'Like a Lawyer': An Incrementalist's Proposal for First-Year Curriculum Reform" (2003) 53(2) Journal of Legal Education 254.

97 For more detail, see Stropus, *supra* note 77.

98 See, for example, Andrew J. Rothman, "Preparing Law School Graduates for Practice: A Blueprint for Professional Education Following the Medical Profession Example" (1999) 51(4) Rutgers Law Review 875 at 877-78.

99 See Margaret Thornton, "Technocentrism in the Law School: Why the Gender and Colour of the Law Remain the Same" (1998) 36(2) Osgoode Hall Law Journal 369 at 373.

100 Tong and Pue, *supra* note 89 at 863fn.

101 Margot E. Young, "Making and Breaking Rank: Some Thoughts on Recent Canadian Law School Surveys" (2001) 20 Windsor Yearbook of Access to Justice 311 at 319.

102 *Ibid.* at 321. It should also be noted that these "select law school graduates" are a self-selected group responding to the magazine's annual questionnaire.

103 See Kirsten McMahon, "The *Canadian Lawyer* 2005 Report Card on Canadian Law Schools" (2005) 29(1) Canadian Lawyer 28.

104 See Kirsten McMahon, "The *Canadian Lawyer* 2006 Report Card on Canadian Law Schools" (2006) 30(1) Canadian Lawyer 33.

105 Young, *supra* note 101 at 324-27.

106 McMahon, *supra* note 103 at 29-30.

107 The rankings in the *Canadian Lawyer* surveys should be viewed with caution. They are presented in report card format, assigning letter grades for such categories as curriculum, faculty, testing, and facilities. A few percentages are provided in the accompanying discussion, but, without raw data, the reader is entirely dependent on the interpretation provided by the author of the article. Kirsten McMahon, in "Making the Grade" (2001) 25(1) Canadian Lawyer 23 at 23, reports a sample size of "almost 700" and, in 2004, she cites a sample size of "almost 350," which she says is "a high response rate," "almost 100 more than last year." See Kirsten McMahon, "The *Canadian Lawyer* 2004 Report Card on Canadian Law Schools" (2004) 28(1) Canadian Lawyer 19 at 19. The response rate is not provided in either of these articles and readers are given no information about respondents other than their law school affiliation.

108 For more detail on nineteenth-century law practice, see Gidney and Millar, *supra* note 15 at 138-40.

109 For a global perspective on the changing legal profession, see Harry Arthurs and Robert Kreklewich, "The Legal Profession in the New Economy" (1996) 34(1) Osgoode Hall Law Journal 1; and Annie Rochette and W. Wesley Pue, "'Back to Basics': University Legal Education and Twenty-First Century Professionalism (2001) 20 Windsor Yearbook of Access to Justice 167.

110 In a response to requests from large firms, the Law Society of Upper Canada offered members of the 2001 graduating class the option of taking the bar admission course before doing their articles. This strategy apparently allowed students to move into the firms with a level of practical training that would enhance their performance as newly minted lawyers.

111 The authors of the Arthurs Report proposed a range of alternative curricula such as scholarly law programs and specialization in Native peoples' rights or environmental law as ways of avoiding "narrow vocationalism" in legal education. See Arthurs, *supra* note 94 at 155.

112 Joost Blom, dean of the Faculty of Law at the University of British Columbia cites the growth of new areas of law – constitutional, First Nations, intellectual property, international trade, information technology, human rights, welfare law, and children and the law – as signals for change in the law school curriculum. See Joost Blom, "Looking Ahead in Canadian Law School Education" (1999) 33(1) UBC Law Review 7 at 9-10.

113 Cassels and Maloney, *supra* note 86 at 109.

114 Toni Pickard, "Is Real Life Really Happening?" (1987) 2 Canadian Journal of Women and the Law 150. Much of the dissent in Queen's University Law School was triggered by a memo circulated in July 1986 by Sheila McIntyre, a law professor hired the previous year on a limited-term contract. In the memo, she described incidents of sexism and anti-feminism in the law school. For more detail on the consequences of her actions, see Sheila McIntyre, "Gender Bias within the Law School: 'The Memo' and Its Impact" (1987-88) 2(2) Canadian Journal of Women and the Law 362.

115 Lani Guinier, Michelle Fine, and Jane Balin, *Becoming Gentlemen* (Boston: Beacon Press, 1997) at 29.

116 See John O. Mudd, "Thinking Critically about 'Thinking Like a Lawyer'" (1983) 33 Journal of Legal Education 704; Emily Calhoun, "Thinking Like a Lawyer" (1984) 34 Journal of Legal Education 507; and Nancy L. Schultz, "How Do Lawyers Really Think?" (1992) 42 Journal of Legal Education 57.

117 Kurt M. Saunders and Linda Levine, "Learning to Think Like a Lawyer" (1994) 29 University of San Francisco Law Review 121. See also Bethany Rubin Henderson, "Asking

the Lost Question: What Is the Purpose of Law School?" (2003) 53(1) Journal of Legal Education 48, for a discussion of current deficiencies in legal education.

118 Thornton, *supra* note 8 at 80.

119 K.N. Llewellyn, *The Bramble Bush: On Our Law and Its Study* (New York: Oceana, 1960) quoted in Stephen Wizner, "Is Learning to 'Think Like a Lawyer' Enough?" (1998) 17 Yale Law and Policy Review 583 at 586.

120 Mary O'Brien and Sheila McIntyre, "Patriarchal Hegemony and Legal Education" (1986) 2 Canadian Journal of Women and the Law 69.

121 Thornton, *supra* note 8 at 88-89.

122 Kennedy, *supra* note 21 at 36.

123 Simone de Beauvoir, *The Second Sex,* translated and edited by H.M. Parshley (New York: Vintage Books, 1974 [1949]). See also Mary Jane Mossman, "'Otherness' and the Law School: A Comment on Teaching Gender Equality" (1985) 1 Canadian Journal of Women and the Law 213 at 214; and Thornton, *supra* note 8 at 14.

124 O'Brien and McIntyre, *supra* note 120.

125 In a course on gender and the law at Osgoode Hall Law School, Mary Jane Mossman asks her students to examine their own values and critique the supposed neutrality of legal knowledge. See Mossman, *supra* note 123 at 216.

126 Once again, the authors of the Arthurs Report remind us that recommendations for an equitable approach to legal education can come from many sources and reflect the needs of multiple constituencies within the profession. See Arthurs, *supra* note 94 at 154.

127 For example, Catherine Weiss and Louise Melling developed their ideas out of a women students' discussion group at Yale University Law School, and Marina Angel grounded her report on women in legal education in her personal experience as a student at Columbia University Law School. See Weiss and Melling, *supra* note 23; and Angel, *supra* note 23.

128 See, for example, Robert Stevens, "Law Schools and Law Students" (1973) 59 Virginia Law Review 551; and David M. White and Terry E. Roth, "The Law School Admission Test and the Continuing Minority Status of Women in Law Schools" (1979) 2 Harvard Women's Law Journal 103.

129 See Taunya Banks, "Gender Bias in the Classroom" (1988) 38 Journal of Legal Education 137; Janet Taber, Marguerite T. Grant, Mart Y. Huser, Rise B. Norman, James R. Sutton, Clarence C. Wong, Louise E. Parker, and Claire Picard, "Gender, Legal Education, and the Legal Profession: An Empirical Study of Stanford Law Students and Graduates" (1988) 40 Stanford Law Review 1209; Weiss and Melling, *supra* note 23; Cassels and Maloney, *supra* note 86; Suzanne Homer and Louise Schwartz, "Admitted But Not Accepted: Outsiders Take an Inside Look at Law School" (1989-90) 5 Berkeley Women's Law Journal 1; Granfield, *supra* note 68; Harrington, *supra* note 24; Thornton, *supra* note 8; and Guinier, Fine, and Balin, *supra* note 115.

130 Guinier, Fine, and Balin, *supra* note 115.

131 Harrington sees the Socratic method as akin to mediaeval jousting, a coming-of-age ritual intended to toughen and empower students. See Harrington, *supra* note 24 at 48.

132 Adrienne Stone, "Women, Law School and Student Commitment to the Public Interest" in Jeremy Cooper and Louise C. Trubeck, eds., *Educating for Justice: Social Values and Legal Education* (Aldershot: Dartmouth Publishing Company, 1997) 56 at 63. Speaking from her experience as law student and teacher, Adrienne Stone argues that few professors rely entirely on the adversarial questioning that is described in earlier descriptions of law school teaching.

133 Weiss and Melling, *supra* note 23.

134 See also Carrington and Conley, *supra* note 23; Menkel-Meadow, "Portia in a Different Voice," *supra* note 64; Jack and Crowley Jack, *supra* note 23; Tarel Quandt, "Learning Exclusion: A Feminist Critique of the Law School Experience" (1992-93) 4 Education and Law Journal 279; and Guinier, Fine, and Balin, *supra* note 115.

135 See Guinier, Fine, and Balin, *supra* note 115 at 28.

136 See, for example, Taber et al., *supra* note 129; and Weiss and Melling, *supra* note 23.

137 For more information, see Gilligan, *supra* note 63.

138 Bruce Feldthusen, "The Gender Wars: 'Where the Boys Are'" (1990) 4 Canadian Journal of Women and the Law 66.

139 *Ibid.* at 74.
140 *Ibid.* at 70.
141 Christine Boyle, "Teaching Law As If Women Really Mattered, Or, What about the Washrooms?" (1986) 2 Canadian Journal of Women and the Law 96.
142 *Ibid.* at 111.
143 For a discussion of recent attempts to incorporate lesbian perspectives in legal pedagogy, see Kim Brooks and Debra Parkes, "Queering Legal Education: A Project of Theoretical Discovery" (2004) 27 Harvard Women's Law Journal 89.
144 Canadian Bar Association, *supra* note 42 at 228.
145 Gilligan, *supra* note 63.
146 Granfield, *supra* note 68 at 4.
147 See, for example, Tarel Quandt's account of the law school experiences of eleven women at Dalhousie University Law School. Quandt, *supra* note 134.
148 Granfield, *supra* note 68.
149 *Ibid.* at 18.
150 Guinier, Fine, and Balin, *supra* note 115 at 30.
151 *Ibid.* at 35.
152 All the women in the study were working in Ontario when they were interviewed, but several of them had attended law school in other provinces, namely, British Columbia, Saskatchewan, Quebec, New Brunswick, and Nova Scotia.
153 The majority of Windsor and Ottawa graduates felt positive about their law school experiences, but many of the women from other law schools reported mixed feelings about their education. Graduates of Osgoode Hall were most likely to register discontent with their law school experience.
154 One embittered Western graduate applauded the decline of the "Womyn in the law" perspective, adding: "There ain't nothing wrong with the Socratic method. More power to it." See McMahon, "Making the Grade," *supra* note 107 at 26. This comment is inappropriate because Western has never used the Socratic method in first-year classes, but it demonstrates the depth of the conflict between conservative and feminist factions.
155 One of the lawyers in this study said she had avoided the Women in the Law group because it was perceived as a radical feminist lesbian group. She puzzled about her attitudes as a young woman, noting that she had since become very involved with gender issues through the Canadian Bar Association.
156 Granfield, *supra* note 68 at 18.
157 This woman had a very bad experience in the conservative, all-male law firm she joined after graduation from law school.
158 Results of a recent survey indicate that most law students come from families where both parents have university degrees and incomes are well above the national average. For more detail, see Chartrand et al., *supra* note 91.
159 See "The Changing Face of the Legal Profession," which is available online at http://www.lsuc.on.ca/news/a/fact.
160 See Chapter 7 herein for a discussion of the problems associated with race.
161 Thirty-four percent of the women in this study were thirty or older when they were called to the bar. Since law school, articles and bar admission examinations typically take four years to complete, the youngest women in this group were twenty-six when they entered law school.
162 This woman suffered a serious health problem requiring emergency surgery during her bar admission year. She had continued to work and commute, ignoring severe pain until she could no longer keep up the pace.
163 Nine of the fifty women in small towns and cities were Windsor graduates whereas only three of the sixty women in Toronto and London attended Windsor's law school. None of the women in outlying areas had attended the University of Toronto Law School.
164 It is interesting to note that the focus on large American law schools continues. A recent study released by Catalyst Research is funded by Columbia, Harvard, California-Berkeley, Michigan, and Yale law schools. See Catalyst Research, *supra* note 60.
165 Fiona Kay's work incorporates random sampling techniques (Fiona M. Kay, Cristi Masuch,

and Paula Curry, *Diversity and Change: The Contemporary Legal Profession in Ontario* (Toronto: Law Society of Upper Canada, September 2004), and Michael Ornstein uses Canadian Census data to examine patterns of diversity in the Ontario legal profession (Michael Ornstein, *The Changing Face of the Ontario Legal Profession, 1971-2001* (Toronto: Law Society of Upper Canada, October 2004).

166 See David Stager and Harry Arthurs, *Lawyers in Canada* (Toronto: University of Toronto Press, 1990) at 110.

167 See Erin Anderssen and Michael Valpy, "Face the Nation: Canada Remade" *Globe and Mail* (7 June 2003) at A10.

168 In 2002, the University of Toronto Law School approved a proposal to increase tuition by $2,000 a year over a five-year period to reach a goal of $22,000 by 2007. The dean of the law faculty defended this move, arguing that it represented the road to academic excellence. See Ronald J. Daniels, "Let's Reach for the Gold in Higher Education" *Globe and Mail* (1 March 2002) at A15. For more detail on increases in law school fees, see Shirley Neuman, "Provost's Study of Accessibility and Career Choice in the Faculty of Law," 24 February 2003, http://www.provost.utoronto.ca/English/Reports.html; Alan J.C. King, Wendy K. Warren, and Sharon R. Miklas, *Study of Accessibility to Ontario Law Schools,* Executive Summary of the Report, October 2004, Law Foundation of Ontario and the Law Society of Upper Canada, http://www.osgoode.yorku.ca/pdf/ExecutiveSummary.pdf.

169 The University of Toronto was the only Ontario law school to establish an escalating fee schedule, acting in advance of the provincial government's decision in 2004 to impose a two-year freeze on tuition fees. Late in 2005, the five remaining Ontario law schools sent a letter to The Honourable Chris Bentley, Minister of Training, Colleges and Universities, demanding equal status with the University of Toronto, arguably to expand their resources and attract the best students. For more information, see Caroline Alphonso, "Close Tuition Gap, Law Schools Ask" *Globe and Mail* (22 December 2005) at A13.

170 The University of Toronto Law School has proudly declared its mission to compete with Harvard and Yale as a North American centre of legal excellence. Law schools such as Ottawa and Windsor can hardly compete when their tuition fees remain stalled at $8,500 a year. See Editorial, "Let Tuition Fees Rise" *Globe and Mail* (29 December 2005) at A18.

Chapter 4: Caught in the Time Crunch

1 See Morris A. Gross, "Can We Re-humanize the Practice of Law?" (1990) 24 Law Society Gazette 207.

2 See, for example, Katherine Harding, "Work-Life Conflict Rampant, Study Says" *Globe and Mail* (15 January 2003) at C10; and Wallace Immen, "Ease the Stress When Crunch Time Strikes," *Globe and Mail* (4 May 2005) at C3.

3 See John Robinson, "Your Money or Your Time" (1991) 13(11) American Demographics 22. Robinson developed the original time crunch index for a national survey of American adults.

4 See Juliet Schor, *The Overworked American: The Unexpected Decline of Leisure* (New York: Basic-Books, 1991); M. Neal, J. Chapman, B. Ingersoll-Drayton, and A. Emlen, *Balancing Work and Caregiving for Children, Adults, and Elders* (Newbury Park CA: Sage, 1993); and A. Scharlach, "Caregiving and Employment: Competing or Complementary Roles?"(1994) 34 Gerontologist 378.

5 The Centre for Research on Families and Relationships at the University of Edinburgh has sponsored a wide range of courses, conferences, and publications. Current information, including papers presented at the Work-Life Balance Conference, which was held in July 2004, is available on their website at http://www.crfr.ac.uk. In the United States, the Alfred P. Sloan Foundation has committed ongoing funding for the Workforce, Workplace and Working Families Program, establishing six regional centres on working families. An up-to-date list of work and family publications is available from the Sloan Work and Family Research Network at http://www.bc.edu/wfnetwork. In Canada, the Centre for Families, Work and Well-being at the University of Guelph provides resources and links at http://www.worklifecanada.ca, and information on federal government policies in this area appears at http://www.hrsdc.gc.ca.

6 See, for example, H. Bohen and A. Viveros-Long, *Balancing Jobs and Family Life* (Temple, AZ: Temple University Press, 1981); Graham L. Staines and Joseph H. Pleck, *The Impact of Work Schedules on the Family* (Ann Arbor: Institute for Social Research, University of Michigan, 1983); Ann C. Crouter "Spillover from Family to Work: The Neglected Side of the Work-Family Interface" (1984) 37 Human Relations 425; and Joseph H. Pleck, *Working Wives/Working Husbands* (Thousand Oaks, CA: Sage Publications, 1985).

7 Kathleen Gerson, *Hard Choices: How Women Decide about Work, Career and Motherhood* (Berkeley, CA: University of California Press, 1985); Arlie Russell Hochschild, *The Second Shift: Working Parents and the Second Shift at Home* (New York: Avon Books, 1989); Harriet Presser, "Employment Schedules among Dual-Earner Spouses and the Division of Household Labor by Gender" (1994) 59 American Sociological Review 348; Rosalind C. Barnett and Caryl Rivers, *She Works/He Works: How Two-Income Families Are Healthier, Happier, and Better Off* (Cambridge, MA: Harvard University Press, 1996); Kerry Daly, *Families and Time: Keeping Pace in a Hurried Culture* (Thousand Oaks, CA: Sage, 1996); and Arlie Russell Hochschild, *The Time Bind* (New York: Harry Holt and Company, 1997).

8 See, for example, Rosanna Hertz and Nancy Marshall, *Working Families: The Transformation of the American Home* (Berkeley, CA: University of California Press, 2001); Phyllis Moen, ed., *It's about Time: Couples and Careers* (New York: Cornell University Press, 2003); Harriet Presser, *Working in a 24/7 Economy: Challenges for American Families* (New York: Russell Sage, 2003); Rosalind C. Barnett and Caryl Rivers, *Same Difference: How Gender Myths Are Hurting Our Relationships, Our Children, and Our Jobs* (New York: Basic Books, 2004); Cynthia Fuchs Epstein and Arne L. Kalleberg, eds., *Fighting for Time: Shifting Boundaries of Work and Social Life* (New York: Russell Sage Foundation, 2004); Barbara Schneider and Linda J. Waite, eds., *Being Together, Working Apart: Dual-Career Families and the Work-Life Balance* (Cambridge: Cambridge University Press, 2004); and Jerry A. Jacobs and Janice Fanning Madden, eds., *Mommies and Daddies on the Fast Track: Success of Parents in Demanding Professions*, special edition (November 2004) 596 Annals of the American Academy of Political and Social Science.

9 Jerry A. Jacobs and Kathleen Gerson, *The Time Divide: Work, Family, and Gender Inequality* (Cambridge, MA: Harvard University Press, 2004).

10 Data for 2003 indicate that Americans worked 1,792 hours on average, and the corresponding figure for Canadians was 1,718. These data are available online at Nation Master, http://www.nationmaster.com/graph-T/lab_hou_wor. For more detail on trends over time in the United States, see John P. Robinson and Geoffrey Godbey, *Time for Life: The Surprising Ways Americans Use Their Time* (University Park: Pennsylvania State University Press, 1997); and Jerry Jacobs and Kathleen Gerson, "Understanding Changes in American Working Time: A Synthesis" in Fuchs Epstein and Kalleberg, *supra* note 8 at 26.

11 See Linda Duxbury and Chris Higgins, *Work-Life Conflict in Canada in the New Millennium: A Status Report* (Ottawa: Public Health Agency of Canada, October 2003) at xii, available at http://www.phac-aspc.gc.ca/publicat/work-travail/report2/index.html.

12 Jacobs and Gerson, *The Time Divide, supra* note 9; and Jacobs and Gerson, "Understanding Changes in American Working Time," *supra* note 10.

13 Melissa A. Milkie and Pia Peltola, "Playing All the Roles: Gender and the Work-Family Balancing Act" (1999) 61(2) Journal of Marriage and the Family 476 at 488. Milkie and Peltola find that women's work-family balance is hindered by marital unhappiness and sacrifices at home.

14 For earlier treatments of these patterns, see J. Pahl and R. Pahl, *Managers and Their Wives* (Baltimore: Penguin Books, 1971) at 177; H. Papanek, "Men, Women, and Work: Reflections on the Two-Person Career" in J. Huber, ed., *Changing Women in a Changing Society* (Chicago: University of Chicago Press, 1973); and R. Abelda, *Glass Ceilings and Bottomless Pits: Women, Income and Poverty in Massachusetts* (Boston: Women's Statewide Legislation Network, 1994). For more recent findings, see Carroll Seron and Kerry Ferris, "Negotiating Professionalism: The Gendered Social Capital of Flexible Time" (1995) 22(1) Work and Occupations 22; and Duxbury and Higgins, *supra* note 11 at 13.

15 Suzanne M. Bianchi, "Maternal Employment and Time with Children: Dramatic Change or Surprising Continuity?" (2000) 37(4) Demography 401; and Annette Lareau, "Invisible

Inequalities: Class, Race and Child Rearing in Black Families and White Families" (2002) 67(5) American Sociological Review 747.

16 Jean E. Wallace, "Work-to-Nonwork Conflict among Married Male and Female Lawyers" (1999) 20 Journal of Organizational Behavior 797.

17 See Pitirim Sorokin, *Sociocultural Causality, Space, Time* (New York: Russell and Russell, 1943; reprinted 1964) at 158; and Edward T. Hall, *The Dance of Life: The Other Dimension of Time* (New York: Doubleday, 1985). These views are presented in more detail in Chapter 5 in this text.

18 See Barbara Adam, *Timewatch: The Social Analysis of Time* (Cambridge: Polity Press, 1995) at 12-42.

19 See Chapter 5 herein for a discussion of billable hours.

20 See John Hagan and Fiona Kay, *Gender in Practice: A Study of Lawyers' Lives* (Oxford: Oxford University Press, 1995) at 103; and Joan Brockman, *Gender in the Legal Profession: Fitting or Breaking the Mould* (Vancouver: UBC Press, 2001) at 34, for discussions of stress and long hours among lawyers in general. For a more explicit treatment of time in lawyers' lives, see Carroll Seron, *The Business of Practicing Law: The Work Lives of Solo and Small-Firm Attorneys* (Philadelphia: Temple University Press, 1996); and Cynthia Fuchs Epstein, Carroll Seron, Bonnie Oglensky, and Robert Sauté, *The Part-Time Paradox: Time Norms, Professional Lives, Family, and Gender* (New York and London: Routledge, 1999).

21 Robinson, *supra* note 3.

22 Judith Frederick, "Are You Time Crunched?" (1993) 31 Canadian Social Trends 6; and Janet Fast and Judith Frederick, "Working Arrangements and Time Stress" (1996) 43 Canadian Social Trends 17.

23 Cara Williams, "Sources of Workplace Stress" (2003) 15(3) Perspectives on Labour and Income 23; and Cara Williams, "Stress at Work" (2003) 70 Canadian Social Trends 7.

24 The 1998 General Social Survey was based on a stratified random sample of 11,000 Canadians, aged fifteen years and older. It contained questions that were similar to those incorporated in the 1992 General Social Survey.

25 Rod Beaujot and Robert Andersen, "Stress and Adult Health: Impact of Time Spent in Paid and Unpaid Work, and Its Division in Families," paper presented at the Conference on Work-Life Balance across the Life Course, International Sociological Association, University of Edinburgh, Edinburgh, 30 June 2003.

26 Janet Fast, Judith Frederick, Nancy Zukewich, and Sandra Franke, "The Time of Our Lives ..." (2001) 63 Canadian Social Trends 20.

27 Anna Kemeny, "Driven to Excel: A Portrait of Canada's Workaholics" (2002) 64 Canadian Social Trends 2.

28 Catherine Lee, Linda Duxbury, and Christopher Higgins, *Employed Mothers: Balancing Work and Family Life* (Ottawa: Canadian Centre for Management Development, 1994) at 10.

29 *Ibid*. at 24.

30 *Ibid*. at 19.

31 *Ibid*. at 11.

32 *Ibid*. at 28.

33 Robinson, *supra* note 3.

34 Frederick, *supra* note 22 at 7. Robinson's original index contained the items: "When I'm working long hours, I often feel guilty that I'm not at home" and "Sometimes I feel that my spouse doesn't know who I am any more." Canadian researchers removed these questions and substituted "I plan to slow down in the coming year" and "I would like to spend more time alone."

35 In response to an e-mail inquiry, Janet Fast indicated that their factor analysis of the time crunch index confirmed its strength as a valid measure of the underlying construct.

36 Analysis of the time crunch data from the 1992 General Social Survey on Time Use reveals a Cronbach's alpha of 0.852.

37 In the original index, Robinson designated respondents as "time crunched" if their scores were greater than three.

38 See SPSS for Windows at http://www.spss.com/spss/.

39 These findings are based on analyses of data from the 1992 and 1998 General Social

Surveys on Time Use. Women with paid work of thirty hours per week or more are considered to be employed full-time.

40 Tests of reliability established this index as a relatively strong measure of the underlying concept of time crunch stress (Cronbach's alpha = 0.676).

41 Lee, Duxbury, and Higgins, *supra* note 28 at 10.

42 The Toronto and London lawyers were interviewed a second time after four years and approximately half of the Ontario lawyers were interviewed three years after their initial interview.

43 Fifteen of the women with high time crunch scores had young children at home.

44 For more detail, see Shari L. Thurer, *The Myths of Motherhood: How Culture Reinvents the Good Mother* (New York: Houghton Mifflin, 1994) at xv.

45 One woman looked very surprised when I asked her for her mother's occupation. She said: "Well, of course, she was a mother."

46 See John R. Gillis, "Never Enough Time: Some Paradoxes of Modern Family Time(s)" in Kerry J. Daly, ed., *Minding the Time in Family Experience: Emerging Perspectives and Issues* (Oxford: Elsevier Science, 2001) 26.

47 Her latest e-mail reported the birth of her daughter, and her comments were heartwarming: "I found the transition [to motherhood] to be a little stressful, but now that I can communicate with her, and understand what her needs are, I tend to be less stressed about not knowing what to do, and laugh a lot more because she is ... well ... pretty funny ... I must say, after typing this out, I gotta tell you that I have a pretty good life."

48 Jacobs and Gerson, *The Time Divide, supra* note 9.

49 Gross, *supra* note 1 at 207.

50 Canadian Bar Association, *Touchstones for Change: Equality, Diversity and Accountability,* Report of the Canadian Bar Association Task Force Report on Gender Equality in the Legal Profession, chaired by the Honourable Bertha Wilson (Ottawa: Canadian Bar Association, 1993) at 101.

51 *Ibid.* at 104.

Chapter 5: Choreographing Daily Life

1 For a description of this lawyer's report of hostile treatment from senior partners on announcing her pregnancy, see Jean McKenzie Leiper, "It Was Like 'Wow'!: The Experience of Women Lawyers in a Profession Marked by Linear Careers" (1997) 9 Canadian Journal of Women and the Law 115 at 136-37. At the time of the first interview, she was at home with her infant son and she said that she would seek out a new firm at the end of the maternity leave.

2 See Barbara Adam, *Timewatch: The Social Analysis of Time* (Cambridge: Polity Press, 1995) at 19, for a discussion of the multidimensional character of time.

3 For a more detailed discussion of these contrasting images, I refer the reader to Barbara Adam's typology. *Ibid.* at 29-30.

4 Carmen Leccardi, "Rethinking Social Time: Feminist Perspectives" (1996) 5(2) Time and Society 169 at 181.

5 Carroll Seron and Kerry Ferris, "Negotiating Professionalism: The Gendered Social Capital of Flexible Time" (1995) 22(1) Work and Occupations 22 at 25.

6 *Ibid.* at 24.

7 Isaac Newton, *Philosophiae Naturalis Principia,* quoted in John Langone, *The Mystery of Time* (Washington: National Geographic, 2000) at 17.

8 Barbara Adam, *Time and Social Theory* (Cambridge: Polity, 1990) at 16; and Adam, *Timewatch, supra* note 2 at 29-42.

9 Edward T. Hall, *The Dance of Life: The Other Dimension of Time* (London: Doubleday, 1985) at 44-58.

10 Adam, *supra* note 2 at 15.

11 See Chapter 4 herein for a description of recent work in this area.

12 See Linda Marks, "Alternative Work Schedules in Law: It's about *Time!*" (1990) 35 New York Law School Law Review 361, for a discussion of work schedules in legal practice.

13 Keith M. Macdonald, *The Sociology of the Professions* (London: Sage, 1995) at 126-27. See Chapter 2 herein for more detail.

14 For one of the earliest attempts to describe time in sociological terms, see P.A. Sorokin and R.K. Merton, "Social Time: A Methodological and Functional Analysis" (1937) 42 American Journal of Sociology 615. Recent departures from these theories appear in Adam, *Time and Social Theory, supra* note 8; Adam, *Timewatch, supra* note 2; and Kerry Daly, *Families and Time: Keeping Pace in a Hurried Culture* (Thousand Oaks, CA: Sage, 1996).

15 See Sarah Rutherford, "Are You Going Home Already? The Long Hours Culture, Women Managers and Patriarchal Closure" (2001) 10(2/3) Time and Society 259.

16 Julia Kristeva, "Women's Time" in Toril Moi, ed., *The Kristeva Reader* (New York: Columbia University Press, 1986) 186 at 194.

17 *Ibid.* at 209.

18 *Ibid.* at 189.

19 *Ibid.* at 205.

20 Carol Watts, "Time and the Working Mother: Kristeva's 'Women's Time' Revisited" (1998) 91 (September/October) Radical Philosophy 6 at 13.

21 *Ibid.* at 14.

22 See, for example, Karin Jurczyk, "Time in Women's Everyday Lives: Between Self-Determination and Conflicting Demands" (1998) 7(2) Time and Society 286.

23 See Karen Davies, *Women, Time and the Weaving of the Strands of Everyday Life* (Aldershot: Avebury, 1990) at 17.

24 Jurczyk, *supra* note 22 at 287.

25 In a discussion of Kristeva's "women's time," Carmen Leccardi suggests that women's history has also been recorded in fragments drawn from their involvement in everyday tasks. Since these tasks have been seen as unimportant, women have often been rendered invisible. See Leccardi, *supra* note 4 at 173.

26 See Pamela Odih, "Gendered Time in the Age of Deconstruction" (1999) 8(1) Time and Society 9 at 17.

27 *Ibid.* at 20. Odih cites Davies' conceptualization of "relational time." For more detail, see Davies, *supra* note 23 at 15.

28 See Margaret Thornton, *Dissonance and Distrust: Women in the Legal Profession* (Melbourne: Oxford University Press Australia, 1996) at 36-37.

29 See Odih, *supra* note 26 at 18.

30 *Ibid.* at 30.

31 Adam describes the complexity of women's time beyond the formal workplace, emphasizing the heightened status enjoyed by work time and the relatively low status assigned to domestic time. See Adam, *supra* note 2 at 94.

32 Jurczyk, *supra* note 22 at 288-89.

33 For additional work in this area, see Arlie Russell Hochschild, *The Time Bind* (New York: Harry Holt and Company, 1997) at 51. Hochschild describes the lives of busy Americans, referring to their time as a form of scarce personal capital to be managed and invested.

34 Jurczyk, *supra* note 22 at 292.

35 Davies, *Women, Time and the Weaving, supra* note 23; and Karen Davies, "The Tensions between Process Time and Clock Time in Care-Work: The Example of Day Nurseries" (1994) 3(3) Time and Society 277.

36 Leccardi, *supra* note 4 at 181.

37 For more detail, see Daly, *supra* note 14 at 148.

38 Carroll Seron, *The Business of Practicing Law: The Work Lives of Solo and Small-Firm Attorneys* (Philadelphia: Temple University Press, 1996) at 38.

39 See Leccardi, *supra* note 4 at 180.

40 Simone de Beauvoir, *The Second Sex*, translated and edited by H.M. Parshley (New York: Vintage Books, 1974 [1949]).

41 Seron, *supra* note 38 at 44.

42 Jurczyk, *supra* note 22.

43 Cynthia Fuchs Epstein, Carroll Seron, Bonnie Oglensky, and Robert Sauté, *The Part-Time Paradox: Time Norms, Professional Lives, Family, and Gender* (New York and London: Routledge, 1999) at 25.

44 For more information, see Derek Lundy, "Far From the Padding Crowd" (2000) 24(4) Canadian Lawyer 34.
45 Susan Erlich Martin and Nancy C. Jurik, *Doing Justice, Doing Gender: Women in Law and Criminal Justice Occupations* (Thousand Oaks, CA: Sage, 1996) at 149.
46 See Michael H. Trotter, *Profit and the Practice of Law: What's Happened to the Legal Profession* (Athens: University of Georgia Press, 1997); and Lisa Lerman, "Blue-Chip Bilking: Regulation of Billing and Expense Fraud by Lawyers" (1999) 12(2) Georgetown Journal of Legal Ethics 205.
47 Ann Kerr, "Lawyers Trying to Slow Down the Meter" *Globe and Mail* (5 January 2004) at B10.
48 See Marks, *supra* note 12 at 363.
49 See Seron and Ferris, *supra* note 5, for a discussion of gender differences in access to time among lawyers practising in small firms.
50 Jurczyk, *supra* note 22 at 292.
51 For a more detailed treatment of this topic, see Jean McKenzie Leiper, "Gendered Views of Time and Time Crunch Stress: Women Lawyers' Responses to Professional and Personal Demands" in Kerry J. Daly, ed., *Minding the Time in Family Experience* (Oxford: Elsevier Science, 2001), 251.
52 See Julie Lesser, "The Balancing Act" (August 2004) Career Verdict: The Magazine for Law Students 23.
53 This woman had her third child four years later and, in her words, "retired from the practice of law" to stay home with her children. She returned to practice a year later and has been working a two-day week since taking that step. Her latest e-mail is very positive. She says: "Everything is terrific. It is a wonderful balance. I got my former nanny back full-time which gives me the flexibility I need."
54 See Seron and Ferris, *supra* note 5 at 25.
55 For more detailed discussion, see Marilyn J. Berger and Kari A. Robinson, "Women's Ghetto within the Legal Profession" (1992-93) 8 Wisconsin Women's Law Journal 71 at 99.
56 *Ibid.*
57 For more detail on this discussion, see McKenzie Leiper, *supra* note 1 at 136.
58 This woman has now established herself in a comfortable practice and has two small children. In her latest e-mail she says: "In the few years since we last spoke, things both professionally and personally have certainly changed for me, but definitely for the better!"
59 See Fuchs Epstein et al., *supra* note 43, for a discussion of the penalties of part-time practice and the possibilities for change. A range of alternative schedules appears in the Canadian Bar Association, *Touchstones for Change: Equality, Diversity and Accountability*, Task Force Report on Gender Equality in the Legal Profession, chaired by the Honourable Bertha Wilson (Ottawa: Canadian Bar Association, 1993) at 102-5.
60 Leccardi, *supra* note 4 at 180.

Chapter 6: Careers and Curricula Vitae
1 *Oxford English Reference Dictionary*, 2d ed. (Oxford: Oxford University Press, 1996) at 220.
2 *Ibid.* at 349.
3 H.L. Wilensky, "Careers, Lifestyles, and Social Integration" (1961) 12 International Social Science Journal 543 at 553.
4 See Barbara Adam, *Timewatch: The Social Analysis of Time* (Cambridge: Polity Press, 1995) at 21, for a discussion of timing and the multidimensional nature of time.
5 Audrey Collin, "Dancing to the Music of Time" in Audrey Collin and Richard A. Young, eds., *The Future of Career* (Cambridge: Cambridge University Press, 2000) 83 at 84.
6 *Ibid.* at 87-89.
7 Phyllis Moen and Patricia Roehling, *The Career Mystique: Cracks in the American Dream* (Lanham, MD: Rowman and Littlefield Publishers, 2005) at 12.
8 *Ibid.* at 8.
9 Michael B. Arthur, Kerr Inkson, and Judith K. Pringle, *The New Careers: Individual Action and Economic Change* (London: Sage, 1999) at 6-7.

10 For a discussion of the true curriculum vitae, see Jean McKenzie Leiper, "Expanding the Curriculum Vitae: Baby Boom Women Face Retirement," paper presented at the annual meeting of the Canadian Sociology and Anthropology Association, University of Western Ontario, London, Ontario, 31 May 2005.

11 Arthur, Inkson, and Pringle, *supra* note 9 at 17.

12 *Ibid.* at 33.

13 See Barbara Adam, *Time and Social Theory* (Cambridge: Polity, 1990) at 50, for a discussion of Newtonian time.

14 See Karen Davies, *Women, Time and the Weaving of the Strands of Everyday Life* (Aldershot: Avebury, 1990) at 31-32, for a discussion of gender differences in the representation of time and space.

15 Joan Gallos, "Exploring Women's Development: Implications for Career Theory, Practice, and Research" in Michael B. Arthur, D.T. Hall, and B.S. Lawrence, eds., *Handbook of Career Theory* (Cambridge: Cambridge University Press, 1989) 110.

16 Judi Marshall, "Re-Visioning Career Concepts: A Feminist Invitation" in Arthur, Hall, and Lawrence, *supra* note 15 at 282. Marshall's feminist model presents disrupted career paths as rich and rewarding alternatives to the classic career instead of deviant patterns.

17 Moen and Roehling, *supra* note 7 at 188-90. See also Sonya Williams and Shin-Kap Han, "Career Clocks: Forked Roads" in Phyllis Moen, ed., *It's about Time: Couples and Careers* (Cornell: Cornell University Press, 2003) 80.

18 Williams and Han, *supra* note 17 at 96.

19 Arthur, Inkson, and Pringle, *supra* note 9 at 17.

20 Cynthia Fuchs Epstein, Robert Sauté, Bonnie Oglensky, and Martha Gever, "Glass Ceilings and Open Doors: Women's Advancement in the Legal Profession" (1995) 64 Fordham Law Review 306.

21 Mary C. Noonan and Mary E. Corcoran, "The Mommy Track and Partnership: Temporary Delay or Dead End?" in Jerry A. Jacobs and Janice Fanning Madden, eds., *Mommies and Daddies on the Fast Track: Success of Parents in Demanding Professions*, special edition (November 2004) 596 Annals of the American Academy of Political and Social Science 130.

22 For more detail, see Joan Brockman, *Gender in the Legal Profession: Fitting or Breaking the Mould* (Vancouver: UBC Press, 2001) at 198; Canadian Bar Association, *Touchstones for Change: Equality, Diversity and Accountability*, Task Force Report on Gender Equality in the Legal Profession, chaired by the Honourable Bertha Wilson (Ottawa: Canadian Bar Association, 1993) at 51; Fiona M. Kay and John Hagan, "The Persistent Glass Ceiling: Gendered Inequalities in the Earnings of Lawyers" (1995) 46(2) British Journal of Sociology 279; Fiona M. Kay, "Flight from Law: A Competing Risks Model of Departures from Law Firms" (1997) 31(2) Law and Society Review 728; and Judy Steed, "Law Firms Suffer as Women Vote with Their Feet" *Toronto Star* (13 June 2005) at D1.

23 Michael Ornstein, *The Changing Face of the Ontario Legal Profession, 1971-2001* (Toronto: Law Society of Upper Canada, October 2004) at 32.

24 Cynthia Fuchs Epstein, Carroll Seron, Bonnie Oglensky, and Robert Sauté, *The Part-Time Paradox: Time Norms, Professional Lives, Family, and Gender* (New York and London: Routledge, 1999) at 24.

25 Jean E. Wallace, "The Benefits of Mentoring for Female Lawyers" (2001) 58 Journal of Vocational Behavior 366 at 384.

26 *Ibid.* at 385.

27 Heather Höpfl and Pat Hornby Atkinson, "The Future of Women's Career" in Audrey Collin and Richard A. Young, eds., *The Future of Career* (Cambridge: Cambridge University Press, 2000) 130 at 138.

28 Fuchs Epstein et al., *supra* note 24 at 6.

29 I have assigned pseudonyms to the women whose careers are described in this chapter and I have disguised some of the details to provide anonymity.

30 For a more detailed description of this perspective, see Williams and Han, *supra* note 17.

31 See Appendix, entitled "Where Are They Now?" for an updated report on the women in this study.

32 Marshall, *supra* note 16, at 285.

33 See Adam, *supra* note 4 at 22, for a discussion of temporality.

34 She is quoted in Chapter 4 herein under the subheading "The Power of Linear Time in Legal Practice."

35 Her description of this stage of her life appears in Chapter 4 herein under the subheading "I Worry That I Don't Spend Enough Time with Family and Friends."

36 In effect, she had reduced her billable hours and taken a lower share of the company profits.

37 Many of these women had delayed childbirth and, like Marilyn, had had only one child, but several women had three or four children.

38 Mary Blair-Loy, *Competing Devotions: Career and Family among Women Executives* (Cambridge, MA: Harvard University Press, 2003).

39 For a thoughtful commentary on this phenomenon, see John Ibbitson, "When a Woman Chooses Her Family over Her Job" *Globe and Mail* (29 April 2002) at A13.

40 Pamela Stone and Meg Lovejoy, "Fast-Track Women and the 'Choice' To Stay Home" in Jacobs and Fanning Madden, *supra* note 21 at 62.

41 For more detail, see Ann Kerr, "In-House Legal Gigs Gain Greater Prestige, Pay" *Globe and Mail* (21 June 2004) at B17.

42 Five of these women had one child and the remaining two had two children. They had all postponed their families until after they had attained partnership status.

43 Her description of a typical working day appears in the second paragraph of Chapter 5 herein.

44 Her comments on the failure of law firms to accommodate women's needs appear in Chapter 5 herein, under the subheading "Women's Attempts to Control Their Time: Shattered Illusions."

45 Marshall, *supra* note 16.

46 It seems more than coincidental that several of the most career-oriented women in this study possessed well-developed senses of humour that had served them well in difficult situations. The interviews with Sheila, Marilyn, Ellen, and Jenny were very entertaining.

47 This is the woman quoted at the beginning of Chapter 5 herein as she described her struggle with the lack of time in her busy life.

48 See Fiona Cownie, *Legal Academics: Culture and Identities* (Oxford and Portland: Hart Publishing, 2004) at 187, for a discussion of identity in the legal profession.

49 Mary Blair-Loy, *supra* note 38.

50 The italicized portion of this quotation appears in Chapter 2 herein, but it is such a powerful statement of identity confusion that I have repeated it here.

51 In a way, Claire's position on the career continuum is misplaced, but her departure from practice occurred after I had written the initial draft of this chapter. I have decided not to move her to the exit end of the continuum because her career is an excellent example of the twisted paths that women often experience. In addition, I have a feeling that she may return to legal practice one day, after her children have grown up and her life has become less stressful.

52 Marshall, *supra* note 16 at 284.

53 For a discussion of the career implications of part-time practice, see Fuchs Epstein et al., *supra* note 24 at 55-74.

54 She is very devoted to her son. I interviewed her in her office during the evening and my notes indicate that her husband and son arrived during the interview. She got some dog treats out of the cupboard so her son could feed the dog at home, saying to me: "I'm the only criminal lawyer in [her community] with dog food and diapers at the office."

55 Her description of this process appears in Chapter 5 herein under the subheading "Women's Attempts to Control Their Time: Shattered Illusions."

56 Apparently, she resisted the urge to change careers because she is still practising in the same location and has continued to tailor her working day around her children's schedules.

57 A twelfth woman has retired and one woman died in July 2006.

58 See Appendix, entitled "Where Are They Now?"
59 Several other women gave the same reason for avoiding medical school.
60 Moen and Roehling, *supra* note 7 at 197.
61 Steed, *supra* note 22.
62 Höpfl and Hornby Atkinson, *supra* note 27 at 138.
63 Jenny is one of these women. After many years of mutual care and concern for their children, she and her husband have decided to divorce.
64 See Chapter 3 herein for a discussion of legal culture and access to social capital.
65 See Noonan and Corcoran, *supra* note 21 at 146-49.
66 For more detail, see Jean McKenzie Leiper, "It Was Like 'Wow'!: The Experience of Women Lawyers in a Profession Marked by Linear Careers" (1997) 9 Canadian Journal of Women and the Law 115.

Chapter 7: Cracking the Codes
1 Kevin Marron, "Equality Struggle Remains in Law" *Globe and Mail* (19 April 2004) at B15.
2 Richard L. Abel, *English Lawyers between Market and State: The Politics of Professionalism* (Oxford: Oxford University Press, 2003) at 128.
3 For more information see Ruby Heap, Wyn Millar, and Elizabeth Smyth, eds., *Learning to Practise: Professional Education in Historical and Contemporary Perspective* (Ottawa: University of Ottawa Press, 2005) at 13.
4 See Gwen Moore, "Comment: Mommies and Daddies on the Fast Track in Other Wealthy Nations" in Jerry A. Jacobs and Janice Fanning Madden, eds., *Mommies and Daddies on the Fast Track: Success of Parents in Demanding Professions*, special edition (November 2004) 596 Annals of the American Academy of Political and Social Science 208.
5 See Erika Rackley, "Reassessing Portia: The Iconic Potential of Shakespeare's Woman Lawyer" (2003) 11 Feminist Legal Studies 25 at 40.
6 For more detail, see Magali Sarfatti Larson, *The Rise of Professionalism: A Sociological Analysis* (Berkeley: University of California Press, 1977); and Keith M. Macdonald, *The Sociology of the Professions* (London: Sage, 1995).
7 Lani Guinier, Michelle Fine, and Jane Balin, *Becoming Gentlemen* (Boston: Beacon Press, 1997); and Robert Granfield, "Contextualizing the Different Voice: Women, Occupational Goals, and Legal Education" (1994) 16(1) Law and Policy 1.
8 See Shirley Neuman, "Provost's Study of Accessibility and Career Choice in the Faculty of Law," 24 February 2003, available at http://www.provost.utoronto.ca/English/Reports.html; and Alan J.C. King, Wendy K. Warren, and Sharon R. Miklas, *Study of Accessibility to Ontario Law Schools*, Executive Summary of the Report, October 2004, Law Foundation of Ontario and the Law Society of Upper Canada, available at http://www.osgoode.yorku.ca/pdf/ExecutiveSummary.pdf. In 2005, fees at the University of Toronto Law School were the highest among Ontario law schools at $15,872, followed by Osgoode Hall with fees of $11,330. For more detail, see Bar Talk, "Here's Your Law Diploma – and a Bankruptcy Expert" *Globe and Mail* (11 January 2006) at B10.
9 Moore, *supra* note 4 at 211.
10 See Barbara Adam, *Timewatch: The Social Analysis of Time* (Cambridge: Polity Press, 1995) at 14.
11 For a discussion of time as social capital, see Carroll Seron and Kerry Ferris, "Negotiating Professionalism: The Gendered Social Capital of Flexible Time" (1995) 22(1) Work and Occupations 22 at 25.
12 Carmen Leccardi, "Rethinking Social Time: Feminist Perspectives" (1996) 5(2) Time and Society 169 at 180.
13 Phyllis Moen and Patricia Roehling, *The Career Mystique: Cracks in the American Dream* (Lanham, MD: Rowman and Littlefield Publishers, 2005) at 184.
14 Joan Gallos, "Exploring Women's Development: Implications for Career Theory, Practice, and Research" in Michael B. Arthur, D.T. Hall, and B.S. Lawrence, eds., *Handbook of Career Theory* (Cambridge: Cambridge University Press, 1989), 110; and Judi Marshall, "Re-Visioning Career Concepts: A Feminist Invitation" in Arthur, Hall, and Lawrence (*ibid.*) at 282.

15 See Cynthia Fuchs Epstein, Robert Sauté, Bonnie Oglensky, and Martha Gever, "Glass Ceilings and Open Doors: Women's Advancement in the Legal Profession" (1995) 64 Fordham Law Review 306; Fiona M. Kay and Joan Brockman, "Barriers to Gender Equality in the Canadian Legal Establishment" (2000) 8 Feminist Legal Studies 169 at 180-86; Fiona M. Kay and John Hagan, "Cultivating Clients in the Competition for Partnership: Gender and the Organizational Restructuring of Law Firms in the 1990s" (1999) 33(3) Law and Society Review 517 at 525; and Mary C. Noonan and Mary E. Corcoran, "The Mommy Track and Partnership: Temporary Delay or Dead End?" in Jacobs and Fanning Madden, *supra* note 4 at 130.

16 See also Sonya Williams and Shin-Kap Han, "Career Clocks: Forked Roads" in Phyllis Moen, ed., *It's about Time: Couples and Careers* (Cornell: Cornell University Press, 2003), 80.

17 See Heather Höpfl and Pat Hornby Atkinson, "The Future of Women's Career" in Audrey Collin and Richard A. Young, eds., *The Future of Career* (Cambridge: Cambridge University Press, 2000) 130 at 138.

18 The phrase assigns a Zen-like meaning to time, a pause for breath that runs counter to all the accepted images of efficiency and career timing.

19 See John Ibbitson, "When a Woman Chooses Her Family over Her Job" *Globe and Mail* (29 April 2002).

20 See Pamela Stone and Meg Lovejoy, "Fast-Track Women and the 'Choice' To Stay Home" in Jacobs and Fanning Madden, *supra* note 4; and Pamela Stone, *Both Sides Now: Why Career Women Are Quitting Jobs and Heading Home* (working title) (University of California Press, forthcoming).

21 Tuition fees for Ontario's professional schools began to rise dramatically in the late 1990s, and, while the full impact of these increases has yet to be determined, an interesting pattern has taken shape. According to Statistics Canada's analysis of the National Graduates Survey (1995-2000), students whose parents held graduate or professional degrees moved into professional programs in increasing numbers, and enrolment levels also rose for students whose parents lacked post-secondary degrees. Students with "middle-educated parents" (that is, those with post-secondary degrees below a graduate degree) were less likely to enter professional programs during this period. The authors of the report speculate that these differences reflect access to funding, suggesting that students from the middle group did not qualify for as much funding as their counterparts from less-educated families. For more information, see Statistics Canada, "Study: Access to Professional Programs amid the Deregulation of Tuition Fees, 1995 to 2002," *The Daily* (27 September 2005), http://www.statcan.ca/Daily/English/050927/d050927a.htm.

22 Salaries for in-house counsel are gradually becoming more attractive. Respondents in the latest national survey reported average salaries ranging from $114,000 to just over $223,000 (independent of perks such as company cars, laptop computers, and pension plans). See Kirsten McMahon, "Corporate Dividends: The *Canadian Lawyer* In-House Counsel Compensation Survey" (2004) 28(5) Canadian Lawyer 20.

23 See Kirsten McMahon, "The 2004 *Canadian Lawyer* Compensation Survey" (2004) 28(11) Canadian Lawyer 35 at 36.

24 See Kirsten McMahon, "The 2005 *Canadian Lawyer* Compensation Survey" (2005) 29(11) Canadian Lawyer 26 at 28.

25 See Abel, *supra* note 2, for an excellent discussion of elite practices in the British legal profession.

26 Constance Backhouse, *Colour-Coded: A Legal History of Racism in Canada, 1900-1950* (Toronto: University of Toronto Press for the Osgoode Society for Canadian Legal History, 1999).

27 Joanne St. Lewis, "Beyond the Confinement of Gender: Locating the Space of Legalized Existence of Racialized Women" in Radha Jhappan, ed., *Women's Legal Strategies in Canada* (Toronto: University of Toronto Press, 2002) 295.

28 Backhouse, *supra* note 26 at 3-4.

29 See Fiona M. Kay, Cristi Masuch, and Paula Curry, *Diversity and Change: The Contemporary Legal Profession in Ontario* (Toronto: Law Society of Upper Canada, September 2004) at 9-10, for a discussion of the evolution of language around the concept of "race."

30 One woman was Aboriginal and two others were, in part, Aboriginal. One woman was Indian and White and another was Chinese and White.
31 Granfield, *supra* note 7.
32 Backhouse, *supra* note 26 at 7.
33 They used disproportionate random sampling to ensure that lawyers from racialized/ethic communities would be represented in the survey, and they designed nine response categories to differentiate between members of these communities. See Kay, Masuch, and Curry, *supra* note 29 at 10-13.
34 *Ibid.* at 38-40 and 113-18.
35 See Radha Jhappan, "Introduction: Feminist Adventures in Law" in Jhappan, *supra* note 27 at 3; and Lise Gotell, "Towards a Democratic Practice of Feminist Litigation? LEAF's Changing Approach to *Charter* Equality" in Jhappan, *supra* note 27 at 135.
36 For more information, see Akitsiraq Law School, http://www.law.uvic.ca/akits.html.
37 See Michael Valpy, "Supreme Court Appointments" *Globe and Mail* (25 August 2004) at A6. For biographical information about Supreme Court of Canada justices, see http://www.scc-csc.gc/aboutcourt/justices.

Bibliography

Abbott, Andrew. *The System of the Professions* (Chicago: University of Chicago Press, 1988).

Abel, Richard L. *English Lawyers between Market and State: The Politics of Professionalism* (Oxford: Oxford University Press, 2003).

Abelda, R. *Glass Ceilings and Bottomless Pits: Women, Income and Poverty in Massachusetts* (Boston: Women's Statewide Legislation Network, 1994).

Adam, Barbara. *Timewatch: The Social Analysis of Time* (Cambridge: Polity Press, 1995).

–. *Time and Social Theory* (Cambridge: Polity, 1990).

Allen, Max. *Moral Fibre: Dress Codes from Purity to Wickedness* (exhibition) (Toronto: Textile Museum of Canada, 17 July 2002 – 19 January 2003).

Alphonso, Caroline. "Close Tuition Gap, Law Schools Ask" *Globe and Mail* (22 December 2005) A13.

Anderson, Ellen. *Judging Bertha Wilson: Law as Large As Life* (Toronto: University of Toronto Press, 2001).

Anderssen, Erin, and Michael Valpy. "Face the Nation: Canada Remade" *Globe and Mail* (7 June 2003) A10.

Angel, Marina. "Women in Legal Education: What It's Like to Be Part of a First Wave or the Case of the Disappearing Women" (1988) 6 Temple Law Review 799.

Arnott Oppen, Alice. *Shakespeare: Listening to the Women* (Henley Beach, Australia: Seaview Press, 1999).

Arthur, Michael B., Kerr Inkson, and Judith K. Pringle. *The New Careers: Individual Action and Economic Change* (London: Sage, 1999).

Arthurs, Harry A. (chair). *Law and Learning: Report to the Social Sciences and Humanities Research Council of Canada by the Consultative Group on Research and Education in Law* (Ottawa: Social Sciences and Humanities Research Council of Canada, 1983) [Arthurs Report].

–, and Robert Kreklewich. "The Legal Profession in the New Economy" (1996) 34(1) Osgoode Hall Law Journal 1.

Backhouse, Constance. *Colour-Coded: A Legal History of Racism in Canada, 1900-1950* (Toronto: University of Toronto Press for the Osgoode Society for Canadian Legal History, 1999).

–. *Petticoats and Prejudice: Women and Law in Nineteenth-Century Canada* (Toronto: Women's Press for the Osgoode Society for Canadian Legal History, 1991).

–. "Revisiting the *Arthurs Report* Twenty Years Later" (2003) 18(1) Canadian Journal of Law and Society 37.

Baker, J.H. "History of the Gowns Worn at the English Bar" (1975) 9 Costume 15.

–. "A History of English Judges' Robes" (1978) 12 Costume 27.

Banks, Taunya. "Gender Bias in the Classroom" (1988) 38 Journal of Legal Education 137.

Bar Talk. "Here's Your Law Diploma - and a Bankruptcy Expert" *Globe and Mail* (11 January 2006) B10.

Barnett, Rosalind C., and Caryl Rivers. *Same Difference: How Gender Myths Are Hurting Our Relationships, Our Children, and Our Jobs* (New York: Basic Books, 2004).

–. *She Works/He Works: How Two-Income Families Are Healthier, Happier, and Better Off* (Cambridge, MA: Harvard University Press, 1996).

Bartky, Sandra Lee. "Foucault, Femininity, and Patriarchal Power" in Katie Conboy, Nadia Medina, and Sarah Stanbury, eds., *Writing on the Body: Female Embodiment and Feminist Theory* (New York: Columbia University Press, 1997) 129.

Beaujot, Rod, and Robert Andersen. "Stress and Adult Health: Impact of Time Spent in Paid and Unpaid Work, and Its Division in Families," paper presented at the Conference on Work-Life Balance across the Life Course, International Sociological Association, University of Edinburgh, Edinburgh, 30 June 2003.

Beauvoir, Simone de. *The Second Sex,* translated and edited by H.M. Parshley (New York: Vintage Books, 1974 [1949]).

Becker, Gary. "Human Capital, Effort and the Sexual Division of Labour" (1985) 3 (Supplement) Journal of Labor Economics S33.

–. *Human Capital* (New York: Columbia University Press, 1994).

Becker, Mary. "Questions Women (and Men) Should Ask When Selecting a Law School" (1997) 11(3) Wisconsin Women's Law Journal 417.

Berger, Marilyn J., and Kari A. Robinson. "Women's Ghetto within the Legal Profession" (1992-93) 8 Wisconsin Women's Law Journal 71.

Berger Morello, Karen. *The Invisible Bar: The Woman Lawyer in America 1638 to the Present* (New York: Random House, 1986).

Berggren, Paula. "The Woman's Part: Female Sexuality as Power in Shakespeare's Plays" in Carolyn Ruth Swift Lenz, Gayle Green, and Carol Thomas Neely, eds., *The Woman's Part: Feminist Criticism of Shakespeare* (Urbana: University of Illinois Press, 1980) 17.

Bianchi, Suzanne M. "Maternal Employment and Time with Children: Dramatic Change or Surprising Continuity?" (2000) 37(4) Demography 401.

Black, Rosie. "Schools of Thought" (1997) 21(1) Canadian Lawyer 17.

Blair-Loy, Mary. *Competing Devotions: Career and Family among Women Executives* (Cambridge, MA: Harvard University Press, 2003).

–, and Amy S. Wharton. "Mothers in Finance: Striving and Thriving" in Jerry A. Jacobs and Janice Fanning Madden, eds., *Mommies and Daddies on the Fast Track: Success of Parents in Demanding Professions,* special edition (November 2004) 596 Annals of the American Academy of Political and Social Science 151.

Blau, Peter, and Otis Dudley Duncan. *The American Occupational Structure* (New York: Wiley, 1967).

Blom, Joost. "Looking Ahead in Canadian Law School Education" (1999) 33(1) UBC Law Review 7.

Bohen, H., and A. Viveros-Long. *Balancing Jobs and Family Life* (Temple, AZ: Temple University Press, 1981).

Bourdieu, Pierre. *Distinction: A Social Critique of the Judgement of Taste* (London: Routledge and Kegan Paul, 1979).

–. *Outline of a Theory of Practice* (Cambridge: Cambridge University Press, 1977).

Boyd, Susan B. "Can Law School Challenge the Public/Private Divide? Women, Work and Family" (1996) 15 Windsor Yearbook of Access to Justice 161.

–. "Challenging the Public/Private Divide: An Overview" in Susan B. Boyd, ed., *Challenging the Public/Private Divide: Feminism, Law and Public Policy* (Toronto: University of Toronto Press, 1997) 3.

Boyle, Christine. "Teaching Law as If Women Really Mattered, Or, What About the Washrooms?" (1986) 2 Canadian Journal of Women and the Law 96.

Brockman, Joan. "Exclusionary Tactics: The History of Women and Minorities in the Legal Profession in British Columbia" in Hamar Foster and John P.S. McLaren, eds., *Essays in the History of Canadian Law,* volume 6, *British Columbia and the Yukon* (Toronto: Osgoode Society for Canadian Legal History, 1995) 508.

–. "Gender Bias in the Legal Profession: A Survey of Members of the Law Society of British Columbia" (1992) 17 Queen's Law Journal 91.

–. *Gender in the Legal Profession: Fitting or Breaking the Mould* (Vancouver: UBC Press, 2001).

–. "Leaving the Practice of Law: The Wherefores and the Whys" (1994) 32(1) Alberta Law Review 116.

–. "The Use of Self-Regulation to Curb Discrimination and Sexual Harassment in the Legal Profession" (1997) 35(2) Osgoode Hall Law Journal 209.

–. "'A Wild Feminist at Her Raving Best': Reflections on Studying Gender Bias in the Legal Profession" (2000) 28(1/2) Resources for Feminist Research 61.

Brooks, Kim, and Debra Parkes. "Queering Legal Education: A Project of Theoretical Discovery" (2004) 27 Harvard Women's Law Journal 89.

Butler, Judith. *Bodies That Matter: On the Discursive Limits of "Sex"* (New York and London: Routledge, 1993).

Cahn, Naomi R. "Styles of Lawyering" (1992) 43 Hastings Law Journal 1039.

Calhoun, Emily. "Thinking Like a Lawyer" (1984) 34 Journal of Legal Education 507.

Canadian Bar Association. *Touchstones for Change: Equality, Diversity and Accountability,* Report of the Canadian Bar Association Task Force on Gender Equality in the Legal Profession. Justice Bertha Wilson (chair) (Ottawa: Canadian Bar Association, 1993).

Carrington, Paul, and James Conley. "The Alienation of Law Students" (1989) 75 Michigan Law Review 887.

Cassels, Jamie, and Maureen Maloney. "Critical Legal Education: Paralysis with a Purpose" (1989) 4 Canadian Journal of Law and Society 99.

Catalyst Research. *Women in Law: Making the Case* (New York and Toronto: Catalyst, 2001).

–. *Beyond a Reasonable Doubt: Creating Opportunities for Better Balance* (Toronto: Catalyst, 2005).

Chartrand, Larry, Dolores Blonde, Michael Cormier, Kai Hildebrandt, Christopher Wydrzynski, and Edward Czilli. "Law Students, Law Schools, and Their Graduates" (2001) 20 Windsor Yearbook of Access to Justice 211.

Clayborne Park, Clara. "As We Like It: How a Girl Can Be Smart and Still Popular" in Carolyn Ruth Swift Lenz, Gayle Green, and Carol Thomas Neely, eds., *The Woman's Part: Feminist Criticism of Shakespeare* (Urbana: University of Illinois Press, 1980), 100.

Collier, Richard, "(Un)Sexy Bodies: The Making of Professional Legal Masculinities" in Clare McGlynn, ed., *Legal Feminisms: Theory and Practice* (Aldershot: Ashgate/Dartmouth, 1998) 21.

Collin, Audrey. "Dancing to the Music of Time" in Audrey Collin and Richard A. Young, eds., *The Future of Career* (Cambridge: Cambridge University Press, 2000) 83.

Coltrane, Scott. "Elite Careers and Family Commitment: It's (Still) about Gender" in Jerry A. Jacobs and Janice Fanning Madden, eds., *Mommies and Daddies on the Fast Track: Success of Parents in Demanding Professions,* special edition (November 2004) 596 Annals of the American Academy of Political and Social Science 214.

Cooper, Jeremy, and Louise C. Trubek. *Educating for Justice: Social Values and Legal Education* (Aldershot: Ashgate, 1997).

Cownie, Fiona, ed. *The Law School – Global Issues, Local Questions* (Aldershot: Darmouth Publishing Company, 1999).

–. *Legal Academics: Culture and Identities* (Oxford and Portland: Hart Publishing, 2004).

Crouter, Ann C. "Spillover from Family to Work: The Neglected Side of the Work-Family Interface" (1984) 37 Human Relations 425.

Daly, Kerry J. *Families and Time: Keeping Pace in a Hurried Culture* (Thousand Oaks: Sage, 1996).

–, ed. *Minding the Time in Family Experience* (Oxford: Elsevier Science, 2001).

Daniels, Ronald J. "Let's Reach for the Gold in Higher Education" *Globe and Mail* (1 March 2002) A15.

Davies, Karen. "The Tensions between Process Time and Clock Time in Care-Work: The Example of Day Nurseries" (1994) 3(3) Time and Society 277.

–. *Women, Time and the Weaving of the Strands of Everyday Life* (Aldershot: Avebury, 1990).

Dingwall, Robert, and Philip S.C. Lewis. *The Sociology of the Professions: Lawyers, Doctors, and Others* (London: Macmillan, 1983).

Dowsett Johnston, Ann. "Judging Canadian Law Schools" (1997) 110 Maclean's 13.

Drachman, Virginia. G., and the Equity Club. *Women Lawyers and the Origins of Professional Identity in America: The Letters of the Equity Club, 1887 to 1890* (Ann Arbor: University of Michigan Press, 1993).

Duxbury, Linda, and Chris Higgins. *Work-Life Conflict in Canada in the New Millennium: A Status Report* (Ottawa: Public Health Agency of Canada, October 2003).

Economides, Kim. "Cynical Legal Studies" in Jeremy Cooper and Louise C. Trubek, eds., *Educating for Justice: Social Values and Legal Education* (Aldershot: Dartmouth Publishing Company, 1997) 26.

Entwistle, Joanne. "The Dressed Body" in Joanne Entwistle and Elizabeth Wilson, eds., *Body Dressing* (Oxford: Berg, 2001) 37.

Erlich Martin, Susan, and Nancy C. Jurik. *Doing Justice, Doing Gender: Women in Law and Criminal Justice Occupations* (Thousand Oaks, CA: Sage Publications, 1996).

Fast, Janet, and Judith Frederick. "Working Arrangements and Time Stress" (1996) 43 Canadian Social Trends 17.

–, Judith Frederick, Nancy Zukewich, and Sandra Franke. "The Time of Our Lives ..." (2001) 63 Canadian Social Trends 20.

Feldthusen, Bruce. "The Gender Wars: 'Where the Boys Are'" (1990) 4 Canadian Journal of Women and the Law 66.

Fineman, Martha Albertson, and Isabel Karpin, eds. *Mothers in Law: Feminist Theory and the Legal Regulation of Motherhood* (New York: Columbia University Press, 1995).

–, and Nancy Sweet Thomadsen, eds. *At the Boundaries of Law: Feminism and Legal Theory* (New York: Routledge, 1991).

Foucault, Michel. *Discipline and Punish: The Birth of the Prison* (New York: Vintage Books, 1979).

Fraser, Robert L., ed. *Provincial Justice: Upper Canadian Legal Portraits from the Dictionary of Canadian Biography* (Toronto and Buffalo: University of Toronto Press for the Osgoode Society for Canadian Legal History, 1992).

Frederick, Judith. "Are You Time Crunched?" (1993) 31 Canadian Social Trends 6.

Freidson, Elliot. *The Profession of Medicine* (New York: Dodd, Mead and Company, 1970).

–. *Professionalism: The Third Logic* (Chicago: University of Chicago Press, 2001).

Fuchs Epstein, Cynthia. *Deceptive Distinctions: Sex, Gender, and the Social Order* (New Haven, CT: Yale University Press, 1988).

–. *Women in Law*, 2nd edition (Urbana and Chicago: University of Illinois Press, 1993).

–, and Arne L. Kalleberg, eds. *Fighting for Time: Shifting Boundaries of Work and Social Life* (New York: Russell Sage Foundation, 2004).

–, Robert Sauté, Bonnie Oglensky, and Martha Gever. "Glass Ceilings and Open Doors: Women's Advancement in the Legal Profession" (1995) 64 Fordham Law Review 306.

–, Carroll Seron, Bonnie Oglensky, and Robert Sauté. *The Part-Time Paradox: Time Norms, Professional Lives, Family, and Gender* (New York and London: Routledge, 1999).

Gallos, Joan. "Exploring Women's Development: Implications of Career Theory, Practice, and Research" in M. Arthur, D. Hall, and B. Lawrence, eds., *Handbook of Career Theory* (Cambridge: Cambridge University Press, 1989) 110.

Garber, Marjorie. *Vested Interests: Cross-Dressing and Cultural Anxiety* (New York: Routledge, 1997).

Gellner, E. *Plough, Sword and Book* (London: Collins Harvill, 1988).

Gerarda Brown, Jennifer. "'To Give Them Countenance': The Case for a Women's Law School" (1999) 22 (Spring) Harvard Women's Law Journal 1.

Gerson, Kathleen. *Hard Choices: How Women Decide about Work, Career and Motherhood* (Berkeley, CA: University of California Press, 1985).

Gidney, Bob. "'Madame How' and 'Lady Why': Learning to Practise in Historical Perspective" in Ruby Heap, Wyn Millar, and Elizabeth Smyth, eds., *Learning to Practise: Professional Education in Historical and Contemporary Perspective* (Ottawa: University of Ottawa Press, 2005) 13.

Gidney, R.D., and W.P.J. Millar. *Professional Gentlemen: The Professions in Nineteenth-Century Ontario* (Toronto: University of Toronto Press, 1994).

Gilligan, Carol. *In a Different Voice: Psychological Theory and Women's Development* (Cambridge, MA: Harvard University Press, 1982).

Gillis, John R. "Never Enough Time: Some Paradoxes of Modern Family Time(s)" in Kerry J. Daly, ed., *Minding the Time in Family Experience: Emerging Perspectives and Issues* (Oxford: Elsevier Science, 2001) 26.

Golding, Martin P., and William A. Edmundson. *The Blackwell Guide to the Philosophy of Law and Legal Theory* (Malden, MA: Blackwell Publishing, 2005).

Gotell, Lise. "Towards a Democratic Practice of Feminist Litigation?: LEAF's Changing Approach to *Charter* Equality" in Radha Jhappan, ed., *Women's Legal Strategies in Canada* (Toronto: University of Toronto Press, 2002) 135.

Granfield, Robert. "Contextualizing the Different Voice: Women, Occupational Goals, and Legal Education" (1994) 16(1) Law and Policy 1.

–. *Making Elite Lawyers* (New York: Routledge, 1992).

Greenwood, E. "The Attributes of a Profession" (1957) 2 Social Work 44.

Gross, Morris A. "Can We Re-humanize the Practice of Law?" (1990) 24 Law Society Gazette 205.

Guinier, Lani, Michelle Fine, and Jane Balin. *Becoming Gentlemen* (Boston: Beacon Press, 1997).

Hagan, John, and Fiona Kay. *Gender in Practice: A Study of Lawyers' Lives* (New York: Oxford University Press, 1995).

–. "Hierarchy in Practice: The Significance of Gender in Ontario Law Firms" in Carol Wilton, ed., *Inside the Law: Canadian Law Firms in Historical Perspective* (Toronto: Osgoode Society for Canadian Legal History by University of Toronto Press, 1996) 530.

Hall, Edward T. *The Dance of Life: The Other Dimension of Time* (London: Doubleday, 1985).

Halliday, Terence C. *Beyond Monopoly: Lawyers, State Crises, and Professional Empowerment* (Chicago: University of Chicago Press, 1987).

Harbage, Alfred, ed. *William Shakespeare: The Complete Works* (New York: Viking Press, 1986).

Harding, Katherine. "Work-Life Conflict Rampant, Study Says" *Globe and Mail* (15 January 2003) C10.

Hargreaves-Mawdsley, W.N. *A History of Legal Dress in Europe* (Oxford: Clarendon Press, 1963).

Harrington, Mona. "Is Time-out for Family Unprofessional?" (1997) 33(2) Trial 70.

–. *Women Lawyers: Rewriting the Rules* (New York: Alfred A. Knopf, 1994).

Harvey, John. *Men in Black* (Chicago: University of Chicago Press, 1995).

Heap, Ruby, Wyn Millar, and Elizabeth Smyth, eds. *Learning to Practise: Professional Education in Historical and Contemporary Perspective* (Ottawa: University of Ottawa Press, 2005).

Hertz, Rosanna, and Nancy Marshall. *Working Families: The Transformation of the American Home* (Berkeley: University of California Press, 2001).

Hinze, Susan W. "Women, Men, Career and Family in the US Young Physician Labor Force" in Nancy Ditomaso and Corinne Post, eds., *Diversity in the Workforce, Research in the Sociology of Work*, vol. 14 (Oxford: Elsevier, JAI, 2004) 185.

Hochschild, Arlie Russell. *The Second Shift: Working Parents and the Second Shift at Home* (New York: Avon Books, 1989).

–. *The Time Bind* (New York: Henry Holt and Company, 1997).

Homer, Suzanne, and Louise Schwartz. "Admitted, But Not Accepted: Outsiders Take an Inside Look at Law School" (1989-90) 5 Berkeley Women's Law Journal 1.

Höpfl, Heather, and Pat Hornby Atkinson. "The Future of Women's Career" in Audrey Collin and Richard A. Young, eds., *The Future of Career* (Cambridge: Cambridge University Press, 2000) 130.

Hunter, Alfred A. *Class Tells: On Social Inequality in Canada*, 2d ed. (Toronto: Butterworths, 1986).

Ibbitson, John. "When a Woman Chooses Her Family over Her Job" *Globe and Mail* (29 April 2002) A13.

Immen, Wallace. "Ease the Stress When Crunch Time Strikes" *Globe and Mail* (4 May 2005) C3.

Jabbari, David. "Reform of Undergraduate Legal Education" in Richard Buckley, ed., *Legal Structures: Boundary Issues between Legal Categories* (Chichester: John Wiley and Sons, 1996).

Jack, Rand, and Dana Crowley Jack. *Moral Vision and Professional Decisions: The Changing Values of Men and Women Lawyers* (Cambridge: Cambridge University Press, 1989).

Jacobs, Jerry A., and Janice Fanning Madden, eds. *Mommies and Daddies on the Fast Track: Success of Parents in Demanding Professions*, special edition (November 2004) 596 Annals of the American Academy of Political and Social Science.

–, and Kathleen Gerson. *The Time Divide: Work, Family, and Gender Inequality* (Cambridge, MA: Harvard University Press, 2004).

–. "Understanding Changes in American Working Time: A Synthesis" in Cynthia Fuchs Epstein and Arne L. Kalleberg, eds., *Fighting for Time: Shifting Boundaries of Work and Social Life* (New York: Russell Sage Foundation, 2004) 25.

–, and Sarah E. Winslow. "Overworked Faculty: Job Stresses and Family Demands" in Jerry A. Jacobs and Janice Fanning Madden, eds., *Mommies and Daddies on the Fast Track: Success of Parents in Demanding Professions*, special edition (November 2004) 596 Annals of the American Academy of Political and Social Science 104.

Jardine, Lisa. *Reading Shakespeare Historically* (London: Routledge, 1996).

Jhappan, Radha, ed. *Women's Legal Strategies in Canada* (Toronto: University of Toronto Press, 2002).

Johnson, T. *Professions and Power* (London: Macmillan, 1972).

Julius, Anthony. "Crack the Lawyer's Voice" (1996) 29 Times Literary Supplement 8.

Jurczyk, Karin. "Time in Women's Everyday Lives: Between Self-Determination and Conflicting Demands" (1998) 7(2) Time and Society 283.

Kahn, Paul W. *The Cultural Study of Law* (Chicago: University of Chicago Press, 1999).

Kay, Fiona M. "Balancing Acts: Career and Family among Lawyers" in Susan Boyd, ed., *Challenging the Public/Private Divide: Feminism and Socio-Legal Policy* (Toronto: University of Toronto Press, 1997) 195.

–. "Crossroads to Innovation and Diversity: The Careers of Women Lawyers in Quebec" (2002) 47 McGill Law Journal 699.

–. *Transitions in the Ontario Legal Profession: A Survey of Lawyers Called to the Bar between 1975 and 1990* (Toronto: Law Society of Upper Canada, 1991).

–. *Women in the Legal Profession* (Toronto: Law Society of Upper Canada, 1989).

–, and Joan Brockman. "Barriers to Gender Equality in the Canadian Legal Establishment" (2000) 8 Feminist Legal Studies 169.

–, and John Hagan. "Building Trust: Social Capital, Distributive Justice, and Loyalty to the Firm" (2003) 28(2) Law and Social Inquiry 483.

–. "Cultivating Clients in the Competition for Partnership: Gender and the Organizational Restructuring of Law Firms in the 1990s" (1999) 33(3) Law and Society Review 517.

–. "The Persistent Glass Ceiling: Gendered Inequalities in the Earnings of Lawyers" (1995) 46(2) British Journal of Sociology 279.

–. "Raising the Bar: The Gender Stratification of Law Firm Capital" (1998) 63(5) American Sociological Review 728.

–, Nancy Dautovich, and Chantelle Marlor. *Barriers and Opportunities within Law: Women in a Changing Legal Profession* (Toronto: Law Society of Upper Canada, 1996).

–, Cristi Masuch, and Paula Curry. *Diversity and Change: The Contemporary Legal Profession in Ontario* (Toronto: Law Society of Upper Canada, September 2004).

–. *Women's Careers in the Legal Profession: A Longitudinal Survey of Ontario Lawyers, 1990-2002* (Toronto: Law Society of Upper Canada, September 2004).

Kaye, Judith S. "Women Lawyers in Big Firms: A Study in Progress toward Gender Equality" (1988) 57 Fordham Law Review 111.

Kemeny, Anna. "Driven to Excel: A Portrait of Canada's Workaholics" (2002) 64 Canadian Social Trends 2.

Kennedy, Helena. *Eve Was Framed: Women and British Justice* (Oxford: Oxford University Press, 1992).

Kerr, Ann. "In-House Legal Gigs Gain Greater Prestige, Pay" *Globe and Mail* (21 June 2004) B17.

–. "Lawyers Trying to Slow Down the Meter" *Globe and Mail* (5 January 2004) B10.

Kidder, William C. "Portia Denied: Unmasking Gender Bias on the LSAT and Its Relationship to Racial Diversity in Legal Education" (2001) 12(1) Yale Journal of Law and Feminism 1.

King, Alan J.C., Wendy K. Warren, and Sharon R. Miklas. *Study of Accessibility to Ontario Law Schools.* Executive Summary of the Report (Ottawa: Law Foundation of Ontario and Law Society of Upper Canada, October 2004). http://www.osgoode.yorku.ca/pdf/ExecutiveSummary.pdf.

Kinnear, Mary. *In Subordination: Professional Women, 1870-1970* (Montreal and Kingston: McGill-Queen's University Press, 1995).

–. "That There Woman Lawyer: Women Lawyers in Manitoba, 1915-1970" (1992) 5(2) Canadian Journal of Women and the Law 411.

Kleefeld, John C. "Rethinking 'Like a Lawyer': An Incrementalist's Proposal for First-Year Curriculum Reform" (2003) 53(2) Journal of Legal Education 254.

Kornstein, Daniel. *Kill All the Lawyers? Shakespeare's Legal Appeal* (Princeton: Princeton University Press, 1994).

Kristeva, Julia. "Women's Time" (translated by Alice Jardine and Henry Blake) in Toril Moi, ed., *The Kristeva Reader* (New York: Columbia University Press, 1986) 186.

Kuehn, Thomas. *Law, Family, and Women: Toward a Legal Anthropology of Renaissance Italy* (Chicago: University of Chicago Press, 1991).

Kyer, C. Ian, and Jerome E. Bickenbach. *The Fiercest Debate: Cecil A. Wright, the Benchers, and Legal Education in Ontario, 1923-1957* (Toronto: Osgoode Society for Canadian Legal History, 1987).

Landes, David S. *Revolution in Time* (Cambridge, MA: Belknap Press of Harvard University, 1983).

Langone, John. *The Mystery of Time* (Washington: National Geographic, 2000).

Lareau, Annette. "Invisible Inequalities: Class, Race and Child Rearing in Black Families and White Families" (2002) 67(5) American Sociological Review 747.

Law Society of Upper Canada. *Guide to Developing a Policy Regarding Flexible Work Arrangements* (Toronto: Law Society of Upper Canada, March 2003).

–. *Preventing and Responding to Workplace Harassment and Discrimination: A Guide to Developing a Policy for Law Firms* (Toronto: Law Society of Upper Canada, March 2002).

Le Goff, Jacques. *Time, Work and Culture in the Middle Ages* (Chicago: University of Chicago Press, 1980).

Leccardi, Carmen. "Rethinking Social Time: Feminist Perspectives" (1996) 5(2) Time and Society 169.

Lee, Catherine, Linda Duxbury, and Christopher Higgins. *Employed Mothers: Balancing Work and Family Life* (Ottawa: Canadian Centre for Management Development, 1994).

Lerman, Lisa. "Blue-Chip Bilking: Regulation of Billing and Expense Fraud by Lawyers" (1999) 12(2) Georgetown Journal of Legal Ethics 205.

Lesser, Julie. "The Balancing Act" (August 2004) Career Verdict: The Magazine for Law Students 23.

Levack, Brian P. *The Civil Lawyers in England, 1603-1641* (Oxford: Clarendon Press, 1973).

Leventen, Carol. "Patrimony and Patriarchy in *The Merchant of Venice*" in Valerie Wayne, ed., *The Matter of Difference: Material Feminist Criticism of Shakespeare* (Ithaca: Cornell University Press, 1991) 59.

Llewellyn, K.N. *The Bramble Bush: On Our Law and Its Study* (New York: Oceana, 1960).

Lundy, Derek. "Far from the Padding Crowd" (2000) 24(4) Canadian Lawyer 34.

Macdonald, Keith M. *The Sociology of the Professions* (London: Sage, 1995).

Macdonald, Roderick A. "Still 'Law' and Still 'Learning'" (2003) 18(1) Canadian Journal of Law and Society 22.

Macfarlane, Julie. "Teacher Power in the Law School Classroom" (1996) 19 Dalhousie Law Journal 71.

McIntyre, Sheila. "Gender Bias within the Law School: 'The Memo' and Its Impact" (1987-88) 2(2) Canadian Journal of Women and the Law 362.

McKenzie Leiper, Jean. "An Unlessoned Girl, Unschooled, Unpracticed: Women in the Legal Profession" paper presented at the Renaissance Law and Literature Conference, Oxford University, Oxford, United Kingdom, July 1998.

–. "Expanding the Curriculum Vitae: Baby Boom Women Face Retirement," paper presented at the Annual Meeting of the Canadian Sociology and Anthropology Association, University of Western Ontario, London, Ontario, 31 May 2005.

–. "Gender, Class, and Legal Education: Standing in the Shadow of the Learned Gentleman" in Ruby Heap, Wyn Millar, and Elizabeth Smyth, eds., *Learning to Practise: Professional Education in Historical and Contemporary Perspective* (Ottawa: University of Ottawa Press, 2005) 239.

–. "Gendered Views of Time and Time Crunch Stress: Women Lawyers' Responses to Professional and Personal Demands" in Kerry J. Daly, ed., *Minding the Time in Family Experience: Emerging Perspectives and Issues* (Oxford: Elsevier Science, 2001), 251.

–. "It Was Like 'Wow!': The Experience of Women Lawyers in a Profession Marked by Linear Careers" (1997) 9 Canadian Journal of Women and the Law 115.

–. "Women Lawyers and Their Working Arrangements: Time Crunch, Stress and Career Paths" (1998) 13(2) Canadian Journal of Law and Society 117.

MacKinnon, Catherine A. *Feminism Unmodified: Discourses on Life and Law* (Cambridge, MA: Harvard University Press, 1987).

–. *Toward a Feminist Theory of the State* (Cambridge, MA: Harvard University Press, 1989).

McMahon, Kirsten. "Making the Grade" (2001) 25(1) Canadian Lawyer 23.

–. "The *Canadian Lawyer* 2004 Report Card on Canadian Law Schools" (2004) 28(1) Canadian Lawyer 19.

–. "The *Canadian Lawyer* 2005 Report Card on Canadian Law Schools" (2005) 29(1) Canadian Lawyer 28.

–. "The *Canadian Lawyer* 2006 Report Card on Canadian Law Schools" (2006) 30(1) Canadian Lawyer 33.

–. "Corporate Dividends: The *Canadian Lawyer* In-House Counsel Compensation Survey" (2004) 28(5) Canadian Lawyer 20.

–. "The 2004 *Canadian Lawyer* Compensation Survey" (2004) 28(11) Canadian Lawyer 35.

–. "The 2005 *Canadian Lawyer* Compensation Survey" (2005) 29(11) Canadian Lawyer 26.

Marks, Linda. "Alternative Work Schedules in Law: It's about *Time!*" (1990) 35 New York Law School Law Review 361.

Marron, Kevin. "Equality Struggle Remains in Law" *Globe and Mail* (19 April 2004) B15.

Marshall, Judi. 1989. "Re-visioning Career Concepts" in M. Arthur, D. Hall, and B. Lawrence, eds., *Handbook of Career Theory* (Cambridge: Cambridge University Press, 1989) 282.

Martin, Sheilah, and Gaylene Schellenberg. *Equality of Women in the Legal Profession: A Facilitators' Manual* (Ottawa: Canadian Bar Association Standing Committee on Equality, 1996).

Menkel-Meadow, Carrie. "The Comparative Sociology of Women Lawyers: The 'Feminization' of the Legal Profession" (1986) 24(4) Osgoode Hall Law Journal 897.

–. "Exploring a Research Agenda of the Feminization of the Legal Profession: Theories of Gender and Social Change" (1989) 43 Law and Social Inquiry 289.

–. "Portia in a Different Voice: Speculations on a Woman's Lawyering Process" (1985) 1 Berkeley Women's Law Journal 39.

Merton, Robert. "The Machine, The Worker and The Engineer" (1947) 105 Science 79.

Milkie, Melissa A., and Pia Peltola. "Playing All the Roles: Gender and the Work-Family Balancing Act" (1999) 61(2) Journal of Marriage and the Family 476.

Mills, C. Wright. *White Collar* (New York: Oxford University Press, 1956).

Mincer, Jacob. *Schooling, Experience, and Earnings* (New York: National Bureau of Economic Research, 1974).

Moen, Phyllis, ed. *It's about Time: Couples and Careers* (New York: Cornell University Press, 2003).

–, and Patricia Roehling. *The Career Mystique: Cracks in the American Dream* (Lanham, MD: Rowman and Littlefield Publishers, 2005).

Moore, Christopher. *The Law Society of Upper Canada and Ontario's Lawyers, 1797-1997* (Toronto: University of Toronto Press, 1997).

Moore, Gwen. "Comment: Mommies and Daddies on the Fast Track in Other Wealthy Nations" in Jerry A. Jacobs and Janice Fanning Madden, eds., *Mommies and Daddies on the Fast Track: Success of Parents in Demanding Professions*, special edition (November 2004) 596 Annals of the American Academy of Political and Social Science 208.

Mossman, Mary Jane. "Gender Bias and the Legal Profession: Challenges and Choices" in Joan Brockman and Dorothy Chunn, eds., *Investigating Gender Bias: Law, Courts and the Legal Profession* (Toronto: Thompson Educational Publishing, 1993), 147.

–. "Gender Equality Education and the Legal Profession" (2000) 12 Supreme Court Law Review 187.

–. "Lawyers and Family Life: New Directions for the 1990s" (Part One) (1994) 2(1) Feminist Legal Studies 61.

–. "'Otherness' and the Law School: A Comment on Teaching Gender Equality" (1985) 1 Canadian Journal of Women and the Law 213.

–. "The Past as Prologue: Women and the Law" in Alvin Esau and Jonathan Penner *Lawyering and Legal Education into the Twenty-First Century: Seminars in Honour of the Seventy-Fifth Anniversary of The University of Manitoba Law School* (Manitoba: Legal Research Institute of the University of Manitoba, 1990) 27.

–. "Portia's Progress: Women as Lawyers Reflections on Past and Future" (1988) 8 Windsor Yearbook of Access to Justice 252.

–. "Women Lawyers in Twentieth Century Canada: Rethinking the Image of 'Portia'" in Regina Graycar, ed., *Dissenting Opinion: Feminist Explorations in Law and Society* (Sydney: Allen and Unwin, 1990) 88.

Mudd, John O. "Thinking Critically about 'Thinking Like a Lawyer'" (1983) 33 Journal of Legal Education 704.

Mumford, Lewis. *Technics and Civilization* (New York: Harcourt, Brace and World, 1963).

Murphy, R. *Social Closure* (Oxford: Clarendon Press, 1988).

Neal, M., J. Chapman, B. Ingersoll-Drayton, and A. Emlen. *Balancing Work and Caregiving for Children, Adults, and Elders* (Newbury Park, CA: Sage, 1993).

Nelson, Robert L. "The Future of American Lawyers: A Demographic Profile of a Changing Profession in a Changing Society" in Richard L. Abel, ed., *Lawyers: A Critical Reader* (New York: New Press, 1997) 20.

Neuman, Shirley. "Provost's Study of Accessibility and Career Choice in the Faculty of Law" (24 February 2003). http://www.provost.utoronto.ca/English/Reports.html.

Noonan, Mary C., and Mary E. Corcoran. "The Mommy Track and Partnership: Temporary Delay or Dead End?" in Jerry A. Jacobs and Janice Fanning Madden, eds., *Mommies and Daddies on the Fast Track: Success of Parents in Demanding Professions*, special edition (November 2004) 596 Annals of the American Academy of Political and Social Science 130.

O'Brien, Mary, and Sheila McIntyre. "Patriarchal Hegemony and Legal Education" (1986) 2 Canadian Journal of Women and the Law 69.

Odih, Pamela. "Gendered Time in the Age of Deconstruction" (1999) 8(1) Time and Society 9.

Ornstein, Michael. *The Changing Face of the Ontario Legal Profession, 1971-2001* (Toronto: Law Society of Upper Canada, October 2004).

Pahl, J., and R. Pahl. *Managers and Their Wives* (Baltimore: Penguin, 1971).

Papanek, H. "Men, Women, and Work: Reflections on the Two-Person Career" in J. Huber, ed., *Changing Women in a Changing Society* (Chicago: University of Chicago Press, 1973).

Parkin, Frank. *Marxism and Class Theory: A Bourgeois Critique* (London: Tavistock Publications, 1979).

Pateman, Carole. *The Disorder of Women: Democracy, Feminism and Political Theory* (Stanford: Stanford University Press, 1989).

Pickard, Toni. "Is Real Life Finally Happening?" (1987) 2 Canadian Journal of Women and the Law 150.

Pierce, Jennifer L. *Gender Trials: Emotional Lives in Contemporary Law Firms* (Berkeley: University of California Press, 1995).

Pitt, Angela. *Shakespeare's Women* (Newton Abbot: David and Charles, 1981).

Pleck, Joseph H. *Working Wives/Working Husbands* (Thousand Oaks, CA: Sage Publications, 1985).

Posner, Richard A. *The Problematics of Moral and Legal Theory* (Cambridge, MA: Belknap Press of Harvard University Press, 1999).

Presser, Harriet B. "Are the Interests of Women Inherently at Odds with the Interests of Children or the Family? A Viewpoint" in Karen Oppenheim Mason and An-Magritt Jensen, eds., *Gender and Family Change in Industrialized Countries* (Oxford: Clarendon Press, 1995) 297.

–. "Employment Schedules among Dual-Earner Spouses and the Division of Household Labor by Gender" (1994) 59 American Sociological Review 348.

–. *Working in a 24/7 Economy: Challenges for American Families* (New York: Russell Sage, 2003).

Pue, W. Wesley. "Guild Training versus Professional Education: The Committee on Legal Education and the Law Department of Queen's College, Birmingham in the 1850s" (1989) 33 American Journal of Legal History 241.

–. *Law School: The Story of Legal Education in British Columbia* (Vancouver: University of British Columbia Faculty of Law, 1995).

–. "Planting British Legal Culture in Colonial Soil: Legal Professionalism in the Lands of the Beaver and Kangaroo" in Linda Cardinal and David Headon, eds., *Shaping Nations: Constitutionalism and Society in Australia and Canada* (Ottawa: University of Ottawa Press, 2002) 91.

–, and David Sugarman, eds. *Lawyers and Vampires: Cultural Histories of Legal Professions* (Portland: Hart Publishing, 2003).

Qualitative Solutions and Research Pty Ltd. *QSR NUD*IST 4 User Guide* (Thousand Oaks: Sage, 1997).

Quandt, Tarel. "Learning Exclusion: A Feminist Critique of the Law School Experience" (1992-3) 4 Education and Law Journal 279.

Rackley, Erika. "Reassessing Portia: The Iconic Potential of Shakespeare's Woman Lawyer" (2003) 11 Feminist Legal Studies 25.

Reinharz, Shulamit. *Feminist Methods in Social Science Research* (Oxford: Oxford University Press, 1992).

Rhode, Deborah L. "Gender and Professional Roles" (1994-95) 63 Fordham Law Review 39.

–. *Justice and Gender: Sex Discrimination and the Law* (Cambridge, MA: Harvard University Press, 1989).

–. *Speaking of Sex: The Denial of Gender Inequality* (Cambridge, MA: Harvard University Press, 1997).

–, ed. *The Difference "Difference" Makes: Women and Leadership* (Stanford, CA: Stanford Law and Politics, 2003).

–. *Theoretical Perspectives on Sexual Difference* (New Haven, CT: Yale University Press, 1990).

Ritzer, George, and David Walczak. *Working: Conflict and Change*, 3d ed. (Englewood Cliffs, NJ: Prentice-Hall, 1986).

Roach Anleu, Sharyn. "Women in the Legal Profession: Theory and Research" in Patricia Weiser Ésteal, and Sandra McKillop, eds., *Women and the Law: Proceedings of a Conference, September 24-26, 1991* (Canberra: Australian Institute of Criminology, 1993) 193.

Robinson, John P. "Your Money or Your Time" (1991) 13(11) American Demographics 22.

–. and Geoffrey Godbey. *Time for Life: The Surprising Ways Americans Use Their Time* (University Park: Pennsylvania State University Press, 1997).

Rochette, Annie, and W. Wesley Pue. "'Back to Basics': University Legal Education and Twenty-First Century Professionalism" (2001) 20 Windsor Yearbook of Access to Justice 167.

Rosenberg, Janet, Harry Perlstadt, and William R.F. Phillips. "Now That We Are Here: Discrimination, Disparagement, and Harassment at Work and the Experience of Women Lawyers" (1993) 7(3) Gender and Society 415.

Rossides, Daniel W. *Professions and Disciplines: Functional and Conflict Perspectives* (Upper Saddle River, NJ: Prentice Hall, 1998).

Rothman, Andrew J. "Preparing Law School Graduates for Practice: A Blueprint for Professional Education Following the Medical Profession Example" (1999) 51(4) Rutgers Law Review 875.

Rubin Henderson, Bethany. "Asking the Lost Question: What Is the Purpose of Law School?" (2003) 53(1) Journal of Legal Education 48.

Rusk, James. "The Report That Reads Like a Novel" *Globe and Mail* (27 December 2005) A11.

Rutherford, Sarah. "Are You Going Home Already? The Long Hours Culture, Women Managers and Patriarchal Closure" (2001) 10(2/3) Time and Society 259.

St. Lewis, Joanne. "Beyond the Confinement of Gender: Locating the Space of Legalized Existence of Racialized Women" in Radha Jhappan, ed., *Women's Legal Strategies in Canada* (Toronto: University of Toronto Press, 2002) 295.

Sackmann, Sonja A., Margaret E. Phillips, M. Jill Kleinberg, and Nakiye A. Boyacigiller. "Single and Multiple Cultures in International Cross-Cultural Management Research" in Sonja A. Sackmann, ed., *Cultural Complexity in Organizations: Inherent Contrasts and Contradictions* (Thousand Oaks, CA: Sage, 1997) 14.

Salokar, Rebecca M., and Mary L. Volcansek. *Women in Law: A Bio-Bibliographical Sourcebook* (Westport, CT: Greenwood Press, 1996).

Sarfatti Larson, Magali. *The Rise of Professionalism: A Sociological Analysis* (Berkeley: University of California Press, 1977).

Saunders, Kurt M., and Linda Levine. "Learning to Think Like a Lawyer" (1994) 29 University of San Francisco Law Review 121.

Scales, Ann C. "The Emergence of Feminist Jurisprudence: An Essay" (1986) 95 Yale Law Journal 1378.

Scharlach. A. "Caregiving and Employment: Competing or Complementary Roles?" (1994) 34 Gerontologist 378.

Scheftel, Florence A. "The Study of Law as a Means of Culture for Women" (1911) 1(2) Women Lawyers' Journal 10.

Schneider, Barbara, and Linda J. Waite, eds. *Being Together, Working Apart: Dual-Career Families and the Work-Life Balance* (Cambridge: Cambridge University Press, 2004).

Schor, Juliet B. *The Overworked American: The Unexpected Decline of Leisure* (New York: BasicBooks, 1991).

Schultz, Nancy L. "How Do Lawyers Really Think?" (1992) 42 Journal of Legal Education 57.

Seidel, J., R. Kjolseth, and E. Seymour, *The Ethnograph: A User's Guide* (Corvalis, OR: Qualis Research Associates, 1988).

Seron, Carroll. *The Business of Practicing Law: The Work Lives of Solo and Small-Firm Attorneys* (Philadelphia: Temple University Press, 1996).

–, and Kerry Ferris. "Negotiating Professionalism: The Gendered Social Capital of Flexible Time" (1995) 22(1) Work and Occupations 22.

Shakespeare, William. "The Merchant of Venice" in Alfred A. Harbage, ed., *William Shakespeare: The Complete Works* (New York: Viking Press, 1986).

Shalleck, Ann. "The Feminist Transformation of Lawyering: A Response to Naomi Cahn" (1992) 43 Hastings Law Journal 1039.

Shapiro, Michael. *Gender in Play on the Shakespearean Stage* (Ann Arbor: University of Michigan Press, 1994).

Shetreet, Shimon. *Women in Law* (London and Boston: Kluwer Law International, 1998).

Sommerlad, Hilary, and Peter Sanderson. *Gender, Choice and Commitment: Women Solicitors in England and Wales and the Struggle for Equal Status* (Aldershot: Ashgate Publishing Company, 1998).

Sorokin, Pitirim. *Sociocultural Causality, Space, Time* (New York: Russell and Russell, 1943; reprinted 1964).

Sorokin, P.A., and R.K. Merton. "Social Time: A Methodological and Functional Analysis" (1937) 42 American Journal of Sociology 615.

Stager, David, and Harry Arthurs. *Lawyers in Canada* (Toronto: University of Toronto Press, 1990).

Staheli, Kory D. "Introducing Students to Legal Practice Materials: Helping Fill a Law School Void" (1998) 16(4) Legal Reference Services Quarterly 23.

Staines, Graham L., and Joseph H. Pleck. *The Impact of Work Schedules on the Family* (Ann Arbor: University of Michigan, Institute for Social Research, 1983).

Statistics Canada. "General Social Survey: Time Use" *The Daily* (9 November 1999) 2. http://www.statcan.ca:80/Daily/English/991109/d991109a.htm.

–. "Study: Access to Professional Programs amid the Deregulation of Tuition Fees, 1995 to 2002" *The Daily* (27 September 2005) 2. http://www.statcan.ca/Daily/English/050927/d050927a.htm.

Steed, Judy. "Law Firms Suffer as Women Vote with Their Feet" *Toronto Star* (13 June 2005) D1.

Stevens, Robert. "Law Schools and Law Students" (1973) 59 Virginia Law Review 551.

–. *Law School: Legal Education in America from the 1850s to the 1980s* (Chapel Hill and London: University of North Carolina Press, 1983).

Stone, Adrienne. "Women, Law School and Student Commitment to the Public Interest" in Jeremy Cooper and Louise C. Trubek, eds., *Educating for Justice: Social Values and Legal Education* (Aldershot: Dartmouth Publishing Company, 1997), 56.

Stone, Pamela. *Both Sides Now: Why Career Women Are Quitting Jobs and Heading Home* (working title) (University of California Press, forthcoming).

Stone, Pamela, and Meg Lovejoy. "Fast-Track Women and the 'Choice' To Stay Home" in Jerry A. Jacobs and Janice Fanning Madden, eds., *Mommies and Daddies on the Fast Track: Success of Parents in Demanding Professions*, special edition (November 2004) 596 Annals of the American Academy of Political and Social Science 62.

Stropus, Ruta. "Mend It, Bend It, And Extend It: The Fate of Traditional Law School Methodology in the 21st Century" (1996) 27 Loyola University Chicago Law Journal 449.

Swainger, Jonathan, and Constance Backhouse, eds. *People and Place: Historical Influences on Legal Culture* (Vancouver: UBC Press, 2003).

Taber, Janet, Marguerite T. Grant, Mart Y. Huser, Rise B. Norman, James R. Sutton, Clarence C. Wong, Louise E. Parker, and Claire Picard. "Gender, Legal Education, and the Legal Profession: An Empirical Study of Stanford Law Students and Graduates" (1988) 40 Stanford Law Review 1209.

Thompson, Jeffery A., and J. Stuart Bunderson. "Work-Nonwork Conflict and the Phenomenology of Time: Beyond the Balance Metaphor" (2001) 28(1) Work and Occupations 17.

Thornton, Margaret. *Dissonance and Distrust: Women in the Legal Profession* (Melbourne: Oxford University Press Australia, 1996).

–. "Technocentrism in the Law School: Why the Gender and Colour of the Law Remain the Same" (1998) 36(2) Osgoode Hall Law Journal 369.

Thurer, Shari L. *The Myths of Motherhood: How Culture Reinvents the Good Mother* (New York: Houghton Mifflin, 1994).

Tobol, Amy Ruth. "Integrating Social Justice Values into the Teaching of Legal Research and Writing: Reflections from the Field" in Jeremy Cooper and Louise C. Trubek, *Educating for Justice: Social Values and Legal Education* (Aldershot: Dartmouth Publishing Company, 1997), 88.

Tong, Dawna, and W. Wesley Pue. "The Best and the Brightest? Canadian Law School Admissions" (1999) 37(4) Osgoode Hall Law Journal 843.

Trotter, Michael H. *Profit and the Practice of Law: What's Happened to the Legal Profession* (Athens: University of Georgia Press, 1997).

Twining, William. *Blackstone's Tower: The English Law School* (London: Stevens and Sons/Sweet and Maxwell, 1994).

–. "What Are Law Schools For?" (1995) 46(3 and 4) Northern Ireland Legal Quarterly 291.

Valpy, Michael. "Supreme Court Appointments" *Globe and Mail* (25 August 2004) A6.

Waldie, Paul. "Black's Judge 'A Fistful of Dynamite'" *Globe and Mail* (29 November 2005) B20.

Wallace, Jean E. "The Benefits of Mentoring for Female Lawyers" (2001) 58 Journal of Vocational Behavior 366.

–. "Motherhood and Career Commitment to the Legal Profession" in Nancy Ditomaso and Corinne Post, eds., *Diversity in the Workforce, Research in the Sociology of Work*, vol. 14 (Oxford: Elsevier, JAI, 2004) 219.

–. "Work-to-Nonwork Conflict among Married Male and Female Lawyers" (1999) 20 Journal of Organizational Behavior 797.

Ward, Ian. "When Mercy Seasons Justice: Shakespeare's Woman Lawyer" in Clare McGlynn, ed., *Legal Feminisms: Theory and Practice* (Aldershot: Ashgate/Dartmouth, 1998) 63.

Watts, Carol. "Time and the Working Mother: Kristeva's 'Women's Time' Revisited" (1998) 91 Radical Philosophy 6.

Weber, Max. *Economy and Society* (London: University of California Press, 1978).

Weiss, Catherine, and Louise Melling. "The Legal Education of Twenty Women" (1988) 40 Stanford Law Review 1299.

White, David M., and Terry E. Roth. "The Law School Admission Test and the Continuing Minority Status of Women in Law Schools" (1979) 2 Harvard Women's Law Journal 103.

Wilensky, H.L. "Careers, Lifestyles, and Social Integration" (1961) 12 International Social Science Journal 553.

Williams, Cara. "Sources of Workplace Stress" (2003) 15(3) Perspectives on Labour and Income 23.

–. "Stress at Work" (2003) 70 Canadian Social Trends 7.

Williams, Sonya, and Shin-Kap Han. "Career Clocks: Forked Roads" in Phyllis Moen, ed., *It's about Time: Couples and Careers* (Cornell: Cornell University Press, 2003).

Willie, Richard A. *These Legal Gentlemen: Lawyers in Manitoba: 1839-1900* (Winnipeg: Legal Research Institute of the University of Manitoba, 1994).

Wilson, Bertha. "Will Women Judges Really Make a Difference?" (1990) 28 Osgoode Hall Law Journal 507.

Witz, Anne. *Professions and Patriarchy* (London: Routledge, 1992).

Wizner, Stephen. "Is Learning to 'Think Like a Lawyer' Enough?" (1998) 17 Yale Law and Policy Review 583.

Yorke, Lois K. "Mabel Penery French (1881-1955): A Life Re-Created" (1993) 42 University of New Brunswick Law Journal 3.

Young, Margot. "Making and Breaking Rank: Some Thoughts on Recent Canadian Law School Surveys" (2001) 20 Windsor Yearbook of Access to Justice 311.

Index

Jean McKenzie Leiper
Bar Codes: Women in the Legal Profession (2006)

Gerald Baier
Courts and Federalism: Judicial Doctrine in the United States, Australia, and Canada (2006)

Avigail Eisenberg (ed.)
Diversity and Equality: The Changing Framework of Freedom in Canada (2006)

Randy K. Lippert
Sanctuary, Sovereignty, Sacrifice: Canadian Sanctuary Incidents, Power, and Law (2005)

James B. Kelly
Governing with the Charter: Legislative and Judicial Activism and Framers' Intent (2005)

Dianne Pothier and Richard Devlin (eds.)
Critical Disability Theory: Essays in Philosophy, Politics, Policy, and Law (2005)

Susan G. Drummond
Mapping Marriage Law in Spanish Gitano Communities (2005)

Louis A. Knafla and Jonathan Swainger (eds.)
Laws and Societies in the Canadian Prairie West, 1670-1940 (2005)

Ikechi Mgbeoji
Global Biopiracy: Patents, Plants, and Indigenous Knowledge (2005)

Florian Sauvageau, David Schneiderman, and David Taras, with Ruth
Klinkhammer and Pierre Trudel
The Last Word: Media Coverage of the Supreme Court of Canada (2005)

Gerald Kernerman
*Multicultural Nationalism: Civilizing Difference, Constituting
Community* (2005)

Pamela A. Jordan
*Defending Rights in Russia: Lawyers, the State, and Legal Reform in the
Post-Soviet Era* (2005)

Anna Pratt
Securing Borders: Detention and Deportation in Canada (2005)

Kirsten Johnson Kramar
Unwilling Mothers, Unwanted Babies: Infanticide in Canada (2005)

W.A. Bogart
*Good Government? Good Citizens? Courts, Politics, and Markets in a
Changing Canada* (2005)

Catherine Dauvergne
*Humanitarianism, Identity, and Nation: Migration Laws in Canada
and Australia* (2005)

Michael Lee Ross
First Nations Sacred Sites in Canada's Courts (2005)

Andrew Woolford
Between Justice and Certainty: Treaty Making in British Columbia (2005)

John McLaren, Andrew Buck, and Nancy Wright (eds.)
Despotic Dominion: Property Rights in British Settler Societies (2004)

Georges Campeau
From UI to EI: Waging War on the Welfare State (2004)

Alvin J. Esau
*The Courts and the Colonies: The Litigation of Hutterite Church
Disputes* (2004)

Christopher N. Kendall
Gay Male Pornography: An Issue of Sex Discrimination (2004)

Roy B. Flemming
Tournament of Appeals: Granting Judicial Review in Canada (2004)

Constance Backhouse and Nancy L. Backhouse
The Heiress vs the Establishment: Mrs. Campbell's Campaign for Legal Justice (2004)

Christopher P. Manfredi
Feminist Activism in the Supreme Court: Legal Mobilization and the Women's Legal Education and Action Fund (2004)

Annalise Acorn
Compulsory Compassion: A Critique of Restorative Justice (2004)

Jonathan Swainger and Constance Backhouse (eds.)
People and Place: Historical Influences on Legal Culture (2003)

Jim Phillips and Rosemary Gartner
Murdering Holiness: The Trials of Franz Creffield and George Mitchell (2003)

David R. Boyd
Unnatural Law: Rethinking Canadian Environmental Law and Policy (2003)

Ikechi Mgbeoji
Collective Insecurity: The Liberian Crisis, Unilateralism, and Global Order (2003)

Rebecca Johnson
Taxing Choices: The Intersection of Class, Gender, Parenthood, and the Law (2002)

John McLaren, Robert Menzies, and Dorothy E. Chunn (eds.)
Regulating Lives: Historical Essays on the State, Society, the Individual, and the Law (2002)

Joan Brockman
Gender in the Legal Profession: Fitting or Breaking the Mould (2001)

Printed and bound in Canada by Friesens
Set in Stone by Robert and Shirley Kroeger, Kroeger Enterprises
Copy editor: Stacy Belden
Proofreader: Megan Brand
Indexer: Gillian Watts